CONTRIBUTORS

ROBERT H. ELLIS, Ed. D.
Assistant Professor of Educational Psychology
State University College; Fredonia, New York

WILLIAM McBLAIR, Ph.D.
Professor of Biology
San Diego State University; San Diego, California

ALISON SWEENEY, Photographer
27 Corte del Bayo; Larkspur, California

On Becoming an Educated Person

AN ORIENTATION TO COLLEGE AND LIFE

VIRGINIA VOEKS

San Diego State University

Fourth Edition

 SAUNDERS SURVIVAL SERIES

W. B. SAUNDERS COMPANY PHILADELPHIA · LONDON · TORONTO

W. B. Saunders Company: West Washington Square
                          Philadelphia, Pa.   19105

                          1 St. Anne's Road
                          Eastbourne, East Sussex BN21 3UN, England

                          1 Goldthorne Avenue
                          Toronto, Ontario M8Z 5T9, Canada

Listed here is the latest translated edition of this book together with the language of the translation and the publisher.

Japanese (*2nd Edition*) — Eihosha, Ltd.
              Tokyo, Japan

Cover illustration courtesy of Nancy Durkin. Photographs for Chapters 5 and 6 and frontispiece courtesy of Jerry Elliott, San Diego State University.

On Becoming an Educated Person: An Orientation to College   ISBN   0-7216-9069-6
                                  and Life

Last digit is the print number: 9   8   7   6   5   4   3   2

For Students Everywhere

*including the many not at a university or college
who yet care about this most human of endeavors*

With Love

Preface

EDUCATION FOR LIFE

Most of us wish to grow, but are not at all sure how to do so. Sometimes our attempts actually make matters worse. Most of us yearn for a more vibrant life, but have little or no idea how to create such living.

New worlds open daily to the wondering delight of those eager to learn and grow. Wherever you are, old delights are built upon and thereby expand to encompass more and more of the life around. Old questions get answered and new questions arise, inviting your exploration and imaginative attention. Some problems fade; some are solved or dismissed; new problems approach and intrigue you. Daily your imagination is challenged. Your fund of information constantly used constantly grows. Skills in thinking, perceiving, integrating, interpreting, refined through your use become ever more usable. These are some signs of a person awake and growing.

This book is written to help you achieve those goals — in formal education and in the rest of your life.

The book has three uses: for identifying and clarifying your goals; for identifying trouble spots — what exactly is going wrong and what can you do about it; for developing your skill in reading, listening, coping with examinations and other trying crises, your skill in reasoning, seeing more clearly, understanding, learning, and remembering. It will stand you in good stead throughout college and university, but not only that.

This book is intended for all of life, not merely the academic. The material is useful for anyone trying to grow. It can help you learn more swiftly and well, whether in classrooms or in outside life. It can help you live more joyously.

Robert Ellis wrote a vital section on creativity (Chapter 1, C, 6) and another on combatting tension, developing ability to relax (Chapter 5, E, 6), as well as some of the paragraphs on views of college, thrill seeking, and other topics. He also prepared for you an exercise to ease anxiety and help you toward serenity and inner peace. It is the Addendum, after the last chapter.

Pointers on effective discussions (Chapter 3, B, 1 through 8) and the uses of additional languages (Chapter 3, D, 2) were prepared for you by my husband, William McBlair. His insight, love for and knowledge of students, and wisdom shine through this book. He helped in countless ways.

To Paul Streeter you also have cause for gratitude. His advice solved many problems. His sensitive, perceptive editing of the manuscript gave dozens of improvements to clarity and grace.

Alison Sweeney created the delightful photographs which illumine words, adding so much vitality and beauty to this edition. We are fortunate too for the encouragement, imagination, and artistic taste given this project by Mary Jane and Kent R. Willson. Kent R. Willson also is responsible for the singularly clear graphs.

Duane Sturges has compiled an excellent index to enable you to find quickly any topic of especial concern to you. There also is a table of contents which can act as a summary of each chapter or as a preview.

Many thanks to Dad and Mother for their inspiration and tender encouragement, to Antoinette Crane for beautiful final typing, and to Tracy Ann Wilder who, with accuracy and sweet patience, alphabetized, pasted, proofed, ran errands, typed, and offered lovely ideas.

All join me in wishing you well. We hope very much our endeavors aid your endeavors and you become ever more nearly the person you most want to be.

VIRGINIA VOEKS
San Diego, California

Contents

Chapter 4

Chapter 6

Chapter 7

On Becoming an Educated Person

Launch yourself with vigor . . .

Chapter 1

Why Go to University or College?

A. EDUCATION AND LIFE

The university has become, for many of its students and graduates, a shattered dream. No doubt you have encountered persons bitter about their college experience. This disillusionment, however, is not new; H. G. Wells highlighted it in a novel almost forty years ago. He noted that universities are concerned, in the minds of many, with "... 'imparting some sort of ultimate wisdom and mental habits unknown to the commonality, initiating them into a mastery of life. . . .

" 'Initiation. That is what you thought they were going to do for you. . . . That is what our poor befuddled, humbugged lower classes believe goes on up here to this day. They really believe that people who have been up here are mentally better than people who haven't. You cannot believe what they imagine! Education — at a University. Excelsior, and there is nothing higher. They look up to it with their mouths open. Crumbs fall to them. University Extension! Oh, generous, beautiful words! You, Stella, were to be one of those precious educated. The concentrated sort, not the extended sort. And now after two years you find

3

you have got nothing whatever, nothing that makes you different, or stronger, or better, Eh?'

" 'That is what I'm telling you,' said Stella."[53]

So it goes — the current tragicomedy played by college students and their professors. The major difference between Stella and many other college students is that Stella awakened after two years. Many awaken only after four, or not at all. Every spring, thousands upon thousands of black-robed figures docilely line up, parade down an aisle, take their sheepskins, and walk to their seats again, often with quizzical, sardonic smiles. To many of them college has been a farce — and a rather humorless farce at that.

Yet, in that same line are other students — radiantly afire with exciting discoveries and deeply serene with new resources. There are students who feel they have had experiences of great value, experiences of greater value than could be communicated well in any language (designed, as languages are, to convey best only the prosaic).

And you? In which group will you be walking when you graduate?

You rather hope, of course, that it will be the latter group. But hopes are not enough. Songs and folklore notwithstanding, wishing does not make it so — not even very intense wishing.

Why is it, then, that some who come to higher education leave with so much, while others grow bitter and leave with so little?

What differentiates these two groups? They do not differ in intelligence one way or the other;[27, 38] they do not differ in background preparation nor in the major they choose.[21-23, 44, 49] They do differ in approach.[28, 38]

Some students approach college and the university as parallel to a fast-food drive-in: Education is to be like a dinner already prepared, packaged, "pipin' hot," ready to be consumed on the spot. Their job is to receive it. These students view education as a product, a thing, not as a process for becoming a different person.

A variation with similarly bleak consequences is that the university is some sort of way station which must be endured for several years before getting on with life. Those adopting this belief imagine college and the university to be modern equivalents to initiation or the manhood rites of a primitive society. Accordingly, they suggest to one and all that anybody who does more than the minimum necessary to navigate the graduation hurdles ("tests of manhood," in their view) is a fool, or an idealist, or worse.

This modern but cynical approach is ultimately self-defeating. A college degree may get you in the front door for your first job interview, and maybe your first job, but what about the rest of your life? You have to start building your life sometime; why not now? At college and the university all sorts of options and opportunities are available; here you are allowed to grow and experiment with only minimal negative consequences if you flounder and change your mind.

You can join this group: These students approach their college as akin to a large, diverse, and somewhat wild garden. They see it as a place where common and uncommon ingredients can be collected by them and by them combined into new and sometimes exotic dishes; it is a place where they can learn the skills and facts and arts for building the traditional and creating the new.

That captures the difference between the bitter and the joyous. One group approaches knowledge passively; waits to be taught; and finds the taste flat, musty, old, reminiscent of cardboard. The other group actively attacks learning and finds it is delightful and satisfying. So we see, the outcome of college depends largely on you — your perspective, beliefs, and approach.

Unfortunately it is not a simple case of hitching up your resolve and becoming an educated person. You must recognize that the university, despite many claims, is not a modern assembly line nor a guarantee of anything. It is a set of opportunities. You can get as much or as little as you desire, but you must get it yourself.

Let us see how you can guarantee results you will value.

B. YOUR GOALS

To solve any problem, the wisest start is to carefully answer this question: What precisely am I trying to do? Where do I want to get? The probability of ever reaching a desired goal is increased greatly by knowing precisely what you are trying to achieve. So also is your efficiency. Efficiency always increases when you answer first "*What* am I trying to do?" and only then ask "*How* can I do it?"

The point seems obvious, almost like common sense. And yet, how many times have you searched for solutions without knowing clearly what you were trying to solve? As with other problems, so it is with education and studying. Thousands go through school (the majority perhaps) without answering in any specific detail that first crucial question — What am I doing here? Often they fail to even consider the question. Until the question is clear and answered, until you clarify your own goals, you cannot begin a systematic effort at growth. Your four years will be spent meandering and ultimately prove fruitless and disappointing.

Small wonder many graduates are bitter, sometimes sardonic and cynical. Everything has been rather pointless for them. They missed what they wanted from college — this they know. But what did they miss? Any why? Twenty years later they still wonder just *what* it was they wanted, or what they want now. That largely, is *why* they missed obtaining it. Vagueness as to your goals may cause you also to lose what you desire.

You deserve a better fate. You can have it too. A good bit of thinking is required; but the results warrant the time and effort.

First ask yourself: What sort of person am I trying to become as a result of these four years' activities? What am I aiming for? These questions do not bear on college years alone, nor on your vocational life alone. Your whole life is influenced by your answer, or your failure to answer. Having asked yourself these questions, answer them in as much detail as you can.

These questions, and all questions involving your scale of values, you must answer for yourself. No one else can do this for you — unless by great good fortune that person knows you extremely well, is an acute observer, is unusually astute, and is willing to spend considerable time on this project. Such a combination is not common, is it? And without that combination, the best anyone else can do is state what that person would try to do: i.e., what that person values, or what other people value. That "best" will not suffice, for your scale of values and his may differ markedly.

Suppose we were to ask you: "What are you trying to do by going to college?" Your reply might be: "Get educated, of course." That seems definite enough. But is it? The more you ponder this reply, the more you can see that the answer really is no answer at all. The question remains: What do you mean by "educated"? Until you answer at least that question alone, do you really know what you are trying to do?

To be of real aid in reaching your goals, your replies must be highly detailed and definite. One way to form more specific answers is to ask not a single question, but a series. After each reply, ask yourself: "And what do I mean by that?" Then answer that question as well as you can.

What do you mean when you say you want to become educated? To help you formulate your own answer, here is one concept of "a highly educated person." You may think of other qualities essential to what you mean by "highly educated;" and you may deem nonessential some included here.

These characteristics are possibilities. They might be the attributes you want. They certainly will help you identify your goals and thus heighten your chances of becoming the woman or man you long to be.

C. ASPECTS OF AN EDUCATED PERSON —POSSIBLE GOALS

1. You Can Equip Yourself for Various Vocations.

Abbots, administrators, astronauts; homemakers, internists, journalists; youth workers and zoologists find advanced education a help in their work. So do persons in hundreds of other jobs.

Exciting positions are available for college and university men and, increasingly, women[20, 50] — though women still are far behind men.[1, 20, 50, 51]

Through university and college work, you can gain needed information and technical skills for a wide variety of jobs. Additionally, you can build habits and personality attributes much needed in a variety of jobs. You can develop effective ways of tackling problems; habits of carrying out long jobs on your own initiative, with little or no supervision; habits of self-reliance, perseverance, discipline, responsibility; ways of thinking and analyzing; skills in listening and talking; skill in accepting and using criticism; understanding of different kinds of people and habits of easy interaction; courage in undertaking difficult tasks, tenacity in carrying them out. These are qualities exceedingly useful throughout life itself and in almost any vocation.

Most of the students in seven large classes we surveyed said they wanted to become fitted for a "better job." Some students listed only this goal. This raises an important question: Were those students attending college solely to get a job? If so, they might be wise to either take a job and start getting on-job experience or attend a vocational training school instead of a university or liberal arts college. If vocational training is your only goal, you will be apt to deem much of your university experience a dreary waste. That is a pity, for you could improve your job chances and at the same time improve your chances for the good life, while finding the process itself profoundly satisfying.

Almost certainly both you and your parents deem enhanced employability a major justification for the time, worry, and expense committed to obtaining a degree.[13] Enhanced employability is a goal attainable through college or university work and quite properly may be one of your objectives.

It is a big mistake, though, to choose a major solely because it appears to further your chances of getting a job. For example, you may have heard that business majors get more job offers than liberal arts and humanities majors at graduation. Consequently, you might be considering business as a major solely because you fear being unemployed at graduation time. But the employment rate for business majors may only appear to be better. A group of liberal arts students and business students were contacted both at graduation and five months later. At graduation, business students had more job offers but five months later there were no important differences in employment, unemployment, or underemployment.[5]

Similarly, other reports show a growing number of businesses are seeking applicants with a liberal arts background rather than the professional degrees.[3, 12] The consensus seems to be that there is a re-emerging appreciation of the generalist within the business community.

You might try a little experiment. Ask people you know, who have gone to college or the university, what they studied while there and what kinds of jobs they have had. You will be surprised at the variety of jobs each person has held and the apparent unrelatedness of their major to their subsequent occupations. Does this mean college is unimportant to your job? No; it means college is more important than any one job. Your university or college experience, if enthusiastically embraced, will prepare you for a large range of jobs and widening ways of living.

For this to happen, please ask yourself: "Is preparation for a particular job my only important objective?"

Is it important to you to achieve other goals too? Do you, for example, care about being someone truly happy — regardless of your particular vocation? Would you like to participate effectively in community and national affairs? Do you want to be a contributing citizen of a democracy? You may wish to prepare also for the large portion of your life not spent on a vocation, and for the large amounts of leisure flowing from our use of machines and our highly industrialized culture.

Your deepest concern perhaps is not earning a good living, but rather earning a good life. If it is, bear that fact in mind. Otherwise you will tend to evaluate any course or topic primarily in terms of whether it furthers your vocational training. At the extreme, you may even evaluate your entire college endeavor in terms only of vocational skills. With such a narrow preoccupation, you will overlook much of what you could be gaining. Even if you continue at the college or university, you will be apt to miss many (perhaps most) of the opportunities for growth afforded you. Perhaps already you have found yourself ignoring many things because "they have nothing to do with being a physicist," or laboratory technician, or whatever your vocational objective may be. Is that all you want to be?

The following goals would facilitate effective participation in most vocations. They also would facilitate your creating a satisfying life — regardless of your later vocation. They are what Sidney Gulick[19] has called "durable satisfactions": characteristics enhancing life regardless of one's job, regardless of one's age, year after year throughout one's lifetime. They are ways of earning a good life. You, we hope, will think of additional ones.

2. You Can Comprehend Better This World, and Eagerly Go on Learning.

You could build a more complete fund of facts, concepts, principles, and ideas. You could develop habits of eagerly enlarging your fund, while in school and long after school is over.

A fund of information and ideas is a set of tools. Using them, you can do wondrous things: You can solve more reasonably the problems you meet; you can interpret more fully the events about you; you can predict more adequately, and even partially control the events to come. Using them, you also can acquire more easily further facts and ideas. Facts, concepts, principles, and ideas can be extraordinarily useful tools.

However, if you merely collect and store them, facts and ideas are pointless. They are of no more value than a basement full of hammers, saws, and lathes, whose owner proudly displays them to visitors, but leaves them to rust the remainder of the time. Similarly, the mere possession of information is almost worthless.

Furthermore, possession of even a tremendous fund of information does not constitute being "educated," as we are using the term. To be educated, one must develop also the following attributes.

3. You Can Increase Your Ability to See Relationships and Make More Meaningful Integrations.

"Integration" refers to a synthesis of materials. It is a sort of tying together of the concepts, data, methods, and ideas available from one source with those available from other sources — from other courses, books and magazines, from newspapers, movies, and plays, from one's life in general.

With skill in making integrations, each new fact or concept makes old ones more meaningful and comprehensible. All aspects of the world are enriched whenever one discovers anything about any aspect of the world. To a person of such facility, a knowledge of literature contributes to understanding individual behavior (psychology), to understanding group characteristics (sociology), to understanding of the areas of the world most extensively considered by philosophers, anthropologists, political scientists, economists. Similarly, an understanding of psychology or sociology, philosophy or anthropology, economics or political science can enable one to read literature with deeper appreciation and comprehension. Through making integrations, your fund of concepts and facts becomes valuable and useful.

The concept of "integration" is fairly simple. The process is not. To illustrate the integrations you could make and the effect of seeing these interrelationships, let us consider some parts of psychology and one bit of literature, Flaubert's *Madame Bovary*.

In that book, Flaubert paints certain episodes from Emma Bovary's childhood and adolescence. Suppose you understand many of the facts and principles of psychology and are skilled in making integrations. Then these portrayals take on deeper color for you. You go between and beyond the lines and see vividly, deeply the effects of these experiences on Emma. You put these together with your knowledge of psychology and get new views of the world about you. The effects of her impoverished home, devoid of beauty to Emma, but providing materials from which the child created elaborate dreams of life-to-be — these you would see keenly. No longer are those pages stuffy descriptions, dull background information. They are laden with gripping drama — when you know and use your knowledge of psychology. You understand more fully what is resulting from Emma's creation of that world of fantasy and from daydreaming as a habitual response to frustration. Much else too you see more clearly and understand more deeply: how Emma responds to the discovery that the dashing prince she married is neither a prince nor dashing — and never will be . . . how the world strikes her when she finally does get a home of her own . . . how her husband (and life) look to her when she moves into this "new" home, the home which was to be a sort of castle, elegant, exciting, and peaceful, but which actually is shabby, despicably ordinary. How these later experiences affect Emma, you foresee and appreciate more keenly when you know the common results of living in fantasy and integrate this knowledge with the material of the novel. If you add to this an understanding of the relationship between frustration and aggression, you will understand with greater acuity the murderous actions to which Emma later resorts. You understand better, also, the world in which you live.

This is the merest hint of how a book takes on added significance and richness when you integrate a knowledge of psychology with the portrayals of a novel. Through such integrations, you catch more of the author's ideas; you build more ideas of your own; you notice more aspects of the world described; and you see more completely what is happening in your own world. You read with deeper appreciation and enjoyment than you otherwise could, for new dimensions have been added.

Literature becomes more meaningful when you integrate it with your knowledge of psychology. Similarly, psychology becomes more meaningful when you integrate it with your knowledge of literature. You can better comprehend psychological concepts, principles, and facts if you have read reflectively such a book as *Madame Bovary* and have developed skill in seeing interrelationships. To illustrate this, let us look at a sentence from a psychology textbook.

"One's vocational and marriage choices are based, in large part, on fantasy."

Now there is a statement which looks trivial, almost puerile — until you start to think about it and relate it to your other knowledge. Suppose in the course of your thinking, you recall Emma Bovary, and *her* marital choice based on fantasy. How did that work out? You remember how she repeatedly compared her husband with her dream and found Charles always sorely lacking, the dream always better, far better. You remember her disappointed bittnerness when the dream exploded. You recall the way she spoke and acted after she discovered her husband was no gallant knight, no extraordinarily gifted man. You recall how she humiliated and taunted him, goading him for years to try the near impossible; and you recall how Charles became, as a consequence, ever less like her dream. You remember Emma's ensuing conquests, her ruthless exploitation of other men — men who might be princes, but never were.

"One's . . . marriage choices are based, in large part, on fantasy." Do we have clues here concerning an underlying difficulty in many homes? Could this account perhaps for some of the disrupting flashes of rage, the damaging onslaughts, we have often witnessed but seldom understood? The sentence from the psychology text *combined* with a knowledge of "Madame Bovary" gives one new leads concerning the nature of the world. That is one result of "making integrations."

"One's vocational . . . choices are based, in large part, on fantasy." If one chooses a vocation in terms of a dream of the job, would not the results resemble those so tragically illustrated in Emma Bovary's marriage? Does this give some clue to why many people are sorely disappointed by their vocations, rebellious toward their employers, beset by feelings of betrayal? With similar bases for their choices and for Emma's, we should expect similar results. This affords new insight concerning one way to avoid the disillusioned bitterness and conviction of betrayal common in our world.

By the same token, we understand how those who allow fantasy to guide their educational choices become so cynical and disillusioned as they complete several wasted years at a university or college.

The foregoing does not mean we can prove the statements in a text by finding parallels in literature. One cannot do that, but what one can do is truly remarkable. By integrating materials from literature and other fields of life with text materials, you can illustrate the statements in the text. You can bring out their meanings. You can see more of the possible implications. Dry facts become alive; new ideas are born.

4. You Can Build Deeper, Widening Interests.

Such habits go far toward precluding the boredom and lostness we observe all about us and (oftentimes) within us. Bob is an illustration.

When alone, Bob habitually switches on the radio or television, though he finds most programs "stupid." He tries to read, but everything seems dull. That is not surprising, for Bob knows almost nothing about philosophy or astronomy, anthropology or botany, economics or geography, or any other broad area of investigation. He scoffs at these. He scoffs at poetry too. The lives of others (history and biographies) he deems stuffy. Occasionally he reads novels, but even they soon pall on him. Books as sources of joy do not exist for Bob. Listening to music, attending speeches, visiting art museums, writing — all these activities he labels "highbrow" and shoves away. What *can* Bob enjoy? By himself, Bob is bored and discontented. Why? He decides he is lonesome.

So he calls some acquaintances, urging them to "do something" with him. But when they do, Bob still is bored, often restless, and discontented. We could predict that. As is well known (well known to psychologists anyway), *the person who is bored alone, usually is bored also when with others.*

This is no jaded appetite! This is an absence of appetites. Bob's dilemma reflects (among other things) a failure to have developed hearty appetites in the first place.

Pitifully enough, Bob is not the extreme individual you might imagine. His dilemma is that of many. His dilemma may even be yours, though exaggerated of course. To better understand you, or what you might become, let us summarize Bob's predicament.

The general pattern is this: The individual has a deep restlessness. He complains to himself or his parents or his friends that there is "nothing to do." He labels many activities "stupid." When alone, he is listless and lonesome.

He is driven to seek others' company. But even when with other people and "on the go," the restless discontent, the insidious boredom creep up on him.

Life in general is pretty dull, he feels; or else (as he often phrases it) he is "missing life."

As an escape, he seeks thrills avidly — thrills from the excitement of breaking rules and customs, suspense from pinball machines or other gambling. But these do not satisfy his nameless craving. Soon he is restless and bored again, often even more "sunk" than before the episode. As a consequence he seeks thrills even more frantically with the blind, unverbalized feeling they *must* relieve his tension and discontent.

At this point, Bob may turn to alcohol or other drugs in an effort to increase his thrills and decrease his anxiety. This alternative is highly likely and highly dangerous for people like Bob who want life to be both fun and easy. Drugs are a dangerous alternative partly because they preclude a solution to Bob's original problem: they suggest life can be enjoyed simply by letting it wash over you, i.e., that life can be enjoyed passively (as long as one stays in a drugged state) and without personal responsibility. Further, one may begin to believe and rely on the altered states of consciousness that drugs induce and, when that happens, you or Bob become less effective in your efforts to lead an interesting and exciting life.

Thrills and drugs do not cure the difficulty. They cannot, since a fundamental trouble of these people is a boredom within one's self and with most of the world, a boredom stemming in part from a paucity of deep interests. Occasionally the individual has many interests, but the interests are shallow, and confined to a few areas only.

Bob's difficulty differs from that of many other people only in degree. Is he so different from you?

Can *you* be happy alone? Really happy? Or are such hours

ones to be endured (not lived), as best one can? Must you flee from solitude to others? And when you find them, what then? Do you know that restless lonesomeness Bob has?

This boredom (or "restlessness" or "lonesomeness" — it has many names) sometimes is pointed to as characteristic of our culture. It is, however, a characteristic of many *people,* and *not* a characteristic of this civilization. It is not the inevitable fate of people born into this or any other society.

How can you avoid having a life like Bob's? (Incidentally, this condition is not improved by merely getting older!) One of the best ways is that suggested in the heading of this section: Develop wide and deep interests. This does not mean, of course, that you should abandon your current interests. Quite the contrary! Keep those, and develop them; but build new ones in addition. Establish the habit of continuously widening and deepening your interests.

A variety of deep interests does not inevitably result from going to college and the university; nor from traveling; nor from any other set of experiences. Neither are we given these by other people, not even professors — no matter how imperiously we demand that they make things interesting. Interesting experiences result when we have deep interests; and possessing deep interests results from our own efforts — from living in certain ways.

Live with intense eagerness for finding out about the world. When reading a text, for example, try to discover from it as much as possible about the nature of the world with which it deals — whether or not you suspect any of this will appear on a later test. When listening to a lecture, be alert for new facts and ideas. When riding on the subway or trolley, idly eavesdropping, try to gain new insights into how others think and feel.

Try observing more closely everything about you. What you learn in school can give you a wealth of clues to new aspects of the world worth watching and examining. Relate what you discover at any particular time to the rest of your life.

Be alive to beauties and little joys.

"If those who seek happiness would only stop one little minute and think, they would see that the delights they really experience are as countless as the grasses at their feet or the dewdrops sparkling upon the morning flowers. . . . It would be wonderful to find myself free from even a small part of my physical limitations . . . to walk around town alone . . . to come and go without a word to anyone . . . to read the newspapers without waiting, and pick out a pretty handkerchief or a becoming hat in the shops. . . . I feel fortunate indeed that it has been possible for me to enjoy sculpture, poetry, happy make-believe in bleak corners of my limitations."—Keller[30]

This gratitude and alert awareness are part of "the miracle of Helen Keller,"[2] blind and deaf from the age of two and yet a person whose life "defies the notion that man is a passive automaton whose sole purpose is to reduce tension by adaptive responses to threatening environmental changes."[2] *Your* life can be richer too. Life is not drab to one fully awake.

Share other people's interests with them — especially when their interests differ from your own (i.e., from those you already have). Besides possibly making a new friend, sharing another person's interests may open up a whole new world to you. That prospect alone is enough for many of us to approach each new face with eager anticipation.

But, you may ask, how does one go about sharing another person's life? If you follow two simple rules you should have no trouble: First, pay attention to the other person when he or she is telling you someting. That sounds simple, but you would be surprised at the number of people who look away when someone else is speaking (even when they are interested in the topic) or who lean back, fold their arms, stretch, and in other ways unintentionally give the impression they are bored. Some people do not listen at all, but merely wait for the other person to stop talking so they can start.

A second point is to listen actively, to form and ask questions about the person's interests. You will find the benefits twofold: You will discover more about another person and his interests; and you also will find yourself growing more interested in the topic as you think and ask questions about it.

The more actively you participate in life around you, the more you enjoy that life. Life becomes interesting and exciting.

Welcome topics falling outside your old interests. Often we say, "That subject doesn't interest me at all"; then we ignore the subject or look into it only grudgingly. Such an approach militates against new interests. New interests grow and flower only when we explore beyond our current confines.

Common today is an invidious misconception: When we know much, things lose their charm. But knowledge kills no charms. In fact, quite the opposite is true. *The more you know about something, the more fascinating it becomes.*

The more you know about botany, for instance, the more interesting botany becomes and the more interesting also the world becomes. Flowers retain all their old charm, while acquiring for you new beauty and new interest. You see parts you may never have seen before — the varied intricacies of veins in petals and leaves; the fragile beauty of little blossoms in the center of composite flowers, such as daisies, sunflowers, and cosmos; the intriguing array of pistils and stamens. You notice relationships between parts and their functions and begin to see the marvel of how life is sustained. You look at a flower and behold a whole new world of almost magical beauty.

Or you study astronomy — and the night sky, glorious when one knows nothing about it, becomes yet more glorious, marvelously fascinating. No longer do you see merely a jumble of faint lights. You see now the soft rose of Mars, the radiance of Jupiter, the glimmering whiteness from dwarf stars, thousands of times heavier than lead. You note the pulsing shimmer from some far-away star, a light now ending its journey of ten thousand years, or even more. You see a pinpoint of light and know it to be not one star, but an unfathomed swirling array of stars, comprising a vast galaxy clear outside our own. This is another world.

Fear not. You can know incalculable amounts about an area and still its charms endure. Far from being tarnished, they are enhanced by deepening knowledge.[41] (The contrary notion is, we suspect, only a rationalization, a wobbly justification for intellectual loafing or a defense for one's *status quo*.).

Go out to meet your world. Discover as much as you can about everything you meet. Avoid insulations between you and life — the obvious physical, psychological, and social ones, but also the subtle insulations such as drugs. Live each hour with verve, a wide-awake perceptiveness, an eagerness to discover and learn and grow. No better way exists for avoiding later boredom and discontent. No route makes current years more deeply joyous.

5. You Can Develop an Increasing Love for All the Arts.

Sculpture, paintings, free verse, sonnets, novels, essays, interior decoration, food combinations, theories — new worlds wait your discovery. You can use these years to explore them, and more.

In our universities and colleges, there are music courses and musicians — symphony orchestras, marching bands, symphonic bands, choruses, choirs, glee clubs, opportunities to learn to play any of several instruments, individual lessons and group lessons. There are many kinds of art courses and artists, science courses and scientists, athletic programs and skilled athletes. There are architecture and clothes designing and on and on, worlds without end.

Everything (almost) our peculiar species can do which creates beauty, or knowledge, you will find offered at our universities and colleges. These are fascinating worlds. The opportunity is yours to learn about them and become able better to appreciate and delight in them — new joys for now and in the years of life ahead.

One world you are certain to touch is that of books. Have you considered the nature of books? Their magic is one boon available to all men. But few can accept it. A modern tragedy is that many persons, far from learning to appreciate books, actually learn to abhor them.

This is tragic, because books are more than useful tools, far more. They hold keys to other worlds, opening the way to exciting new realms of experience. They can be wondrously enlightening and stimulating, deliciously amusing, deeply refreshing. But all this has been better expressed (in books) by some of the world's most gifted men. Let us listen to them for a moment.

"The world of books is the most remarkable creation of man. Nothing else that he builds ever lasts. Monuments fall, nations perish, civilizations grow old and die out; and, after an era of darkness, new 'races' build others. But in the world of books are volumes that have seen this happen again and again, and yet live on, still young, still as fresh as the day they were written, still telling men's hearts of the hearts of men centuries dead."[8]

"All that mankind has done, thought, gained or been: It is in magic preservation in the pages of books." So Carlyle speaks, across the miles and years, to us.

Mark Twain provocatively reminds us: "The man who does not read good books has no advantage over the man who can't read them."

As you doubtless have observed, what people are like to you depends largely upon you and your interactions with them. As with people, so it is with books: What any book is like to you depends rather more upon you than upon it. When we pick up a book with the half-verbalized set, "I dare you to tell me

anything sensible" or "I dare you to amuse me," we will find
that book dull. One gets nowhere that way. Suppose on the
other hand, we turn to a book asking, "I wonder what new
ideas I can create with the help of this man and his book?" Or,
"I wonder how this person has analyzed that problem?" Or,
"What neat expressions will I discover here?" With such an
approach any book becomes provocative and enlightening.

To find books interesting and worth reading, we must meet
them half way, or even more than half way. We must read as a
collaborator with the author — not as an antagonist, nor yet as
a receptacle!

The same point holds for music, for paintings, for practically all aspects of the world. *How* to meet artists half way,
how to collaborate with them, these you can learn.

In universities and colleges you are certain to meet students and professors who deeply enjoy various forms of
beauty. Usually they will be eager to give you leads on how you
too can derive deeper appreciation and enjoyment from those
aspects of the world.

Our worlds are filled with many sorts of beauty, could we
but see them. You can go to college in such a way that you
discover these new realms and learn to love them.

6. You Can Actualize Your Creativity.

Many of us never realize our potential creativity because
we have the mistaken notion that creativity is the domain of a
few gifted geniuses; so we do not try. Furthermore, we have
been led to believe that whatever creative potential we might
have had was quashed by an unresponsive school system; and
so we do not try. There is also the rumor that creativity and
genius carry with them the shadow of madness, and so we do
not try. Such reactions are unfortunate for there is evidence
that each of us is capable of great feats of creativity.[48] You,
indeed, have performed creative feats countless times. Consider the following.

To create is to generate new syntheses or insights, new
understanding about ourselves and the world around us. Thus,
learning is a creative act. Each time you learn something new,
each time you come to understand a little better, you perform
an act of creation.

Creativity is a process whereby the unusual, the unexpected, and the strange are made comprehensible. The painter, the
dancer, the sculptor who, through their art, help us to under-

stand better some aspect of the human condition perform thereby a creative act. The biologist, astronomer, ecologist, philosopher who, through their science, help us to better understand reality also perform creative acts.

In order for each of us to gain through experience, to learn and to mature, we must create personal meaning for what happens to us. To translate experience into knowledge, you must create.

The major differences between your daily creativity and the creativity of the renowned scientist, scholar, and artist is one of scale: Our personal creativity results in small new insights just for us while theirs may result in huge new understanding for all of us. That difference in scale need not inhibit you but should inspire you to examine the process of creativity so you can use your creativity with added precision and success.

How do persons with extraordinary innovation go about attacking and solving problems? One of their most obvious traits is persistence: No matter what their profession, occupation, or mode of expression, they are enduring and uncommonly hard workers.[35] Many work on a single problem for years before achieving a breakthrough (and sometimes they never achieve the breakthrough). Besides being tenacious, they are independent, self-sufficient, hopeful;[15] they are optimistic a solution can be found.[15] These traits are absolutely essential, for when you propose new ways of seeing, doing, and thinking you must be prepared to go against the many who are content with the way things are.

Curiosity is associated with creativity. The nature of this curiosity was clarified recently, through prolonged study of creative artists. We learn that the most successful are those who spend the most time and energy searching for problems.[15] That makes a lot of sense, in hindsight, for the quality of the question determines (in large part) the quality of the answer. Curiosity can not be passive if it is to be productive and lead to a creative life; our curiousity must be an active, problem-seeking, problem-welcoming approach to life.

A creative process has several stages. It begins with recognition or feeling that something is not right. The creative person takes this as a cue to jump in and try to clarify and define the problem.[15] A noncreative person turns in the other direction and flees, for he finds uncertainty and the ambiguity associated with problems quite unpleasant; he does his best to avoid that feeling of instability. A potentially creative individual must realize several things: that the ambiguity must be tolerated, and that any effort to clarify and define a problem ultimately saves time, resulting in less total time spent on the problem.[15] The preparation stage sets the stage for completing the act of creativity.

Once you are pretty sure you have a good understanding of the problem, you need to start coming up with possible solutions. We have not discovered yet the key to unlocking the source of these ideas, but we do know how to help the process along a little. Whereas you were being analytical and systematic while trying to clarify the dimensions of the problem, you now must be noncritical, spontaneous when you want ideas to flow. Let go, relax, and allow your imagination a free rein. Accounts abound of creative people who struggled with a problem long and hard, then forgot about their problem, relaxed, even went on vacation, and a solution popped into the person's head.

Creativity does not stop with the imagination stage. You must take your potential solution and try it out; the solution may look good and yet in trying it out, you find you misunderstood the problem. It is imperative, therefore, that you always test your ideas to see if they do solve your problem.

To be creative is within your capability. It requires a few preliminaries like courage and independence so you are not deterred unduly by the laughter of your friends and others. It requires a commitment to hard, persistent, systematic work. It also requires an ability to shift from an analytical, critical style of thought to a spontaneous, imaginative style. Others, with no greater potential than you, have developed their creativity to provide a more interesting and meaningful life for themselves and for others. You can have that kind of life.

7. You Can Grow in Compassion and Understanding of All Other People.

Compassion and understanding of each other are two most distinctively human potentialities. Probably you value those qualities in their own right. In addition, they lead toward other cherished goals: They enable you to live more joyously and more harmoniously with your fellow men; and also (delightful result) they enable you to be more at peace with yourself. Deep compassion and a real understanding of many other individuals almost preclude extensive dictatorships, and are prerequisite to a true democracy.

Writings by Keefe,[29] C. S. Lewis,[32, 33] and Albert

Schweitzer[46] illumine beautifully the nature of compassion, what it is and is not, what difference compassion and understanding make.

Studying psychology can help you learn to understand people better, see more clearly their problems, their limitations, and their assets. So also can philosophy, economics, business administration, sociology, anthropology, physiology, zoology, neurology, geography, political science, literature, art, and history. All of these and others too can help you understand people better. They can, that is, if you study these areas partly in an effort to gain deeper insights into the nature of your fellow men, their actions, dreams, and problems — and their achievements. These are far more remarkable than is commonly realized.

Extraordinary achievements are the result not merely of great talent, as is almost invariably assumed, but of extraordinary effort, devotion, and a willingness to work extremely hard.[6, 7, 47] Edison notified us long ago that genius is 99 per cent hard work, 1 per cent talent. Alexander Dumas pointed out: "I achieve the impossible working as none else ever works. . . ." Michelangelo remarked: "If people only knew how hard I work to gain my mastery, it wouldn't seem so wonderful at all." (To some, of course, it would seem more wonderful.)

Accounts by individuals sketching how they manage to paint, or write, or carry out illuminating research, how they manage to beautifully re-create music, to invent, or to live in any other way with grace and creative skill, make clear these are unspeakably difficult human feats when done superbly. They are triumphs of the human spirit.

Creative endeavors of all kinds are remarkable human feats. Recently we have acquired invaluable information concerning creativity — what creativity involves,[9-11, 14-18] what the creative person does,[36-42] what these individuals are like.[24-26, 31] We can understand better these people, and those parts of ourselves.

In the university and college you not only will study about such people, you will meet many such individuals and can talk with them; you can learn first-hand to understand them, and what they are achieving. You will meet many different sorts of persons, with different skills, different information, different kinds of abilities, different kinds of achievements. You could develop better understanding of all these richly varied persons, and what they are doing.

Further, by understanding what those people are trying to do and by developing insight into how they are attempting to accomplish their goals, you too can become more creative in your work and in your personal life.

8. You Can Gain New Appreciation of Individual Differences.

The capacity to appreciate persons different from ourselves is not identical with compassion and understanding. Nor is it faintly synonymous with toleration. Valuing individual differences goes far beyond the blandly tolerating "live and let live" philosophy.

When this is developed to a high degree, we appreciate the worth of each human being, we recognize the uniqueness of individuals, and (crucially important) we consider this uniqueness outstandingly precious. Instead of merely tolerating differences in people, we value these differences; we strive to maintain and encourage at least some aspects of the uniqueness of individuals. This is rare — even in our society — and is of great worth.

To understand deeply the worth of "valuing individual differences," we should have to study the natures of democracy and autocracy, and study also their importance. We cannot do that in this little book, but in many of your college courses you will have opportunities to examine these matters. Let us glance, however, at some of the repercussions in your world when people fail to value individual differences.

Don is a college student. He enjoys the writings of Molière, Proust, and Shakespeare. He appreciates the artistry of Shostakovich and Cézanne. Almost certainly Don will be labeled an intellectual and, in less happy times, "egg head," "un-American," "pointy head."

David writes poetry which to him is beautiful and a joy to write. Some other people too find in it new and unique beauties. However, since his writing meets the unfulfilled needs of only a minority, it is often labeled "silly" and "highbrow."

Joan wants to be a mechanical engineer — a dream laughed at by most of her friends and associates. Even her parents regard this as wholly unsuitable.

Nancy intends to be a research chemist. People are appalled. Both girls are excellent in math, delight in detail, and have amply the other qualities needed for their preferred vocations. Nonetheless, pressure is put on Joan and Nancy to do something "more appropriate."

It isn't just the young who have problems with conventions. Professor B is trying to introduce a new course. It is a course which perhaps only one person of a hundred deeply needs in order to better utilize certain prized capacities. The welfare of thousands of people may be enhanced if that 1 per cent can develop their potentialities as fully as possible. Yet for introducing this course, Professor B is labeled "undemocratic" and "out of touch with reality." (Alice, of course, was deemed wholly mad by the Queen of Hearts and her entourage; but that was in Wonderland.)

These labelers would maintain that they themselves are strongly democratic. But are they really? Whitman wrote a haunting lament: "Democracy, the destin'd conqueror, yet treacherous lipsmiles everywhere, And death and infidelity at every step."[54] That is a poetic exaggeration; treacherous lipsmiles are not everywhere. Yet episodes like those in the paragraphs above do occur many times each day. And who, in such cases, is undemocratic? Is it really the labeled? Or is it the labelers?

The foregoing examples illustrate the opposite of valuing individual differences. In each case, the labelers fail to value individual characteristics. Further, they scoff at individual differences, attaching to them all manner of opprobrious adjectives. They try to make individuals conform to one pattern, their pattern. Consciously or unconsciously, they work toward making people into carbon copies of each other. Converting people into carbon copies appears outstandingly characteristic of various Communist societies, of Hitler's Germany, of all authoritarian regimes.

The essence of democracy, on the other hand, consists in part of a recognition of individual differences, a high evaluation of many of these differences, and actions in accord with this recognition and evaluation. Without these, all shreds of democracy die. With them, democracy can grow.

Valuing individual differences also makes it possible for you to be you. Suppose differences in people were minimized. Suppose everyone actually did conform to a comprehensive set of standards. Then, whether the standard for conformity was that of the current majority, or your own standard, or any other, *you* would not exist. You would be indistinguishable from everyone else. You, and all people, would be individuals only in the sense that oranges are individuals — they occupy different positions in time and space.

Were there few individual differences, life would be horribly boring. Can you imagine what that world would be like? Suppose there were a world with people as much alike as so many ants in a hill. Even if all the ants were like *any one of us*, would not life be infinitely monotonous?

You help create the social climate. If you value the results of there being many individual differences, and dislike the opposed results, it behooves you to develop your own appreciation for such differences and to actively encourage these differences. Your associates, in turn, can more readily appreciate individual differences when you do so. College work will furnish you many opportunities for perceiving the value of difference, and learning to act in accord with these perceptions. But here again, you must be alert for these opportunities to profit from them.

9. You Can Learn New Skills in Thinking.

Skill in thinking does not inevitably appear merely because you were born with that potentiality. Much practice is required in order to develop clear thinking.

Nor are you doomed forever to sloppy thinking merely because currently you are maladroit. Thinking can be impaired; and thinking can be improved.[34, 43, 52]

Unique opportunities to practice these skills are furnished in college. While studying, for example, or listening to a lecture, or participating in a discussion, you could practice the skills which comprise clear thinking: skill in analyzing data and formulating a variety of alternative interpretations for the data; skill in evaluating hypotheses and devising sounder modifications of them; skill in identifying pitfalls in thinking; skill in avoiding these pitfalls; skill in seeing what leads to what. You could learn to doubt honestly and without fear. You could learn to ask pertinent questions of yourself and to derive your own answers.

Through practicing and developing these skills, you free yourself from having to rely so heavily upon other people's thinking (skillful or otherwise). You free yourself from being harnessed to their conclusions, when you are able to form your own conclusions with soundness and swiftness. You become a remarkably adept thinker.

10. You Can Grow in Responsibility for Your Own Life.

To what extent do you rely on others' thinking and delegate responsibility to them? If you watch yourself and your own living, you may be quite enlightened by what you find. Note the variety of situations in which you wait for someone to tell you what to do and how to do it and insist upon having detailed instructions. When trying, for example, to decide upon a vocation, or to devise ways to study, or to smooth out difficulties in interpersonal relations, how often do you seek directions from others, instead of figuring these things out for yourself? Do not include here the times you seek information or collaboration, a pooling of skills. Include only the times you seek *conclusions,* asking that the decisions be made for you.

Sometimes we even seek solutions to personal problems, and then seek advice as to the proper choice among the conflicting recommendations. We may go so far as to assume it is the advisers' "fault" when things work out poorly for us — although we are the ones responsible for turning that part of our life over to them.

How we depend upon others even for our opinions; sometimes to an incredible degree. In this connection, there are many little investigations you could conduct. For example: In conversation, watch for such phrases as "Well, Dr. So-and-So said...," "My wife read...," or "Walter Cronkite said...," and then note how often such statements are made *in place of* formulating any opinion of one's own or are made in order to "prove" some contention. "I read it in the newspaper." "I saw it on T.V." Ipso facto, truth; no need to think.

Our position often is not as different as we like to imagine from that of a dependent child. We have merely switched, and added, parents. We have adopted new authorities to do our thinking for us.

Like children, too, we want something but do not want the inseparable correlates of the something. Do we want liberty? But shrink from the correlated obligation of making our own decisions? Do we want the right to vote? But do not want to bother about getting pertinent information and thinking about it? Often we want the pleasures and privileges of being free adults, but fail to develop the skills requisite for that freedom.

We want to live our own lives, pursue our own goals, make our own decisions, but neglect the necessary skills of accepting responsibility and thinking clearly.

Insofar as we lack skills in thinking and in accepting responsibility, we have but two choices when facing a problem: We can trust to luck and fate. (You know how that alternative works out.) Or we can ask for instuctions, waiting for others to tell us what to do and how to do it. These "others" may be clumsy thinkers too; they may be as poorly informed as we — or more so; they may know little about us and care little or nothing about our problem; but accept their advice and conclusions we must. We must accept their statements and interpretations for the simple reason that we have no other choice, unless we have learned the skills necessary for making our own decisions. Dismally oppressive though dictators may be, they would be indispensable — in private life and public.

To develop skill in being responsible requires continuing sustained practice. But to the extent you succeed, you become more fully human. You become more autonomous, freer.[4, 45] You can solve your problems more satisfactorily. You no longer need wait (often in vain) for someone else to tell you what to do. You will become increasingly adept in weighing the factors important to *you* and making your own decisions. You will develop a new ability to work independently, on your own initiative. You could even live your own life and have real freedom.

11. You Can Develop Qualities Fitting You Better for Many Occupations.

You need not choose among the ten qualities set forth above. They fit together and coexist in harmony. Further, they all can be developed simultaneously.

At first glance some of the ten may seem frills. They may seem conducive mainly (or only) to a fuller, richer life. Each does contribute toward those ends. But that is not all. Each objective also serves sound practical purposes as well.

Each of the ten contributes toward equipping you better for a large array of vocational objectives and a large array too of other occupations.

As an example, let us look at the fourth quality mentioned: "You can build deeper, widening interests." How does that help equip you for any job? Offhand, it seems a luxury, whipped cream on the cake. It does give life zest (and that has practical side effects); but additionally, wide interests have other noteworthy practical advantages.

Every fact you learn ties in with somebody's vivid interests. No matter how trivial the fact or how remote from everyday events, it will have bearing on somebody's hobbies and curiosities. Thus the more you learn about everything, the better your chances of knowing something about anything of interest to anybody you meet in the years ahead. If the 'some-body' happens to be your boss and he or she has come to dinner, clearly it would be convenient if you could let him take the lead and choose topics of conversation of interest to him, with you and your spouse being able to join him wherever he chose to go, joining with sensible, knowledgeable remarks and understanding listening. An evening with such conversation is one way to ensure that your boss has a delightful and delighted few hours in your company. This can help get promotions and smooth out other difficulties — handy in any job.

Or suppose you are a foreman. Or an ambassador. Or a contractor. A broker, impresario, agent for an artist. Or a diplomat, or statesman, or personnel manager, or politician. All of these jobs involve interacting with people on a one-to-one basis. Albeit the jobs differ in many ways, each of them entails talking to individuals on an individual basis part of the time. Such interactions are facilitated greatly if you can find a relatively lighthearted area to talk about, or some matter of mutual concern not directly job-connected. You can establish rapport and start a friendship, and then turn to business. This enhances the chances for succes on the strictly business part.

Consider any job in which other persons are prospective clients or customers — for example, being a nurse, doctor, lawyer, receptionist, salesperson, dentist, real estate or insurance agent. If you can put the other person at ease, he is more apt to come to you again. One way to put a person at ease is to know what he is talking about if he happens to bring up his interests. You may be surprised how reassuring this is, and how welcome. To talk even a bit about what he cares about can warm his outlook toward you and what else you have to offer.

Sharing a person's interests (albeit quietly and not necessarily overtly) is nearly indispensable for being able to understand that person in depth and comprehend well his circumstances and conditions. In some jobs, such as the medical professions, understanding is needed to help the client most effectively. This does not mean you participate in the activity with the client. It does mean that you know what his interests entail, not merely what they are.

Another aspect: In construction work, clerical jobs, teaching, typing, dental hygiene, in almost every job, there are coffee breaks or lunch hours. You can spend the break talking about the job, and many people do. This gets mighty dull and tedious. You become satiated with work and really want to get away from it all at least for fifteen minutes — or forever. If you can share your fellow workers' other interests, really knowing what they are talking about so you can listen appreciatively and communicate easily, coffee breaks become truly refreshing. Relations with your colleagues are bound to improve — become warmer, more tranquil, and fun. And your hours on the job go by more productively and pleasantly.

Consider the part of your life not spent on the job. Consider being a neighbor. Clearly, you can have happier relations with neighbors if you can share their enthusiasms and concerns. Consider being a friend. Again, you can have deeper, happier relationships and more variety when you have more various interests. You also can be more helpful. When friends tell you about some problem they are having, you will know what it is all about. If they ask your advice, you might have some worth profferring.

If you have wide enough interests, it is likely that for almost everybody you meet, at least one of their interests will be one of yours. At parties and neighborhood get-togethers, you will have far more to talk about than just your jobs, the children, or gossip. You can share their vivid enthusiasms.

Suppose you have a husband or wife. Here too you can share more of your life when you have multifaceted interests. You also can have fuller understanding and appreciation of each other. If you concentrate on one interest only, a job and one hobby, or no hobbies at all, clearly you will be lonely. No matter how many people are around and how many interests each of them has, you will have little or nothing to share with them. You can listen to them, but their conversation will mean little. You can talk, but your talk will be drab.

Are you a parent? Do you intend to have children? An oft-heard cry from all ages: They don't understand me. One way to become more understanding is to develop wide interests: Learn participating together in many kinds of areas and participate in many kinds of activities. Participating together in a variety of enjoyed, healthy activities shows you new dimensions in each other; making the other person more interesting to you and you to them. Happy times are created, closeness, trust.

You may also become more understanding when you learn in many areas. The more you learn, the better your chances of being able to answer your tots' questions, and the questions of older offspring too. The more you learn, the wider your interests become and the more richness and depth you bring to later activities, walks in the woods, leaf-pressing, tide-pool searches, trips to museums.

So we see that developing wide interests is no mere luxury, nor important just for the sake of a more colorful life and self-actualization. Building wide and widening interests turns out to be a highly practical matter contributing much to more perfect fulfillment of a wide variety of daily interactions.

This same kind of analysis can be made for each of the qualities presented in this chapter. Each quality helps fit you better not merely for one vocation but for many vocations and many occupations. And not only that: each quality prepares you also for a life of greater beauty.

12. In Sum, You Can Earn a Better Life.

Nameless longings, vague discontents haunt some lives. You know this. You witness daily strife erupt from bitter misunderstanding. You see cynicism, lostness, a sense of futility wreck human living.

"There is a more excellent way!" Jesse Jackson reminds us. You can follow it. By putting together the eleven qualities discussed in this chapter, yours can be a different life.

Your world can be a fascinating place of challenging experiences and new delights. Through your college work and ways of living, you can develop new sensitivity to beauty in all of its many forms. You can build such a breadth and depth of interests that no hour could fail to touch some of them. You can learn the thrill of discovery and of creativity. Fresh worlds would open.

You can develop new skill in coping with your world. You can learn to think with greater clarity and speed. You can gain greater abilities to apply information, to see new relationships, to judge the reasonableness of arguments, and to solve myriad problems. You can build a more complete fund of concepts, facts, and ideas with which to comprehend your world, your fellow men, and yourself.

Your interpersonal relationships can have new peace and joyousness, based firmly upon these more complete understandings and a deepening, genuine sympathy which make life a joy to you and you a joy to others.

New skills in living and a new enthusiasm for life can be yours. You can earn a good life — whatever your job may be.

These things can happen. Note, though, university and college guarantee no such personal development.

Universities and colleges furnish opportunities. The best imaginable can do no more. What will be your responses? Your responses determine the result.

D. A NEW SPIRIT

No college or university can give one an education. Becoming educated does not follow inevitably from anything done by anybody else. Becoming educated depends upon you and what you do. Education is an on-going process, and the result of that process, built day by day through the way you live.

Theodore Roosevelt once remarked, "What I am to be, I am now becoming." That is true for you too. What sort of person you will be is influenced by every response you currently make. What you are like on Graduation Day depends upon all the habits you practice now: the way you study, and how much; the way you listen; the way you read, take tests, participate in other activities; the way you respond to your colleagues; in brief, the way you live each hour. And how you do all these depends in part upon the clarity with which you identify your own objectives, and the constancy with which you practice the skills comprising these goals.

These facts will appall many people, and by some will be rejected as sheer nonsense — for there are people who, because of their own inner make-up, must believe that events are due mainly to other people and their actions.

Actually, it is a happy circumstance that the outcome of college rests upon you. It means your life is in your hands. You need not trust in luck; nor even in other people's generosity, skill, and wisdom. They do not determine whether you become highly educated nor what sort of life you have. You do.

The next chapter shows ways you can attain some dreamed-of goals, becoming more truly an educated person.

BIBLIOGRAPHY FOR CHAPTER 1

1. Amer. Assoc. Univ. Professors. Faculty lose ground economically. Academe, 9, 6–7, 1975.
2. Anon. Helen Keller (1880–1968). J. Amer. Med. Assoc., 205, 584, 1968.
3. Anon. Business is opening doors to more liberal arts graduates. World of Work Rep., 2, 141–143, 1977. Also in Career Devel. Rev., 1, 37, 1978.
4. Bar-Tal, Daniel; and Bar-Zohar, Yaakov. The relationship between perception of locus of control and academic achievement. Contemp. Educ. Psychol., 2, 181–199, 1977.
5. Cappeto, Michael A. Liberal arts vs. business administration. J. Coll. Placement, 37–39, Fall, 1977.

6. Chambers, J. A. Relating personality and biographical factors to scientific creativity. Psychol. Monogr.: Gen. and Applied, 78, #584, 1964.

7. Chambers, J. A. Creative scientists of today. Science, 145, 1203–1205, 1964.

8. Day, Clarence. The Story of the Yale University Press Told by a Friend. New Haven, Conn.: Yale Univ. Press, 1920.

9. Dentler, R. A.; and Mackler, B. Originality: Some social and personal determinants. Behav. Sci., 9, 1–7, 1964.

10. Dreistadt, Roy. The use of analogies and incubation in obtaining insights in creative problem solving. J. Psychol., 71, 159–175, 1969.

11. Eisenman, Russell. Creativity, awareness, and liking. J. Consulting Clin. Psychol., 33, 157–160, 1969.

12. Fowler, Elizabeth M. Business retraining of Ph.D.'s. New York Times, page D-15, July 26, 1978.

13. Gallup, George. Teens believe college is good investment. The Daily Californian, page 5A, August 30, 1978.

14. Gershon, A.; Guilford, J. P.; and Merrifield, P. R. Figural and symbolic divergent-production abilities in adolescent and adult populations. Rep. Psychol. Lab., Univ. Southern California, No. 29, 1963.

15. Getzels, J. W.; and Csikszentmihalyi, M. The Creative Vision. New York: John Wiley and Sons, 1976.

16. Gibson, James W.; Kibler, Robert J.; and Barker, Larry L. Some relationships between selected creativity and critical thinking measures. Psychol. Reports, 23, 707–714, 1968.

17. Guilford, J. P. Factors that aid and hinder creativity. Teachers Coll. Rec., 63, 380–392, 1962.

18. Guilford, J. P.; Merrifield, P. R.; Christensen, P. R.; and Frick, J. W. Some new symbolic factors of cognition and convergent production. Educ. Psychol. Measmt., 21, 515–541, 1961.

19. Gulick, Sidney L. Consider the long view: A square report. Invited Address, San Diego State College Chapter of Phi Kappa Phi, (mimeo.), 1969.

20. Handler, Philip. Women scientists: steps in the right direction. The Sciences, 18, 6–9, 1978.

21. Heath, Douglas H. Growing up in College. San Francisco: Josey-Bass, Inc., 1968.

22. Heath, Douglas H. Prescription for collegiate survival: Return to liberally educate today's youth. Liberal Educ., 43, 338–350, 1977a.

23. Heath, Douglas H. Academic predictors of adult maturity and competence. J. Higher Educ., 48, 613–632, 1977b.

24. Hoffman, L. Richard. Conditions for creative problem solving. J. Psychol., 52, 429–444, 1961.

25. Houston, J. P.; and Mednick, S. A. Creativity and the need for novelty. J. Abnorm. Soc. Psychol., 66, 137–141, 1963.

26. Israeli, Nathan. Creative art: A self-observation study. J. Gen. Psychol., 66, 33–45, 1962.

27. Johansson, C. B.: and Rossman, J. E. Persistence at a liberal arts college: A replicated five-year longitudinal study. J. Counseling Psychol., 20, 1–9, 1973.

28. Kamens, D. H. The college "charter" and college size: Effects on occupational choice and college attrition. Sociology Educ., 44, 270–296, 1971.

29. Keefe, Carolyn (Ed.) C. S. Lewis: Speaker and Teacher. Grand Rapids, Mich.: Zondervan Publishing House, 1971.

30. Keller, Helen. The Faith of Helen Keller. Kansas City, Mo.: Hallmark, pp. 20 and 24, 1967.

31. Krop, Harry. Effects of extrinsic motivation, intrinsic motivation, and intelligence on creativity: A factorial approach. J. General Psychol., 80, 259–266. 1969.

32. Lewis, C. S. The Four Loves. New York: Harcourt Brace Jovanovich, Inc., 1960. Also, The Great Divorce. New York: Macmillan Company, 1946, 16th printing, 1970.

33. Lewis, C. S. God in the Dock. Grand Rapids, Mich.: Eerdmans, 1970.

34. Lyle, Edwin. An exploration in the teaching of critical thinking in general psychology, J. Educ. Res., 52, 129–133, 1958.

35. Maddi, S. R. The strenuousness of the creative life. In Taylor, I. A.: and Getzels. J. W. (Eds.) Perspectives in Creativity. Chicago: Aldine Publishing Co., 1975.

36. Maier, Norman R.; and Burke, Ronald J. Studies in creativity: II. Influence of motivation in the reorganization of experience. Psychol. Reports, 23, 351–361, 1968.
37. Maier, Norman R.; Thurber, James A.; and Janzen, Junie C. Studies in creativity: V. The selection process in recall and in problem-solving situations. Psychol. Reports, 23, 1003–1022, 1968.
38. Marks, E. Student perceptions of college persistence, and their intellective, personality and performance correlates. J. Educ. Psychol., 58, 210–221, 1967.
39. Mednick, M. T. Research creativity in psychology graduate students. J. Consult. Psychol., 27, 265–266, 1963.
40. Mednick, M. T.; Mednick, S. A.; and Jung, C. C. Continual association as a function of level of creativity and type of verbal stimulus. J. Abnorm. Soc. Psychol., 69, 511–515, 1964.
41. Meltzer, Herbert L. The unexpected. The Sciences, 18, 12–13, 1978.
42. Merrifield, P. R.: Guilford, J. P.; Christensen, P. R.; and Frick, J. W. The role of intellectual factors in problem solving. Psychol. Monogr., 76, No. 529, 1962.
43. Murphy, Gardner. Creativeness. Menninger Quart., 11, 1–6, 1957.
44. Pantages, Timothy J.; and Creedon, Carol F. Studies of college attrition: 1950–1975. Review Educ. Res., 48, 49–101, 1978.
45. Riesman, D. The Lonely Crowd. New Haven: Yale University Press, 1950.
46. Schweitzer, Albert. The Teaching of Reverence for Life. (Translated from the German by Richard and Clara Winston.) New York: Holt, Rinehart and Winston, 1965.
47. Taylor, C. W.; and Ellison, R. L. Biographical predictors of scientific performance. Science, 155, 1075–1080, 1967.
48. Taylor, Calvin W.; and Ellison, Robert L. Moving toward working models in creativity: Utah creativity experiences and insights. In Taylor, Irving A.; and Getzels, J. W. (Eds.) Perspectives in Creativity. Chicago: Aldine Publishing Co., 1975.
49. Tinto, V. Dropouts from higher education. Rev. Educ. Res., 45, 89–125, 1975.
50. United States Departments Commerce, Labor. In the professions, women are moving up. U. S. News and World Report, 85, 59–61, Sept. 4, 1978.
51. United States Department of Labor. Women haven't closed gap with men in earnings, jobs. The Daily Californian, page 5A, Sept. 14, 1978.
52. Voss, James F. (Ed.) Approaches to Thought. Columbus, Ohio: Charles E. Merrill Publishing Co., 1969.
53. Wells, H. G. Babes in the Darkling Wood. New York: Alliance Book Corporation, 1940, pp. 196–197.
54. Whitman, Walt, Leaves of Grass. New York: Doubleday & Co., Inc., 1924.

Daylight is best . . .

Chapter 2

Learning More — Outside Class

A. A PLAN OF ACTION

To use more fully and beneficially our inner resources — those are major objectives. But how can we achieve them? "Most of us feel as if we live habitually with a sort of cloud weighing on us, below our highest notch of clearness in discernment, sureness in reasoning, or firmness in deciding. Compared with what we ought to be, we are only half awake. Our fires are damped, our drafts are checked, we are making use of only a small part of our possible mental and physical resources." — William James.[37]

How can you more nearly live up to your capacities? How can you prepare a fuller life, laying the groundwork for a more joyous and satisfying adulthood? How can you even raise your grades?

Psychologists and educators studied these problems. They examined the procedures used by successful students and neglected by unsuccessful ones. They investigated the pronounced changes occurring when "unsuccessful" students started practicing some of these techniques and procedures and developed new study habits. Results from that research and from the extensive experimental work in learning are offered here for your use.

These are ways you can make fuller use of your resources, develop your present abilities, and ultimately become more nearly the person you long to be. They are
ways of profiting more from the university and college —
both in terms of becoming a more educated person and in
terms of making higher grades.

A warning: The actions itemized below cannot be
achieved simply by resolving to do so. This disheartens
many a student. When good resolutions do not lead to immediate success, we conclude erroneously we are "stupid,"
incapable of doing what we resolve, or else that the suggested methods are worthless. Then we give up. That pitfall
must be avoided.

Being unsuccessful in your first several attempts does
not mean you are stupid. It means only this: To learn to
study effectively, one must develop complicated skills;[24]
and to develop any skill requires action and considerable
practice — in addition to firm resolutions.

To help you start, the numbered headings list various
ways of studying more effectively. Under each heading are
suggestions for how to develop the habit stated in the heading. These actions enable you simultaneously to make high
grades and become a more educated person.

B. WHY STUDY?

1. By Knowing Your Goals, You Reach Your Goals Better.

Before the question "How should I study?" you should
answer another question: "Why should I study? Toward
what ends?"

Reaching any goal is facilitated by knowing clearly
what you are trying to do. Chapter 1 discusses the point.
We mentioned it again to remind you: This is the place to
start.

The first step in studying more productively is to formulate your goals. If you skipped Chapter 1, please go back
to it and read it now. When you know why you are studying, immediately you know better how to study.

Later, when you are weary and find yourself asking
"Why bother?", look again at the life you wish to build, at
the person you aim to become. You will be lifted and stead-
ied.

2. Do Not Adopt Blindly Other People's Objectives.

People differ greatly in what sort of life they regard as worth living. They differ in what sort of persons they want to become. Even your closest friends have value systems somewhat different from yours. Therefore, what is best to them and right for them will not always be what is best to you and right for you. This means you cannot blindly adopt their objectives as your own, nor satisfactorily pattern your life wholly after theirs.

3. Formulate Your Own Objectives, in Detail, and Remember Them.

Work out for yourself what *you* are trying to achieve through studying and attending classes. Outline your goals for college in general; formulate also some of the sub-goals for each of your courses. Jot down these objectives, add to them, and save them for reference. Whenever a sense of futility sweeps upon you and you wonder why you are studying, what you are trying to achieve through study and other arduous activities, refer to your list of goals. See if those goals do still matter to you and are worth much effort. If they are, live accordingly — giving to them the efforts, devotion, and skills they merit.

4. Not All Goals Are Attained Best by Attending University or College.

Colleges and universities have much to offer. Nonetheless, to expect them or any other set of institutions or procedures to be all things to all people is unreasonable. There are other lives that are also worth living, lives not particularly facilitated by attending college. Dancing is a wonderful thing; so is painting pictures. However, to give everyone dancing lessons or art lessons would be a foolish squandering of resources and inappropriate to the nature of the individual.

Neither should everyone attend college. Many circumstances exist which make it wise to withdraw from college, or never start, a few of which have been indicated (pages 6 and 8). If you find yourself exceedingly discontented with college or the university, perhaps that life is an inappropriate undertaking for you and dropping it would be your most rational course of action. Your goals may be met best through some other kind of endeavor, not involving college and university work.

Another possibility: If you are deeply discontented with college or the university, perhaps you are approaching your education in inappropriate ways. Perhaps you should modify how you study, listen, write.

To help you do this is the concern of this book.

C. A PLACE TO STUDY

1.   A Quiet Room Is Not Essential for Concentration.

To eliminate distractions, where you study makes little difference. How you study and how you approach studying are crucial. Eliminating distraction is dealt with in Chapters 6 and 7. For now you might note merely this: Any room will be free of distractions when you develop enthusiasm for learning and break habits such as fear and resentment. Otherwise, no room (regardless of how quiet it may be) will be free of distractions.

2.   Start with One Special Place for Study.

When first learning how to study intensively and with high efficiency, pick one special place to study. Trying to study in many different places hinders learning to study.

Therefore, when first developing skill in studying, try to do all your home study in the same room, at the same desk, in the same chair. If practicable, use them only for studying.

These suggestions sound a bit trivial, don't they? Their results, however, are far from trivial. When you follow them, fairly soon just sitting down in that chair at that desk will make you feel like studying; you will require far less time for warming up.

You need not go on forever studying in one place only. After you become skillful studying in one place, you readily can learn to study in another place, and another and another. Finally you will be able to study easily and well almost anywhere, under almost any circumstances.

Under some circumstances, shifting your study room is a distinct help. For example, when there is a great deal of the same sort of thing to do, our performance is apt to progressively deteriorate;[15, 42]* changing rooms can reduce this deterioration and facilitate learning and retention.[15] If you are studying many hours at a time and becoming jaded, try shifting to a new room or different chair. This can refresh you and enable you to continue efficiently; sometimes for several hours more.

3. Keep Pictures of Favorite People Away from Your Desk.

When such pictures are present, either they distract you or else you become negatively adapted to them. That is, you learn to ignore them.

Negative adaptation is fairly simple to acquire. But do you want to, in this case? Do you want to become indifferent to even the pictured sight of your favorite person? Probably you do not. Yet neither do you want such pictures to catch your attention and arouse thoughts unrelated to what you are studying. The solution is obvious: Simply do not have those pictures around your study desk.

4. Have the Tools of Your Profession Handy.

Just as a doctor has an office equipped with the tools of his profession, so also you will find it convenient to have an "office" equipped with the tools of yours. Some of the most useful tools to have within reach are these: dictionary, pen, ink, pencils, eraser, notebooks, pad for miscellaneous notes, and textbooks.

When getting your supplies, do not omit that last item — textbooks. Many of us are in narrow financial straits. However, in view of the immense amounts of time, money and energy we invest in going to college, failure to buy the texts is an unwise economy. Purchase of texts is an investment that pays larger dividends — both in terms of getting educated and in terms of getting grades.

At the end of the term, consider keeping your text-

---

*Throughout this edition, as in the prior editions, almost all references are to research done with people. The few exceptions are noted specifically.

books rather than turning them in for a rebate. They make extremely handy reference books during the years to come. Of all the books in that field, the one you used as a text is probably the one you know best — and therefore one of the ones you can use most effectively. To a remarkable degree you know what is in it and what is not; you know where various facts and charts are to be found in it; you are familiar with and at home with the style of writing; you are peculiarly adept in using it. When subsequent questions arise, you can use your old textbooks quickly and effectively as an aid in answering the questions. In addition, when you save your textbook, you save your marginal notes. Marginal notes are valuable (at least to the writer). Even when you do not save your texts, your notes aid learning and reviewing. However, when you know you are going to keep your books, you can make marginal notes such that the book becomes of yet greater use to you — both at the time and in later years: notes such as "but in contrast see page 22," or "examples given on page 14," notes indicating cross-references or making tie-ins with other courses, notes of questions you have, indications of things you wish to check upon, passages marked which you especially wish to be able to find again, ideas of your own extending what is written. Such notes can be invaluable.

5.   Use Sufficient and Even Lighting.

Quality of lighting affects the ease and speed with which you read, draw, write, and study, thereby affecting the quality of your work. Additionally, quality of light affects personality.

Standard fluorescent light is satisfactory for some people,[48] but wholly inadequate for others. They tire quickly,[81] become more nervous and wrought-up under cool-white fluorescent lights, hyperactive on occasion, more easily distracted and irritable.[14, 52, 53] With shielded full-spectrum fluorescents, they are calmer, steadier, less easily distracted, and show significant improvements in academic achievement.[52, 58] Daylight can be nearly ideal; shielded full-spectrum fluorescent lights closely parallel it.

Avoid letting light shine directly from a bulb onto your books.[22, 81] After two hours working under a direct light, the loss in clear vision is almost four times as great as with indirect light. After three hours, the loss is about nine times as great. In fact, three hours of work under a direct light has brought an average loss of 81 per cent in clear vision.[22]

Have ample light. A minimum intensity for studying is three foot-candles. (That is the amount of light about four feet below a 50-watt bulb in an ordinary lamp.) Light intensities greater than this are better. Increasing intensities up to 15 or 20 foot-candles increases visual acuity[67, 75, 77] and decreases tension and fatigue developed during reading.[23] Avoid, however, having the light excessively bright (e.g., 200 foot-candles), as this too can cause decrements in speed of reading.[76]

To further reduce eyestrain and increase visual acuity, light the page evenly, so no shadows are cast on it by your hand or by any other object. Also, be sure to arrange the light so it does not glare on your paper nor shine in your eyes. The situation is similar to that in night driving. Headlights from oncoming cars cast far more light on the road than do your lights alone, but often you see less well. When headlights shine into your eyes, you may be unable to see the road at all — despite the additional light now falling on the road. Lights glaring on your paper or shining in your eyes while reading have a similar effect, decreasing greatly your visual acuity.

For similar reasons, try to light the entire room as evenly as possible, with no marked differences between the desk area and other parts of the room. *Even* illumination and freedom from glare are as important as lighting of proper intensity.[73, 74]

A bulb remarkably free from glare is the tungsten "soft-white." It gives an even, diffuse light which reduces eyestrain and general physiological stress.

Eyestrain also can be eased by wearing glasses, when needed. Not always does one realize when glasses are needed, so a check on your eyes by an oculist or ophthalmologist is worthwhile if your eyes often become strained or weary from even small amounts of reading.

6. Avoid Too Much Muscular Relaxation.

Most people should study at a desk using a chair not of the lounging type. Experimenters have demonstrated repeatedly that slight amounts of muscular tension generally lead to increased efficiency and accuracy in mental work.

For example, when people gently but firmly squeezed a

hand dynamometer (an instrument designed to measure strength of grip), they learned lists of nonsense syllables in fewer trials. They also had better recall after three hours than people who had learned the lists without this slight added muscular tension.[6] Similar results have been found for solving simple arithmetic problems,[6] and learning to recognize various visual forms.[69]

Do not conclude that the greater the tension the better. You probably have observed that one can be too "keyed up" and too tense for effective learning. It is small amounts of tension which facilitate learning.[6, 69] Note also, it is tension of the skeletal muscles which is beneficial, not tensions of the anxiety or fear type.[5, 12]

7. Under Most Circumstances, Study Alone.

Studying independently is generally more effective than studying with a companion. Concentration is simpler.[63, 64] Temptation is lessened. We handle more easily our inclination to stop and talk, or stop wholly and go play. Alone you tend to business more readily — usually.[51, 80]

However, in four special circumstances, another person may be helpful:

If both of you already have mastered the material very well, quizzing each other may be more effective than self-quizzing only.

If the material is so difficult you cannot figure it out alone, collaboration with some other student may be profitable.

If you feel isolated and desolate when alone, a partner who works quietly and without interrupting (if you can find such a person) sometimes eases anxiety and conflict.

Finally, for review and a finishing polish, about three to eight persons meeting on the days before examinations can afford mutual benefit. Syntheses made by one person may not have been accomplished by another. Examples and implications one person has worked out may have caused another to stumble. Questions troubling you, some other student in your group may be able to answer; and you may be able to help him on matters clear to you but troublesome to him. Here again, for this to work well, you each must have studied in advance and have gained respectable mastery of the subject.

D. THE USE OF BOOKS FOR BECOMING EDUCATED

1. Reading Books as Most People Read Newspapers Results in Little Gain.

Do you read texts in much the same casual way you read newspapers? If you have read the newspaper today, this little experiment might be enlightening. Ask yourself what was in the paper; then notice closely what happens. Do you start to tell of some event, but slip over almost all of the facts?

"Someone said something about some senator who did something wrong." That is what one person remembered from the morning newspaper. What had the senator reputedly done? Who was the senator? Are you reasonably sure it was a senator? Who said he had done "it"? Under what conditions was the accusation made? These questions drew blanks. "I'm not much good at details," my informant said, "only at remembering the general idea." But did he have the "general idea" even? Or did he have merely vague impressions and remnants of an emotional tone? To have an accurate "general idea," we must remember precisely at least some of the pertinent details. Details give the idea meaning.

If we read texts and newspapers in similar ways, we should expect similar results. If anything, our impressions from the textbook will be even more incomplete and inaccurate than from the newspaper, for textbooks present many more complicated relationships. How can the results of our reading be any more useful than the "somebody said some senator did something wrong" memory?

2. How Often You Read Something Is Immaterial; How You Read It Is Crucial.

Often we just plow through pages, over and over again. Sometimes we combine this re-reading with desultory (or else frantic) attempts to memorize certain scattered details. We mark a few sentences and read them ten or twenty additional times. When quite clever at this, we sometimes can spot on a test certain sentences which look like something we have seen before and can spot other sentences which do not. At best we can answer a few true-false items correctly, provided the items are of the superficial recognition type. Is *this* something you care about tremendously?

It is quite possible for us to re-re-read a text in these ways and still fail to learn anything we value. We even can fail to learn anything that helps on an examination. How many times have you head this bewildered cry? "I read the book four times! And I flunked the test! It's not fair." Often to this anguished accusation is appended: "And Doug only read it *once* but *he* got an A!"

Some such reports undoubtedly are correct. How often one reads something makes little difference in the outcome. A person *could* walk through the Louvre one hundred times and still learn almost nothing about the pictures there — he could have gained little understanding of various uses of color, or combinations of forms, or placement of figures to achieve various effects; he could have negligibly increased his appreciation of beauty and his awareness of it. You can imagine circumstances under which this would happen. How many times the person walks through the museum is relatively insignificant. The crucial matter is this: What did he do while there?

As with art exhibits, so it is with books. *Not how often* you read a book, *but how* you read it is the major determinant of the outcome.

How can you read with greater retention and other satisfying results? The secret is this: Practice the habits you wish to make skills. In reading, as in all of life, do what you want to learn. Dewey made this suggestion and it is a wise one, for whatever you actually do, you learn. Moreover, you learn *only* what you actually do. These propositions afford basic clues on how to read effectively. More specific suggestions are presented below.

3. Read in the Way You Converse with an Esteemed Friend.

Some people approach books with a bored lethargy verging on contempt. Instead of doing that, start with an intent to make the very most you can from whatever you read. Treat the author as you do your friends.

When talking with a friend, you listen attentively and eagerly. You watch for contributions of value and are sensitive to them. You actively respond to his ideas with ones of your own. Together you build new syntheses.

You can read with similar expectations and results. Expect the author to present facts you had not known before, to offer ideas of which you had not thought, to give new slants on old problems and to formulate new problems. When alert to these things, you will see them. Reading then becomes refreshing fun, and stimulating.

As with your friend, supplement what the author presents with your own ideas and facts. Ask questions of him, and look for clues to the answers.[61] Make as many tie-ins as you can among the parts of what you are learning,[55, 59] and between what you already know and what you are learning.[20, 28, 79] Try to reconcile differences and build new syntheses.[11, 36] In short, each time you study, practice collaborating with the author.

See authors as your friends, joyful and eager to share with you their thinking and observations. They worked long hours to make this sharing possible, so that you could know worlds you otherwise might not meet. When you regard authors in this light, reading is transformed. Books become fascinating. All reading becomes an occasion of new growth and learning.

4. Read with a Zest to Discover the World and to Find Partial Answers to Your Questions.[11, 46, 48]

In the preceding section, a new way of reading was offered to you. This section presents one special application of those principles.

Have you ever asked a colleague studying, what he was doing? If you have, he probably made some such reply as this: "I'm doing psych." Another student, also studying a psychology text, might say: I'm discovering how we see colors." Or, "I'm getting new information on what happens when we use ridicule to try to improve behavior." Perhaps your colleague is "doing anthropology." He could have replied, "I'm finding various conditions which lead the Zuni Indians to become marvelously cooperative and the conditions which lead some other groups to be fiercely aggressive and competitive." Or, "I'm being introduced to a new culture — and learning how radically different 'human nature' is when the individual lives in a different social context." Instead of "doing philosophy," one could be "finding out what two rather brilliant thinkers conceive to be the ideal state."

The differences in these words are small. The differences in the reflected activities are large. Does the "studying" of the first person have anything in common with the
"studying" of the second? Not much, we surmise, beyond
such insignificant resemblances as sitting at a desk, looking
at a book, turning pages.

Will there be much similarity in what these two persons
become as a consequence of studying? Since what they are
actually doing differs greatly, the results also will differ
greatly. The habits they learn, the skills they develop, the
information they acquire, will be scarcely comparable.

Try studying with the second outlook and organization — that of an explorer seeking to learn and understand.
If you try out this new system of studying, you probably
will find yourself learning much more while expending less
time. You may even discover that studying can be a joy.

5.　Think — Do Not Merely Memorize or Rehearse.[11, 21, 22, 27]

What is meant by thinking? In large part, thinking is composed of these skills: adroitly finding implications of facts
and principles, seeing the concepts and principles which
underlie and are implicit in various materials, discovering
for yourself new relationships.

You can increase those skills while reading. Here are
some ways you can do that, and thus read with more retention and greater edification.

Before reading the body of the text, read the pertinent
parts of the table of contents or the main headings of the
chapter. From these, build a framework within which to
place the facts and ideas presented in that chapter.

As you read, make some sort of written or mental outline. Written outlines have the merit of getting the main
framework on a page or two where you can see it as a
whole. However, any kind of outline will help bring out the
nature of the total picture as well as clarify how the details
fit together. Incidentally, your outline need not follow the
author's organization, if some other organization is more
meaningful to you.

Establish logical connections between the facts or ideas
presented in the text and the facts and ideas already at your
command from previous courses or observations in your
daily world. How can you build logical connections? To

help you do so, the rest of this section gives some ways of making logical connections.

Formulate underlying principles — generalizations which can be inferred from and which integrate various facts presented in the text and elsewhere.[17, 18] Apply these principles to diverse problems which occur to you.

Whenever you meet a new concept or principle, note with care any examples given, what they have in common with each other and what about them is different from each other and irrelevant to the categorization. When negative cases are given (examples of what the concept does not mean), study them too.[16, 57] Find also your own examples. Forming new concepts is aided greatly by studying examples of the concept.[10, 19, 32]

Make abstractions more concrete and meaningful.[28, 41, 62] Look for new examples, illustrations, tie-ins, supporting data, and possibly refuting evidence. Look for them in stories, articles, news reports, anything you read or hear, in drawings and movies, and in your life in general.

Re-interpret your current impressions in terms of the new information and ideas you meet in college. If you are learning anything really worthwhile in school, the world outside should look different to you as a result.

In every way you can devise, apply the results of your study. Tie in what you are studying with other parts of your life. Tie the rest of your life in with what you are studying. These possibilities are, really, the whole point of going to university and college: to get the knack of living adult life with more skill and grace and wisdom, to become more thoroughly the human being you most want to be.

Develop the art of asking yourself questions; then answer them! Do you know how to ask yourself questions? An excellent question is your favorite: "So what?" Be sure, however, not to stop after asking the question; answer it too.

Other questions you can profitably ask are these: If this material is true, then what follows? What can I infer from those facts? To what problems is this information or concept pertinent? How does this accord, or fail to accord, with my current beliefs? If this were the case, how would I behave differently? What ideas would I reformulate? What opinions would I revise? What difference would there be in the way I view various situations? (Pick out specific situations about which to ask this question.) What does this fact or idea mean for a specific point of view? Does it fit? If not, how can the point of view be revised so that the facts and principles do fit? What is the evidence for and against some idea?

Take time to answer each of your questions. Try to answer them yourself before calling upon your friends, or teachers, or others to answer them.

In everything you read, try to anticipate what is coming next. When you can repeatedly forecast parts to come, you have become highly skilled in seeing the implications of what you are reading.

Whenever you come to something you did not forecast, see if you now can infer that fact or principle from something else you know. If you cannot do so, be certain to make a visible note of that point, for apparently it is a fundamentally new one to you.

After meeting several new facts and concepts, stop reading and draw your own conclusions. Then check on how well these conclusions fit with information presented later.

Watch for apparent inconsistencies in the material you study, mark them, and in your leisure try to reconcile these discrepancies.

Each of these is a way to understand and remember far better what you read. They also are all ways of learning to think more quickly and more clearly.

6. Practice Making Intelligent and Intelligible Statements.

From your reading, make notes in your own words. If ever you are to be able to talk, or write, or even think about the matters you now are studying, if you are to use them in any way different from that of a parakeet, you must be able to express that material in your own words. It is logical, therefore, to practice that skill from the start. Besides, writing something helps you remember it.[34]

Summarize and recite the material to yourself. Make lists of related facts and rehearse them, silently or aloud.[7-9, 40] After each paragraph you read, ask yourself, "Now what was that all about?" And answer the question as best you can. If you fail to recall some fact, mark it (e.g., by a check in the margin) and try to tie it in better with other material. As you become increasingly skillful in this, you can read longer and longer sections, finally reading several

pages or even a chapter, before stopping and rehearsing.
Practicing recall helps you make subsequent recalls more
readily and more accurately.[72]

Retention can be facilitated by spending the major part
of your study time rehearsing (as contrasted with straight
reading). In a classic experiment,[26] the value of rehearsal is
demonstrated vividly. The amount the students learned (in
the same length of time) increased progressively as the
amount of rehearsal increased from zero per cent of the
total study time, to 20 per cent, to 40 per cent, to 60 per
cent, and even to 80 per cent. As you can see from Figure
1, the advantage of frequent rehearsal over frequent reading

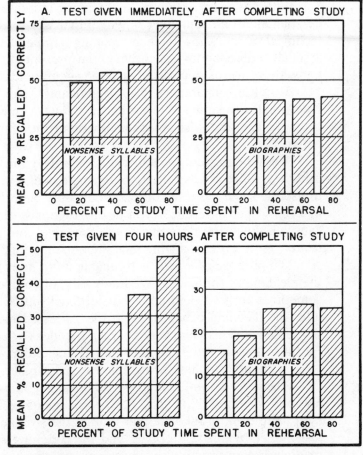

Figure 1.   Effects on retention of spending various proportions of study time in rehearsal rather than in silent reading.
These data are for eighth-graders. Substantially the same
trends hold for younger children and for college students.[26]

is much greater for memorizing nonsense syllables than for learning facts in short biographies. For both kinds of material, however, learning and retention are at least somewhat facilitated by spending a rather large proportion of time in active rehearsal.

7. Develop a More Adequate Vocabulary.[3, 25, 78]

Rare words are used by some people merely to gain prestige; but this is not their only use. When a skilled thinker and careful writer uses some rare word, he usually is attempting to communicate a meaning not expressed adequately by a common word. You miss these meanings whenever you fail to familiarize yourself with the words used.

With any word, knowing its meaning increases your understanding of all sentences in which that word occurs. With technical words, knowing their meaning is imperative for even a rough understanding of the material presented. You must know these words in order to develop accurate ideas.

A better vocabulary also significantly aids memory. Knowing the meaning of terms enables you to remember concepts better and also to remember surrounding material better.[38]

A new, enlarged vocabulary can clarify your thinking in other ways also.[39] Less often, for example, will you be obliged to use the same word for different concepts, and thus muddy or even forget differences you at one time saw clearly. You can tack down the differences you perceive, and thus make neater, more precise distinctions in your thinking.[33]

The purpose of words is to enable us to infer from them the meaning of sentences. We know this, of course. Still, we sometimes forget it and go at our job backwards: We try to infer the meaning of words from the "guessed meaning" of the sentence. This is no way to grasp the ideas of any author. Further, that system, and the limited vocabulary which results, virtually preclude being able to read rapidly.

Whenever an unfamiliar word appears, you are stopped abruptly — though you may not be conscious of this. Your eyes jump back to take another look at the strange thing you just met. Obviously, stopping and backtracking slow down reading. If new-to-you words occur often, stopping and backtracking can become a habit. You will automatically go back and re-read phrases even when they do not include unfamiliar words. Thus you lose all chance of becoming a very rapid reader.

Consulting a dictionary takes time. However, you can look up many words in the time wasted in repeated encounters with unfamiliar words. Also, you soon will need to look up fewer and fewer words, and with your new enlarged vocabulary, you will have a new speed in reading and a new comprehension.[31]

Limited in your expression by your limited vocabulary, you say what you can. With a more complete vocabulary, you can communicate your own ideas more adequately. You can say what you mean — not some discouragingly rough and misunderstood approximation. This is a boon in writing term papers, taking examinations, listening to lectures, and in conversation.

One of our modern poets and novelists (Rumer Godden) noted:[4] "If books were Persian carpets, to assess their value one would not look only at the outer side, the pattern and colourings, one would turn them over and examine the stitch, because it is the stitch that makes a carpet wear, gives it its life and bloom. The stitch of a book is its words." A person who has "never explored words, never searched, sifted through his knowledge and memory, his dictionaries, the thesaurus. . .to find the right word, is like someone owning a gold mine who has never mined it, someone living near a mountain who never walks to the top of it to see the view, someone putting his gift into a cage when it might fly free."[4]

E. MORE ABOUT USING BOOKS

1. Read All Headings.

Students sometimes skip headings, believing them to be extraneous material or intended merely as a guide for locating material. Headings, however, are an integral part of the text. They give one an idea of what is coming next, serving as an orientation and making the meanings of the author easier to follow. With some books, skipping the headings will cause one wholly to lose the thread and become utterly unable to comprehend the text. Material which would have been simple becomes enormously difficult.

If you customarily skip headings and cannot break this habit all at once, be sure to try reading the headings first. You may warmly welcome this preview and overview of the material to be presented, giving a framework into which you can fit the details.

2. Use the Graphs, Tables, and Pictures.

Most of us skip such materials, after noting gleefully that there are fewer pages to read than we had first thought. This is a pity, for graphs and tables can be a great help. They can clarify enormously what some fact means; they can bring out new implications of the fact; they can present clearly some facts difficult or even impossible to state simply in words. When you give them a chance, graphs and tables do remarkable things.

3. Read Selectively, Varying Your Speed with the Kind of Material.

For most effective use of your time, do not read all materials at the same rate.[36, 45] When reading a novel to get the outline of its plot, you need not dwell long on any sentence. You can learn to skip right along. On the other hand, when reading highly technical work, go more slowly. That kind of material often is highly condensed and you need more time per page to catch the author's meanings. Similarly, practice covering the familiar rapidly, the unfamiliar more slowly.

Bracket, or in some other way note, the important sentences. By "important" sentences we do not mean merely those you believe will be covered on a test. We mean all principles, facts, and concepts which are new to you. Anything you did not infer from other material at your command is new to you and is important.

Subtle dangers lurk here. Caution: Some extremely important matters take only a few words to express. A short sentence, a mere sub-point within the particular framework used, may present a concept enlightening and revolutionary when understood.

Also, the fact that a passage sounds eminently reasonable does not mean you already knew what it is presenting. Many students believe that whenever they are saying, "Obviously," "Quite so," or the like, in response to some passage, its contents must be common facts and ideas which they understand thoroughly and can recall easily. This is a mistake.

Plausibility does not mean commonness nor does it mean familiarity with the facts or ideas.

Similarly, suppose all the words look familiar, and the sentences are graceful, easy to read. Do these mean you understand the passage and probably can recall that material accurately? Not at all. What all of these phenomena really mean is this: The author is a skilled writer.

Watch for this. Confusion on these matters can slip up on one and cause havoc.

4. When Some Passage Is Incomprehensible, Re-Read It in a New Way.

Sometimes a paragraph makes no sense at all when we first read it. Then we re-read it, in much the same way we read it the first time, and with much the same results. We may read the paragraph over and over, a dozen times or more, and still not understand it. We begin to feel mildly feebleminded. Sometimes we feel like a fool for having tried to understand such difficult material. We may even get so wrought up that the rest of the chapter too is almost wholly incomprehensible.

Instead of that, try this system: When some passage is incomprehensible, re-read it, but not in the same way you first read it. This time stop after each sentence and ask yourself what that sentence means. Usually you will be able to translate the first sentence into something you understand. Then go on to the next sentence. Read it and ask yourself what it means. Often the whole passage becomes clear when tackled in this way, sentence by sentence.

However, if the passage still is unclear, mark it and temporarily skip it. Simply go on to the rest of the chapter, and come back later to the unclear part. Usually when you return with new information at your disposal and a new internal organization, the points no longer are obscure. You may even wonder why they seemed so difficult before. (Incidentally, this same technique works delightfully well with mathematics problems which at first seem impossible to solve.)

Although exceedingly effective, every now and then this system does not help to any appreciable extent — or at least, not sufficiently. If it does not, you might see the professor during an office hour or bring the question up in class. The chances are high that if you had this difficulty after seriously trying to fathom the meaning of the passage, others will have run into similar difficulties. By active participation, and the answer from a classmate or the professor, the likelihood is heightened that this new information will be grasped and retained.

If several passages in a row are incomprehensible, this may be a sign of fatigue. Take a rest or study something else for a while. Arranging to have different kinds of study follow each other improves learning[60] and reduces fatigue.

5. Develop Skill in the Mechanics of Reading.

Not always,[50] but often,[30, 49] scholastic achievement is related to skill in reading. Some people can read 500 words per minute; that is one or two pages in a single minute. Some people can read much faster than that and with high comprehension. How do they do it? In part their ability consists in having developed considerable skill along the lines sketched above; and in part it consists in having developed skill in the mechanics of reading. In contrast to more average readers,[71] the more skillful read by phrases,[29, 46] their eyes progressing along the line in quick even jerks with only a few brief fixation points[43] and virtually no backtracking.[29, 43] They make few, if any, lip movements.[80]

If you can read 500 words per minute, with high comprehension, probably you already have developed those habits or ones equally effective. If, however, you read slowly, probably you are weak in some or all of them. Some people, for example, read one letter at a time. When they come to "cat," they sound out c-a-t. Probably you do not do this. You can read a whole word at a time. But perhaps you can read *only* one word at a time.[70] Just as you learned to read a word as a whole, instead of letter by letter, so also you can learn to read a phrase as a whole instead of word by word. This enormously increases reading speed and can increase your comprehension too.

Many universities and colleges have reading laboratories, free to anyone enrolled at the school. The members of these laboratories are outstandingly adept in helping people develop new skills in reading. In a few months, many students have doubled or even tripled their speed of reading, with little or no loss in comprehension.[13, 66] So also have other adults.[56] For some people, the increase in speed of reading is accompanied by a significant increase in vocabulary and comprehension[54, 68] as well as grade point average.[68] These gains not only were maintained, but in at least one study they had increased after a lapse of 60 weeks with no further formal training.[68] You too can take advantage of these opportunities. No college student need continue to spend ten or fifteen minutes, nor even five minutes, merely reading an ordinary page.

6. Check on Possible Structural Defects in Your Eyesight.

Difficulties in reading and chronic eyestrain can stem from various defects, such as muscular imbalance, astigmatism, myopia, or hypermetropia.[2, 35]

If your head aches and your eyes ache while you are at the movies or reading love stories, as well as while studying, possibly something is wrong with your eyes. If you have trouble reading for long periods, becoming exhausted or nauseated after a few hours or even less, perhaps you need glasses.

One's eyes change from year to year: Glasses may not be needed at one stage of life and badly needed at another; lenses appropriate one year may not be most appropriate a few years later. Even astigmatism can change from year to year. You can be free of astigmatism and then develop one, or have an astigmatism and then grow free of it. Astigmatisms and other difficulties sometimes go undetected for years. An optometrist or ophthalmologist can tell you whether you have these and can prescribe corrective lenses.

7. If Reading Difficulties Persist, a Clinical Psychologist or Other Specialist May Be of Help.

Despite patiently practicing all these suggestions, some students still cannot read with speed or high comprehension.

Persistent troubles with reading often reflect deep emotional distress.[44, 70] Severe emotional distress is extremely difficult to remedy without assistance. Fortunately you do not need to, for expert assistance is available. Psychologists and other specialists in this field can help you resolve these problems and build new, more satisfying habits.

BIBLIOGRAPHY FOR CHAPTER 2

1. Aström, Björn; and Nilsson, Lars-Goran. Overt repetition as a means of controlling rehearsal. Scand. J. Psychol., 18, 53–58, 1977.
2. Ball, R. J. Visual functioning in reading disability. Education, 82, 175–178, 1961.
3. Bendig, A. W. Comparison of the validity of two temperament scales in predicting college achievement. J. Educ. Res., 51, 605–609, 1958.
4. Best, M. A. Rumer Godden. Book-of-the-Month Club News, page 5, September, 1969.
5. Bevan, William; and Maier, Richard A. Emotional tension and the generality of its effects upon intellectual performance. J. Personality, 26, 330–336, 1958.
6. Bills, A. G. The influence of muscular tension on the efficiency of mental work. Amer. J. Psychol., 38, 227–251, 1927. With Stauffacher, J. C. The influence of voluntarily induced tension on rational problem solving. J. Psychol., 4, 261–271, 1937.
7. Buschke, Herman. Encoding for short-term storage. Psychonomic Bull., 1, 14, 1967.
8. Buschke, Herman. Verbal noise and linguistic constraints. Psychonomic Science, 12, 391–392, 1968.
9. Buschke, Herman; and Hinrichs, James V. Controlled rehearsal and recall order in serial list retention. J. Exper. Psychol., 78, 502–509, 1968.
10. Calfee, Robert C. Recall and recognition memory in concept identification. J. Exper. Psychol., 81, 436–440, 1969.
11. Capretta, Patrick J.; Jones, Reginald L.; Siegel, Laurence; and Siegel, Lila C. Some noncognitive characteristics of Honors Program candidates. J. Educ. Psychol., 54, 268–276, 1963.
12. Chansky, Norman M. Threat, anxiety, and reading behavior. J. Educ. Res., 51, 333–340, 1958.
13. Chansky, Norman M.; and Bregman, Martin. Improvement of reading in college. J. Educ. Res., 51, 313–317, 1957.
14. Colman, Richard S.; Frankel, Fred; Ritvo, Edward; and Freeman, B. J. The effects of fluorescent and incandescent illumination upon repetitive behaviors in autistic children. J. Autism Childhood Schiz., 6, 157–162, 1976.
15. Dallet, Ken; and Wilcox, Sandra G. Contextual stimuli and proactive inhibition. J. Exper. Psychol. 78, 475–480, 1968.
16. Denny, J. Peter; and Benjafield, John G. Concept identification strategies used for positive and negative instances. Psychonomic Sci., 14, 277–278, 1969.
17. Dirkes, M. Ann. Learning through Creative Thinking. Buffalo, N.Y.: Discriminators of Knowledge, 1977.
18. Dirkes, M. Ann. The role of divergent production in the learning process. Amer. Psychologist, 33, 815–820, 1978.
19. Dominowski, R. L. Role of memory in concept learning. Psychol. Bull., 4, 271–280, 1965.

20. Eagle, Morris N. The effect of learning strategies upon free recall. Amer. J. Psychol., 80, 421–425, 1967.
21. Erdelyi, Matt; Buschke, Herman; and Finkelstein, Shira. Hypermnesia for Socratic stimuli. Memory Cognition, 5, 283–286, 1977.
22. Feldhusen, J. F.: Treffinger, D. J.; Van Mondfrans, A. P.; and Ferris, D. R. The relationship between academic grades and divergent thinking scores derived from four different methods of testing. J. Exper. Educ., 40, 35–40, 1971.
23. Ferree, C. E.; and Rand, G. Good working conditions for the eyes. Personnel J., 15, 333–340, 1937.
24. Gadzella, Bernadette M.; and Goldston, John. Effects of study guides and classroom discussions on students' perceptions of study habits. Percep. Motor Skills, 44, 901–902, 1977.
25. Garms, Joe D. Predicting scholastic achievement with nonintellectual variables. Diss. Abstr., 28 (8-B), 3460, 1968.
26. Gates, A. I. Recitation as a factor in memorizing. Arch. Psychol., 6, No. 40, 1917.
27. Gibson, James W.; Kibler, Robert J.; and Barker, Larry L. Some relationships between selected creativity and critical thinking measures. Psychol. Rep., 23, 707–714, 1968.
28. Giorgi, Amedeo. Learning as a function of meaning levels with American and German Ss. Psychol. Rep., 23, 27–39, 1968.
29. Glock, M. D. The effect upon eye-movements and reading rate at the college level of three methods of training. J. Educ. Psychol., 40, 93–106, 1949.
30. Gowan, J. C. Intelligence, interests, and reading ability in relation to scholastic achievement. Psychol. Newsltr., N.Y.U., 8, 85–87, 1957.
31. Hall, W. E.; and Robinson, F. P. An analytical approach to the study of reading skills. J. Educ. Psychol., 36, 429–442, 1945.
32. Haygood, Robert C.; Sandlin, J.; Yoder, D. J.; and Dodd, D. H. Instance contiguity in disjunctive concept learning. J. Exper. Psychol., 81, 605–607, 1969.
33. Henle, Paul. (Ed.) Language, Thought, and Culture. Ann Arbor, Mich.: Univ. Michigan Press, 1958.
34. Higgins, E. Tory; and Rholes, William S. "Saying is believing." J. Exper. Soc. Psychol., 14, 363–378, 1978.
35. Hirsch, M. J. The relationship of school achievement and visual anomalies. Amer. J. Optom., 32, 262–270, 1955.
36. Husbands, K. L.; and Shores, J. H. Measurement of reading for problem solving: A critical review of the literature. J. Educ. Res., 43, 453–465, 1950.
37. James, William. Principles of Psychology. New York: Henry Holt & Co., 1890. Re-issued by Dover Publications, Inc., 1950.
38. Jenkins, Joseph R.; and Bausell, R. Barker. Cognitive structure variables in prose learning. J. Reading Beh., 8, 47–66, 1976.
39. Jenkins, James J. Language and thought. In Voss, James F. (Ed.) Approaches to Thought. Columbus, Ohio: Charles E. Merrill Publ. Co., 211–237, 1969.
40. Johnston, James J. Answer changing behavior and grades. Teaching Psychol., 5, 44–45, 1978.
41. Katz, Albert N.; and Denny, J. Peter. Memory-load and concreteness in the order of dominance effect for verbal concepts. J. Verbal Learning Verbal Beh., 16, 13–20, 1977.
42. Keppel, Geoffrey; Postman, Leo; and Zavortink, Bonnie. Studies of learning to learn: VIII. The influence of massive amounts of training upon the learning and retention of paired-associate lists. J. Verbal Learning Verbal Behav., 7, 790–796, 1968.
43. Klare, George R.; Shuford, Emir H.; and Nichols, William H. The relationship of style difficulty, practice, and ability to efficiency of reading and to retention. J. Appl. Psychol., 41, 222–226, 1957.
44. Letson, Charles T. Speed and comprehension in reading. J. Educ. Res., 52, 49–53, 1958.
45. Letson, Charles T. The relative influence of material and purpose on reading rates. J. Educ. Res., 52, 238–240, 1959.

46. Lewis, N. How to Read Better and Faster. (Rev. Ed.) New York; Thomas Y. Crowell, 1951.
47. Lion, Judith S.; Richardson, E.; and Browne, R. C. A study of the performance of industrial inspectors under two kinds of lighting. Ergonomics, 11, 23–34, 1968.
48. McCollom, Ivan N.; and Badore, Nancy Lloyd. Exploring Psychology. New York: Thomas Y. Crowell Company, 1973, pp. 428–431.
49. McDonald, Arthur S. Influence of a college reading improvement program on academic performance. J. Educ. Psychol., 48, 171–181, 1957.
50. McQueen, R. Diagnostic reading scores and college achievement. Psychol. Rep., 3, 627–629, 1957.
51. Markus, Hazel. The effect of mere presence on social facilitation. J. Exper. Soc. Psychol., 14, 389–397, 1978.
52. Mayron, Lewis W.; Ott, John; Nations, Rick; and Mayron, Ellen L. Light, radiation, and academic behavior. Academic Therapy, 10, 33–47, 1974.
53. Mayron, Lewis, M.; and Kaplan, Ervin. Bioeffects of fluorescent lighting. Academic Therapy, 12, 75–90, 1976.
54. Miller, J. O., Jr. A comparison of a self-improvement and teacher-oriented approach to reading improvement at the college and university level. Diss. Abstr., 28 (12-A), 4955–4956, 1968.
55. Montague, William E.; and Wearing, Alexander J. The retention of responses to individual stimuli and stimulus classes. Psychonomic Sci., 9, 81–82, 1967.
56. Morton, J. An investigation into the effects of an adult reading efficiency course. Occup. Psychol., 33, 222–237, 1959.
57. Nelson, Barbara A.; and Chavis, Glenn L. Cognitive style and complex concept acquisition. Contemp. Educ. Psychol., 2, 91–98, 1977.
58. Ott, John N. Influence of fluorescent lights on hyperactivity and learning disabilities. J. Learning Dis., 9, 417–422, 1976.
59. Pollio, Howard R.; and Gerow, Joshua R. The role of rules in recall. Amer. J. Psychol., 81, 303–313, 1968.
60. Proctor, Robert W. Attention and modality-specific interference in visual short-term memory. J. Exper. Psychol., 4, 239–245, 1978.
61. Pyper, John Romney. Attentional factors in learning from written texts. Diss. Abstr., 29 (2-A), 486–487, 1968.
62. Reed, Homer B.; and Dick, R. Dale. The learning and generalization of abstract and concrete concepts. J. Verbal Learning Verbal Behav., 7, 486–490, 1968.
63. Sanders, Glenn S.; and Baron, R. S. The motivating effects of distraction on task performance. J. Per. Soc. Psychol., 32, 956–963, 1975.
64. Sanders, Glenn S.; Baron, Robert Steven; and Moore, Danny L. Distraction and social comparison as mediators of social facilitation effects. J. Exper. Soc. Psychol., 14, 291–303, 1978.
65. Schulz, R. W.; Miller, R. L.; and Radtke, R. C. The role of instance contiguity and dominance in concept attainment. J. Verbal Learning Verbal Behav., 1, 432–435, 1963.
66. Schwartz, Marvin. An evaluation of the effectiveness of the reading training given in the U.S. Naval school, pre-flight. USN Sch. Aviat. Med. Res. Rep., Proj. No. NM 14 02 11, Sub. 12, No. I, ii + 8 pp., 1957.
67. Simonson, E.; and Brozek, J. Effects of illumination level on visual performance and fatigue. J. Opt. Soc. Amer., 38, 384–397, 1948.
68. Smith, D. E. P.; and Wood, R. L. Reading improvement and college grades: A follow-up. J. Educ. Psychol., 46, 151–159, 1955.
69. Smock, C. D.; and Small, V. H. Efficiency of utilization of visual information as a function of induced muscular tension. Percept. Mot. Skills, 14, 39–44, 1962.
70. Strang, Ruth. Reading and personality formation. Personality, 1, 131–140, 1951.
71. Taylor, Earl A. The spans: Perception, apprehension and recognition: As related to reading and speed reading. Amer. J. Ophthal., 44, 501–507, 1957.
72. Thompson, Charles P.; Wenger, Steven K.; and Bartling, Carl A. How recall facilitates subsequent recall. J. Exper. Psychol., 4, 210–221, 1978.
73. Tinker, M. A. Cautions concerning illumination intensities used for reading. Amer. J. Optom., 12, 43–51, 1935.
74. Tinker, M. A. Trends in illumination standards. Illum. Engr., 43, 866–881, 1948.

75. Tinker, M. A. The effect of intensity of illumination upon speed of reading six-point italic print. Amer. J. Psychol., 65, 600–602, 1952.
76. Tinker, M. A. Length of work periods in visual research. J. Appl. Psychol., 42, 343–345, 1958.
77. Tinker, M. A. Brightness contrast, illumination intensity and visual efficiency. Amer. J. Optom., 36, 221–235, 1959.
78. Trembly, Dean. Laws of learning general and specialized vocabularies. Proceedings 74th Annual Conv. APA, 229–230, 1966.
79. Tulving, E.; and Osler, Shirley. When is recall higher than recognition? Psychonomic Bull., 1, 15, 1967.
80. Wrenn, C. G.; and Larsen, R. P. Studying Effectively. Stanford Univ., Calif.: Stanford Univ. Press, 1943, pp. 1–3.
81. Zaccaria, A.; and Bitterman, M. E. The effect of fluorescent flicker on visual efficiency. J. Appl. Psychol., 36, 413–416, 1952.

Share your interests with a friend . . .

Chapter 3

Learning More — in Class

What you do at the university or college will change your entire life. How you live these years, what you learn, and what you don't learn, will shape the rest of your life.

The information you acquire now is a large part of your lifetime fund. The habits you build now are habits you carry with you throughout life — or struggle to destroy. Whether they are useful or hampering, they will be your foundation.

This chapter deals with time in classrooms, starting with lectures. Much of life is listening: Your benefits from future speeches, seminars, talks, TV and radio newscasts, conventions, sermons, panel discussions, symposia, even conversations will rest securely upon whatever skills in listening you develop.

A. PROFITING MORE FROM LECTURES

An excellent way to swiftly gather patterns of facts, ideas, and viewpoints is through lectures. During your college and university years, and subsequent years, you have the opportunity to hear experts on many topics; with great good fortune, on hundreds of topics. Many of these lectures will be wasted. They will, that is, unless you recognize this danger and strive to avert it.

How can you make lectures worthwhile? Let us put the question differently: How can you be changed by a person's talking to you for an hour? Suppose you already know all the facts the speaker presents. Even then you can be growing: You can be seeing new relationships from the particular contexts in which those facts are introduced. You can be getting leads on sources of information. You can be exploring ideas which had not occurred to you before. You can be developing a somewhat different and more comprehensive picture of the world. All of these you can be doing. Sometimes, though, we do none of them and leave the classroom almost unchanged.

Whenever we leave a class-meeting unchanged, we have squandered a bit of life. This section points a way to living that part of your life more fully.

1. Listening Is a Complex Skill.

Listening comprehendingly and retentively is not an innate ability some lucky people have and some do not. Nor does it inevitably materialize merely because we have a capacity for it.[43, 59, 88] Effective listening is a set of intricate skills which, to possess, we must learn and practice and polish.[72, 117] This can be facilitated by various arrangeable conditions.

2. Sit As Near the Front of the Classroom As Is Comfortable for You.

Ease in concentrating and understanding can be greatly influenced by your position in the classroom. If currently your attention wanders, shift to a different part of the room.

Try sitting near the front. The many inevitable noises are not as distracting there nor do they blur as many words and phrases. You understand the words better and therefore can understand the ideas better.

For many students, sitting near the center of a room has resulted in better learning (as measured by high grades) than sitting near the back of a room or on the aisles.[55] Perhaps the majority feel more secure when surrounded by their colleagues than when on the fringes. However, avoid crowding, if possible. With somewhat scattered seating, rather than shoulder to shoulder seating, listeners can focus better attention on the speaker.[46]

Small classes may help you too, especially if you feel lost or overwhelmed in large classes.[36, 50, 121]

3. Before Class Begins, Get Set for That Class.

You do not have to lose the first ten minutes of each class trying to get organized. You can become oriented toward that class before the hour begins. For example, go over your notes from the previous day's meeting just before the class begins, review the reading assigned for that day. Both of these help you get ready for that class.

Classes taken at 1:00 or immediately after lunch seem to cause trouble. One is apt to be distracted, particularly disoriented, and sluggish. The blood and oxygen are not zipping to the brain in optimum quantities but going instead to the digestive tract in larger-than-usual proportions.[48] This is fine for digesting lunch, but not much help to thinking. With some students this phenomenon is so pronounced they tend to go to sleep—more so in "one o'clocks" than usual.

If you are such a student, try eating early in the period available for lunch, eat a light snack, and then eat again after classes are finished. And take special care to spend the last few minutes before class getting prepared for that class. If the course is a difficult one or particularly important to you, postpone lunch.

Some professors compile a reading list or make textbook assignments for the term. When reading assignments have been made for particular dates, try to complete them before the lecture. The more pertinent information you have before the lecture begins, the better you retain what is presented.[94]

Through your reading, you gain a framework with which to integrate the lecture material. You recognize what facts and principles in the lecture are already available in the textbook; thus you do not spend time taking notes on those points. You also recognize what material in the lecture is not in your textbook and thereby are alerted to make notes of that material.

If you read the textbook before the lecture, you know what parts of the text were unclear to you; during lecture you can watch for clarifications and will notice better whatever clarifications are given. Sometimes too you are given a chance to ask questions after a lecture, or possibly during it. Use that time to ask about any parts of the text which still bewilder you.

Reading the pertinent parts of your textbook before

going to class prevents needless questions. Some parts of the lecture might well be unclear if you have not studied the assignment, but are wholly apparent when you have prepared yourself properly.

4. Should You Take Notes?

Much needless confusion has resulted from assuming this question has one best answer equally applicable to all lectures. That simply is not the case.

As you know, things classified under the same heading may differ greatly. Golf and bowling are both sports — but not all the activities necessary for skill in one are desirable in the other. Keeping your eye on the ball is fine for golf, but it does not improve bowling. So it is with studies. *You must modify your procedure in accord with the particular course you are taking and the particular skills you are trying to acquire.*

In some courses, taking many notes is virtually imperative; in others, a few notes suffice. When the lecturer repeats the textbook, probably no notes are necessary. That material already is accessible. At the other extreme when the lecturer presents a host of new facts and ideas, many notes may be necessary in order to deeply understand the material — or even to understand it at all.

In lectures, as in reading, do not be lured by a plausible, graceful presentation into believing you already know and understand the material and so need no notes. "Understanding" the ideas while a skillful lecturer is presenting them is one thing; understanding them when alone is something quite different.

5. To Profit Fully from Some Courses, Many Notes Are Essential.

Anything important which is clearly expressed can be remembered by attentively listening to it once — or at least so we seem to believe. The belief is encouraged by some conversations which contain little we had not previously known. The belief is further fortified by T.V. advertisements, and by speeches filled with oversimplifications and repetitions. Such material we can remember, of course, without notes. But not all lectures are like those conversations, advertisements, and speeches.

Would you remember most of the material from a complex book, after reading it once as fast as you could? Such a feat you might deem miraculous. Yet that is what many of us attempt with lectures! We feel strangely disappointed when we do not understand and recall in detail a lecture heard but once. Why do we try to do with lectures what we know cannot be done with books?

There is nothing magical about converting words from visual stimuli into auditory ones. When new-to-you, complex ideas and a wealth of condensed information are presented in a lecture, do not expect to recall the material, far less understand its implications, from hearing it once. Such accomplishments require reviewing and reflective study. In order to have the materials you need for this reviewing and study, take notes on such lectures.

6. Make Written Notes of Everything You Deem Ridiculous, or Conflicting with Your Present Desires and Beliefs.

Material which conflicts with your desires or beliefs is particularly apt to be overlooked,[97] misconstrued,[83, 97] or forgotten.[79, 98]

For example, a large number of college students listened to a 10-minute speech containing facts favorable and other facts unfavorable to a well-known political position.[41] Immediately thereafter, they took an objective test on that material. A questionnaire had shown that some of these students favored the position discussed, and that others were opposed. Both groups remembered best the parts of the speech which fit their own views. Three weeks later the students were given a second test on the speech. By then, their tendency to remember accurately only those facts harmonizing with their beliefs was even more pronounced than it had been immediately after the speech. The implications are obvious.

Deviant ideas or facts (and they may be facts, not opinions) are not only difficult to remember. They are difficult to understand without thinking about them. Clearly, you cannot think about something unless you can remember it. This behooves us to make careful, detailed notes of anything we do not believe.

7. You Need at Least Some of the Details of the Lecture, As Well As the "General Idea."[61]

The basic ideas are meaningless (even when remembered!) and lack significance except in terms of the details they imply. Jotting down some of the illustrations,[67] for instance, clarifies the main idea and helps fix it in your memory by showing a few of its implications.

Record the details of any experiments given. Again this increases the meaningfulness of the "main" points. Such notes are valuable too if later you wish to pursue the subject further, or get to wondering what sorts of evidence exist for some viewpoint.

Duplicate any diagrams described or shown on the chalkboard. You can copy the diagrams as your professor draws them and they will clarify your notes greatly. Similarly, copy any tables or charts put on the chalkboard. If the material is important enough for the instructor to copy, it is a good thing for you to copy.

Record numerical data, as well as significant names of persons. Make your notes full, so you will have enough information for a clear reading later.

8. Note the Framework of the Lecture, As Well As What You Construe Are Main and Minor Points.

Oftentimes some of the main points are not statements, but are implicit in the particular ways in which the materials are integrated. In other words, the framework itself constitutes, tacitly, many ideas.

This does not mean there is only one way to organize facts. It means more nearly the opposite: There are many ways to organize facts and the organizations themselves have meanings. After class, try integrating the material in new frameworks of your own creation.

9. Be Accurate.

In taking condensed notes, do not omit such words as "usually," "sometimes," "very," or "somewhat." Omitting such words changes the basic meaning of the sentence. Avoid also substituting "is" for "tends to be." Such a substitution radically changes the whole sentence and its implications.

Avoid the common mistake of interchanging parts of a sentence. For example, suppose the lecturer says: All hostile aggression stems from frustration. Do not write: Frustration always results in hostile aggression. That could be false, while the original statement was true.

When several conditions are listed as being necessary for some specified outcome, be certain to record them all. If the lecturer states that $2 + 5 + 8 = 15$, getting down in one's notes that $2 + 5$ gives 15 is not merely incomplete; it is downright wrong and highly misleading.

Abbreviate what you can, but make sure your short cuts are understandable.

Accuracy and completeness are facilitated by using some system of shorthand. You can devise your own system. Use symbols and abbreviations you already know, supplemented by ones of your own creation. For example, abbreviate common words by the first few letters, use contractions, and leave out unnecessary vowels. Use the same abbreviation for the same word each time. Do not bother about writing complete sentences. In taking notes, the trick is to do as little writing as possible while still getting down as many of the facts and principles as possible.

10. Jot Down Reminders of Questions Which Occur to You.

Jot down reminders also of any disagreements you may have. During the lecture is not an appropriate time to think about these questions, for almost certainly you would miss hearing some subsequent ideas. But after class, try to answer your questions. Talk with the instructor after class or during office hours. Try to answer the question yourself: Look up relevant material, re-read pertinent parts of your textbook, talk the matter over with friends.

11. When First Learning to Take Notes, Most People Have Difficulty Writing and Listening at the Same Time.

This difficulty does not last forever. With practice of the two skills (note-taking and attentive listening), you can easily do them simultaneously. You can learn this even as many people, after much practice, have learned to knit and converse well at the same time. First practice the two skills separately; then practice them combined.

12. After Taking Notes, How Should You Handle Them?

Rote copying of notes is almost pointless. Reworking notes has great value. Rewrite parts that are legible the next hour, but will be illegible the next day. Fill in gaps. Add points you still remember but did not have time to record during the lecture. These things can best be done shortly after the lecture.

Then, answer the questions you have noticed in the margin of your notes. Find examples of the facts and principles presented. Ideally, use your notes in the ways suggested in connection with studying books.

Suppose, after taking notes, you never looked at them. Taking them still would not have been a waste of time. For one thing, you would have started building skill in note-taking, and that skill is indispensable in some situations for fully utilizing the opportunities afforded for becoming educated. In addition, the mere act of writing something enables many people to remember it better — even though they do not look at their notes again.

13. During Class Be Active.

Learning is facilitated immensely by active participation.[19, 119, 122] Rather than passively sitting, waiting to become educated, be as responsive and attentive as you can be.[9] Listen with the intent to understand and remember the material presented.[11, 106] Listen as though you were going to take a quiz immediately after class, without any opportunity to see or hear the material again.[49, 108] This technique brings heartening gains; sometimes twice as much is remembered as under usual listening conditions.[108]

In numerous ways, you can be active and growing: Look for examples or other applications of the material presented; answer aloud or to yourself the questions raised by your teacher or classmates; compare other people's answers with your own; try to anticipate how the lecturer will develop a point. You can be re-examining old beliefs and looking at your world through new eyes. You can be following the ideas as well as the words of the lecturer. There is much you can do and learn during lectures.

Each of these actions develops your skill in seeing meanings; so at the same time you are mastering the subject matter, you are perfecting skills in thinking. Thus, you grow in two ways at once.

14. Before Devising Counter-Arguments, Be Certain You Understand the Ideas Presented — Especially When They Differ from Yours.

It is these strange, new viewpoints and facts that furnish you with bases for new actions . . . for new interests . . . for new ways of looking at old problems . . . for new conceptions of the world. These, in turn, are the bases for growth.

You did not enter the university hoping to end the same as you began. You hoped to improve yourself. You hoped to change. So when someone presents a fact or opinion very different from what you believe, note it with care. This is what you came for. After class think about the new fact or opinion, discuss it with your friends, try to understand it and see in what senses it is true.

When you are sure you understand the material, try to think of counter-arguments. Then see if you can devise a way to make the apparently disparate data fit.

B. PARTICIPATION IN DISCUSSIONS

In some courses a discussion section is scheduled on a particular day. Format varies, but these courses frequently are taught with two or three lectures per week and one discussion class per week. When properly prepared for, the discussion section can be a valuable adjunct.[14, 36, 47, 120] So also can discussions on a less formal basis.[62, 113]

1. Read the Assignments Before Class.

As we already learned in section A of this chapter, distinct benefits accrue from completing assigned reading before going to lecture. It is desirable to complete assignments before any class meeting, but it is imperative before a discussion session.

No matter how well informed nor how widely read you are before starting this course, nor how brilliant and charming, you still need the particular material presented in the textbook. Those particular facts, concepts, definitions, principles, explications, and development give you and your colleagues something in common. They make the foundation you can build on together. Consciously or unconsciously, students assume each other knows at least that much; they allude to the material in the textbook directly or indirectly. The point of their comment depends partly upon knowledge of that material. Besides, it is maddening in a discussion to have to take time out to explain to someone something he would have known perfectly well had he read the text.

2.   Read Other Material That Is Relevant.

Useful relevant material includes: definitions of terms used in the assignment;[64] writings referred to in the assignment; newspaper articles, magazine articles, other references pertinent to the reading material.

Sometimes the lecturer has cited relevant material during the lecture. Look it up and read it.

You need not do all of these things. Even if you do only some, you increase your knowledge and understanding. You give depth to the text material. You will know something of how information is acquired and how it is synthesized. You also will be able to remember more of the pertinent information, thus enhancing test performance as well as discussions.

Make notes of what you discover during your reading of assignments and during your reading of supplementary material. Bring your notes with you to all classes in which you anticipate discussion, so you can add to and modify them during the discussion.

3.   Jot Down Questions You Wish to Ask During the Discussion.

Questions about the meaning of terms are a good place to start. By starting here, you will find many facts become clear that had been hazy. Much of what you are learning at first is how to converse in the field being studied.

Make a list of apparent discrepancies in what you have read and heard. Sometimes stating a discrepancy with great clarity makes the discrepancy disappear. The ones that do not disappear are good topics to bring up in class discussion. Mention in class that you have tried to clear up the discrepancy and so far have not been able to. You will find, usually, there are others in the class who need help here; also, quite likely someone has an answer for you. Or part of an answer. The partial answer gives you added ideas for an answer. Often you can pool resources and work out together a really good solution.

Make a practice of writing down questions which occur to you when you are reading, when you are listening to lectures, when you are mulling over the subject. Collect these questions into a separate list. Make notes of possible answers. Bring this list to class and use it during the discussion. Ask your questions in class.

Doing all this gives you opportunities to become far clearer on what you are studying and what it means. This question and answer system will also help prepare you for examinations. Best of all, however, you experience the joys of a joint enterprise in learning.

4. Go Over Your Lecture Notes Seeking Anything You Would Like Explained.

Try to write an explanation or partial explanation before you go to the discussion section. Thereby you see better what you still need to know. Also, when someone in class is clarifying something for you, you will understand what is being said and what it means. Further, your request for clarification or amplification can be succinct and to the points you wish clarified or amplified. You will find you are saving valuable time, yours and others. Vagueness and wandering interspersed with "you know" or "like" are sure indications of faulty preparation or no preparation at all.

One way to prepare a partial explanation or amplification of your own before class is to tell your roommate, friend, or spouse the subject that is troubling or confusing you. Often in telling someone else, you suddenly see where your confusion lies.

It is sometimes better to have this experience happen

with a limited audience. If neither you nor your friend can figure out what is amiss, you quite likely have a good topic to bring to discussion section.

Your textbook also may have clues to answer your questions, either in the parts assigned or in some other section. Search the index for likely clues. Go back over the table of contents and scan the various headings that seem relevant. Often the searching process itself leads you to the beginning of the explanation or amplification you desire.

Sometimes, returning to the subject later, you suddenly see what you need to do to find what is amiss. Or, you suddenly see an explanation which escaped you before. If you don't, in the discussion class you will be confident you are not being frivolous and that what you ask for is information not readily apparent.

5. A Few Rules Might Be Handy.

During discussion, listen for ways that others' contributions are clarifying things for you and answering your questions — even though you had not yet asked the question aloud. Quite often several other persons have questions similar, or even identical, to yours.

When the discussion bogs down, you may be able to help as a third party who sees things from a different angle. Cooperation increases the utility of the discussion for everyone.

Do not take too much time or too little time in class. If it seems you are taking too much time, offer to meet the instructor after class to get further amplification. Often by then it either will not be needed, or a meeting will prove to be a really great opportunity for mutual discussion and much learning.

Do take enough time to ask your questions so someone can answer what you want answered. However, if others are asking your questions, and the answers you hear are right for you, you may attend several discussion sessions without speaking up. But you will be participating. You will be learning, albeit silently.

Use class discussion to help relate the new material to material already learned.

Listen to the questions other students ask. Almost always you will get insights on what is troubling you. One sometimes doesn't listen to these other questions, but one should.

6. You Need Not Limit Your Discussions to Class Time.

Get acquainted with other members of the class. Learn their names and start friendships. Continue the discussions after class. Meet somewhere, such as a lounge or cafeteria, to talk about the subject matter and exchange help on an informal basis. Many students find these informal learning situations highly valuable. Your classmates become colleagues and companions. You have a sense of companionship with them even when they are not present.

This has a seldom foreseen, happy side effect: When studying for examinations, you know others who also are studying for this particular examination. You will find this, somehow, a decided comfort and support, even when you are not needing to telephone someone for information or help.

Your professors or instructors of the discussion section might meet with your informal group once or twice during the term just to chat and exchange ideas. If it doesn't occur to them, suggest it — and invite them.

7. Bring to Class Relevant Journal Articles and References.

Take with you newspaper clippings, quotations, whatever you think important for class discussion. Other students will be grateful and so will the instructor. When you are working in the library and have this in mind, your library work is more interesting and becomes more directly related to the subject matter of the course. Also, you will encourage the instructor of the discussion section, who also enjoys joint enterprises in the scholarly world.

8. The Discussion Session Can Be Used as a Practice Testing.

This is excellent preparation for the written test. Try to prepare yourself well enough so you can answer the questions other students ask of the instructor. Jot down your answers and check them with the instructor's answers. This gives you a quick check on your knowledge. You discover where your information is accurate and where there are gaps — a huge help in your preparation for the written test.

You will profit from discussion sessions to the extent you, and others, participate in ways detailed above. Without some such preparation and participation, discussions become quite futile — people simply taking turns expressing prejudices. With preparation, you build and clarify.

C. PROFITING FROM TELEVISED COURSES

Many universities and colleges are offering courses through television — sometimes by closed circuit to campus classrooms, and sometimes to homes. Difficulties in obtaining sufficient numbers of professors to keep pace with enrollments make likely an increasing number of televised courses.

1. TV Instruction Can Be Highly Effective.

The TV lecturer can be one of the most skilled and most informed on campus. Through TV, he or she can contact many more students than otherwise would be possible. When TV presentations are taped, guest lecturers can be brought in who otherwise would not be able to address this class. Special film strips can be smoothly incorporated, which otherwise could not be presented at all or presented only clumsily. Displays can be constructed and filmed which would be too unwieldy or too expensive to present to one "live" class only. Various other audio-visual aids can be employed effectively.

Whether these advantages are utilized depends upon the imagination and resources of the instructor and also upon the imagination and responsiveness of the students.

In general, students with TV instruction grasp subject matter as well as students with more familiar instructional procedures.[24, 85, 105] Retention also is high — in both short-range and long-range measurements.[24] Televised instruction appears to be as effective for communicating subject matter as the other modes of instruction.

The impacts on interest are chaotic at the college and university level. Sometimes the students like the TV instruction as well as other instructional procedures,[24, 109] sometimes better,[109] sometimes less well,[42] with no clear trend being discernible. For some students, interest in that particular course or even in that whole area is heightened during the term with TV; with other students it is impaired relative to the interest engendered through other techniques of instruction. Individual differences are large.

2. Televised Courses Pose Some Difficulties.

The main difficulty from the students' point of view seems to be keeping attention focused upon the lecturer and the subject. What is going on up there on the screen may seem terribly remote sometimes and far removed from our own world. We wait to be "entertained," in accord with habits practiced throughout childhood. We daydream. We become listless and bored.

The techniques suggested for profitable listening to lectures can all be used to advantage here. (See Section A.) Since with televised instruction there often is no professor to check on how you are doing, or what you are doing, you need to take even more initiative and more responsibility for your education than is true in more conventional situations. Notable opportunities for growth are afforded if you meet the challenge.

3. The Impersonality of TV Can Be Alleviated.

With televised instruction especially, students seem to feel that the TV instructor is on another planet, a world removed from theirs with no point of contact. They cannot see and talk with the instructor; the instructor cannot see and really talk with them. They feel isolated.

The sense of isolation is mitigated by remembering that though the TV professor cannot see you, he or she does know you exist and is talking to you. Usually the professor has met many hundreds of students, and is addressing all those sorts of individuals. If you resemble any of them, the lecturer will be presenting the lectures partly in terms of you — though you cannot be seen. Even if you are uncommon in your major interests and attributes, probably he or she will have met someone sometime resembling you. They will be remembering this, trying to slant the lectures in terms of you and your presumed existence. They will be trying to answer at least some of the questions they suspect you have...exploring some of the paths they have reason to believe will be new and interesting to you...showing you phenomena, and introducing concepts, and communicating facts not likely to be readily available to you elsewhere. They may never have an opportunity to meet you face to face, but will nonetheless be addressing you and hoping the You they think is there really is there.

D. LEARNING ADDITIONAL LANGUAGES

1. Other Languages Are Useful.

Three hundred and sixty-nine million of the people of the world speak English;[31] 95 million speak French; 120 million, German; 246 million, Russian; 670 million, Mandarin; 278 million, Hindustani; 225 million, Spanish; 134 million, Arabic; 113 million, Japanese.[31] One million people speak Esperanto,[31] a language constructed as an auxiliary language on roots from all the Greco-Latin languages, thus heightening its learnability. Many educated persons (and even many millions not educated, by your standards) speak two or more languages. English is a great language, but it may not be sufficient today for your purposes in an increasingly multinational community.

Being able to talk with persons of varying experiences and language enriches both participants. Being able to read what they have taken the trouble to write makes one more of a human being. Comprehending what they are saying opens the way to better comprehension of the world and more complete understanding. Wonderful benefits accrue from knowing additional languages.

We know too that increased skill with one language facilitates learning or perfecting another language.[3, 68, 99] With new languages as with much else, getting started is the hardest part.

Should you desire to learn another language, the task is not as difficult as you might suppose. Especially if you are a good student in other areas, learning a foreign language should go well.[3, 12, 25, 110]

2. Other Languages Sometimes Are Required.

In the academic world, as student and scholar, you sometimes need to read in other languages. In conversing with students and scholars from other lands, you need to be able to speak in languages other than English. In maintaining some friendships, you need to write other languages. In all aspects of foreign commerce, fluency in other tongues opens doors and opportunities.

Persons who are bilingual, trilingual, or multilingual are in great demand for working at the United Nations. Language skills also are demanded of persons working with multinational businesses. Customs agencies, school systems, diplomacy, social work, and welfare departments, in southern California, Arizona, New Mexico, Texas, Florida, Hawaii, New York City, and elsewhere, all require many bilingual people. Our State Department needs people fluent in other languages. The State Department operates a large language school[115] in which those who have begun language studies at a university can become more proficient. Those already proficient teach in these courses. All three branches of the military and also the Commerce Department depend greatly upon university-educated people who have learned a foreign language.

Preferably, you should learn to read, write, and speak one of the major languages of the world[31] in addition to English. Most universities offer Spanish, French, and Russian — to name three major European languages. Arabic, Mandarin, Japanese and many others are sometimes also available. Upon graduation, if you have learned one of these three European languages and one of these three non-European languages, you can look forward to high level employment by any of the groups mentioned, as well as others. Splendid opportunities await anyone skilled in languages, in this country and abroad.

3. Various Techniques Facilitate Learning Languages.

Practice labeling the objects around you in the new language.[29, 34, 41a] As you sit in your home, glance around the room labeling everything you can. As you walk down the street, list the things you see. Describe them as best you can.

Summarize the events you observe, in whatever sentences you can construct.

If the language has genders, label objects using the article as well as the noun — taking care to practice this correctly. One sometimes strongly tends to repeat old errors (rather than correct them) as well as to make new errors on successive rehearsals if one does not check accuracy with the original list.[87]

When starting a new language, make your own vocabulary lists — grouping together similar entities.[21, 38, 73, 86] For example, make separate lists for nouns, verbs, adjectives, phrases, idioms, putting the new words in one column and the English "equivalent" in a second column. Visualize the object denoted (or the activity, person, or quality) and label it aloud with your new word.[8, 45, 78] Tie it in with your major interests.

Cover one column and try to reproduce the English; cover the Egnlish and try to reproduce the other column. Going from language 1 to language 2 is a different process from starting with language 2 and going to language 1. If you wish to be skillful in both, practice both.

Contrast simple sentences depicting some action (e.g., I carry the book; he sits in the chair). Building sentences helps you remember the component parts.[52, 53] In addition, go through the action depicted by the sentence, or imagine it, while you say the sentence. Such activities while first learning a new language enhance both learning and retention.[5-8, 76] Using this system, adults far exceed children in rapidity of acquiring a language.[8]

Whenever you become proficient with some new word or phrase, omit translating it. You not only can but should omit translating word by word as soon as you are able; you thereby save time, learn to think in the new language, and lay the groundwork for swifter, more complete communication in your new language.

When proficient with the entire language, you will not need to translate at all but will simply read and speak and listen to it as you do the language you learned first. In the meantime, though, while you are first learning, it is wise to think the nearest English equivalent as you are reading the new language.

Considerable practice and rehearsal are needed to master any language.[91] If you make little lists of conjugations or of words in your new language and their English equivalents (and vice versa: lists of English and new language equivalents), you can carry these around with you and practice them in moments apt to be lost while waiting — waiting for a friend to turn up, waiting for a lecture to begin, waiting for a subway or trolley or bus, waiting for a dentist or doctor. Amazing amounts can be learned during these stray moments, and learned delightfully easily and well.

Similarly, you can prop a list near where you wash or comb your hair, have one in the car to study while waiting at drive-throughs, keep one on the dresser where you can glance at it and practice while dressing, tape one over the sink to practice while doing dishes, have one on the stereo or TV set. The possibilities are endless.

This is a highly effective way to learn, since spaced practice on this kind of material is fare more effective than massed practice. It also is relatively painless — freeing you from spending so many hours at a desk.

Your lists should be short for best results. Six or seven words, or even less, work fine and, indeed, work better than longer lists. This is one of many places where concordant data are available from the earliest experiments published on learning (the astounding work of Ebbinghaus), through the many intervening years,[81, 82] to the present time.[53, 86, 107] The data show that one learns more items per unit time when the learning is done with short lists than with long lists.

The first-acquired items of a list may be acquired at the same rate, a rate independent of length of list.[26] This suggests an additional technique: When you have all but two or three items learned from a list, begin a new list and put these recalcitrant items on it.

A foreign language is the kind of material apt to be retained when learned just prior to sleep rather than at other times of day.[63, 92, 100] Hence, another handy place to keep some of your lists is by your bed. By reading a list just before retiring, you can practice the vocabulary while falling asleep and learn large parts of it.

You need not limit yourself to vocabulary. Your lists may be of irregular verbs, or conjugations, or infinitives falling into the same conjugation, and so on. Here again, possibilities are wide for a student with ingenuity.

Straightening out differences in words (or objects) is easier when they are written near each other and are stripped of irrelevancies.[118] When a language has several words which look or sound much alike to you but have different meanings, or when the language has one or more words which look or sound like an English word but mean something different from it, make a list of them. Study them so you see clearly exactly wherein they differ.[69] Practice these words with special care.

Notice parallels with your own language, as well as differences.[89] As a starter, note words similar to yours and words very different, and note exactly what the similarities are and what the differences are.

Identify the sounds of your language which do not occur in the new language, and note exceedingly carefully the sounds of the new language which do not occur in yours. These new sounds you will need to practice with special care.

Note similarities of grammar and differences; note similarities of word order and differences. The meanings of language do not rest solely on vocabulary, but depend heavily on structure too. The importance of structure to meaning is at least dimly apparent to anyone who knows that school music is different from music school, and that the professors of education are not the same as the education of professors. The importance of structure is jarringly clear to anyone who has found the meaning of every word in a sentence of a new language and still did not know the meaning of the sentence — a phenomenon disconcertingly common when you do not understand the structure of the language.

Practice conversing. This is fun, and profitable. If your wife or husband, roommate, or some other close friend is studying the same language you are or already knows it, this would be an ideal companion with whom to practice. You have a chance to be together, at least for a few minutes, doing something light-hearted and constructive. If by some lucky chance you know someone from the country who speaks the language you are learning, converse with him or her in your new language — as best you can. Your new friend will be pleased, quite probably, to hear even a mangled version of a beloved first-learned language. And you, of course, will learn a great deal more than the language.

Be active. Especially when first learning an additional language, being active far surpasses passivity. The above studies imply this, as do others. For example, incidental learning is increased when you guess at the meaning of a new-language word, rather than merely read its English equivalent;[11] but when you are intent upon learning, seeing the equivalent and pronouncing the new word aloud is as good or better.[11] Similarly, practicing the more active art of speaking a new language before being trained in listening exceeds the reverse order, both for acquiring skills in speaking and for acquiring skills in listening comprehension.[70, 71]

A general principle runs through all this: Make as many associations as you can between the new label and your old label. The more associations you have to a word or nonsense syllable (and most new languages are close to being nonsense syllables), the better your chances of recalling that word or syllable.[17, 33, 65, 116]

Learning a language adapts itself beautifully to spaced practice. While brushing your teeth, or waiting to pick up the children, or walking to classes, or dropping off to sleep, you can practice the new vocabulary and practice building sentences with your new language. The few minutes before dinner is served, the few minutes at the gas station, all the stray moments too short to do much of anything else, are long enough to gain added skill in your new language. Astounding skill is attainable this way.

4. Supplementary Aids Abound.

For many languages, records are available which aid understanding the spoken language and perfecting pronunciation. Heightened skill in discriminating sounds helps you produce those sounds.[3, 18]

Some universities and colleges have facilities to record what you say. Studying playbacks of what you yourself have said speeds development of speaking the new language and understanding it when it is spoken to you.[80]

Recently,[84] an analysis was made of French, setting forth the words most useful in that language. Words were assessed on several bases, including their frequency in everyday speech and writing, the range and number of contexts in which they appeared, and their coverage — i.e., their capacity to replace other words. A list was compiled of the 3,626 words having highest usefulness by these criteria. This could be handy for people having little time to learn a language.

Books are available in both English and another language. Reading in the new language a sentence or paragraph or page, depending upon your skill, and then reading the English translation gives you a mode of checking on your accuracy and progress. It also affords practice with the language in a sensible context, and is far more delightful than many conventional modes of studying. Some translations, you will discover if you try this technique, are hilarious — even when done by a professional.

5. Speaking Does Not Enable You to Read.

Reading, speaking, and writing a language are related[4, 57] but somewhat different skills.[3, 15, 37] Practice them all if you wish to attain them all. Ability to read a language does not enable you to write or speak it with grace or precision. Nor will being able to speak a language guarantee your being able to read it. You must have experience with each to master each.[60, 70, 104]

In what order should these various skills be practiced? No easy answer is available because individual differences are so immense. For some people, particularly those with low aptitude,[4, 95] hearing the words pronounced and receiving training in listening and speaking before studying the printed words is a good way to begin a new language — especially if what one is interested in is skill in speaking. This should not be continued long, as the advantage seems to hold primarily or only in the early stages of learning.[4, 96]

For other students, practicing visual learning first and then relearning aurally works better than the reverse.[4, 96, 104] That is, learning the word or phrase first by seeing it, then by hearing it, works out better than learning it first by hearing it only. This should surprise nobody who remembers how many years go by of hearing a language daily before a child has a vocabulary of more than a few hundred words and grammar even faintly acceptable to educated adults. For the good student especially, this procedure of seeing the new word and its meaning, then hearing it, is superior.[4, 96] It appears superior also for low ability students who are beyond the initial stages of learning.[96]

The advantage is marked for the reading-writing skills and when the word is not pronounced in the way expected.[96] Greater positive transfer occurs from the visual to the audio skills and also from the audio skills to the visual when one uses visual-then-audio training than occurs with audio-then-visual training.[4]

The most effective system of all, however, may be simultaneously seeing and hearing the new word,[28, 102] rather than having many repeated trials of first one and then the other.

Take your lists of new words, look at them, read them aloud to yourself, carefully pronouncing each word while looking at the word. Read aloud your sentences illustrating various principles of grammar. This combines seeing with hearing, thus speeding learning, and lends itself nicely to impromptu studying at all sorts of odd moments, as described.

E. USING SPECIAL LEARNING AIDS

Various special aids are available for students having difficulty or simply desiring a supplement to the more usual materials and methods of learning. Most notable are teaching machines and programmed texts, the effective development of which was pioneered largely by A. A. Lumsdaine and his associates.

1. Teaching Machines and Programmed Texts Can Supplement Lectures.

Teaching machines are special devices which present a series of statements and questions, usually in some special order to facilitate understanding of the material. The student reads the statements and the questions, answers them sequentially (either mentally or more overtly), and then manipulates the machines to reveal the answer and the next question.

These devices have some special assets.[13, 30, 56, 114] Teaching machines respect individual differences in learning rates, the student being able to go through the material at his own preferred pace, rapidly when things are going well, more slowly when matters are obscure or difficult. The machine stops when the student wants to stop and ponder; it proceeds when he wants to proceed. The machine provides also an immediate check on knowledge and understanding; it keeps the learner active and lets him learn by trying his own answers first. Students enjoy using these machines and can employ them effectively to obtain relatively large amounts of information in relatively short amounts of time, with good retention.[25, 27, 74]

However, these devices have drawbacks, particularly when used as the sole or primary mode of instruction and study. Some students find them stultifying and frustrating and profit little from their use.[1, 16] The information gained may be very fragmentary, with a loss of integration of ideas, little opportunity or tendency to see relationships between facts, and little transfer of the acquired information or skill to new situations.[93, 112]

Programmed texts are available and useful. These are similar to teaching machines, except that the material is in book form. They can be effective aids to learning.[44, 77, 101, 111] but are not always.[1, 2, 16] For some people, programmed texts heighten habits only of rote memorizing, discourage thinking, and require more time than ordinary texts for acquiring the same amount of knowledge.[39, 90] Others welcome the opportunity for self-pacing and learn well.[20, 75, 103] If you are looking for some addition to your textbook, either for a review or for a preview introducing you to the material, you might find these a helpful and refreshing supplement.

Here again the questions are presented sequentially, and you can write your answer, think it to yourself, or simply read the answers. All of these methods can work, but writing your answer seems best for difficult material, whereas for relatively easy or already well-understood material, the latter two methods can be used efficiently.[54, 74] When learning new material, answer the question yourself before checking the answer; this is far more effective than simply reading the answer.[10]

2. Tutors Are a Valuable Aid.

We often solicit help from our friends. The assistance that tutors offer is similar, but usually more extensive and expert.

If you are having special difficulty with some particular course, or some particular phase of some course, remember skilled assistance is available and can help a lot.[20, 22, 23, 30] You need not, or course, use a tutor for the entire term, if at all, but only for those aspects elected.

3. Recordings and Other Special Aids Can Assist the Blind.

An organization called Recordings for the Blind recorded 33,429 books by 1976 in 16 different languages. These include the book you are reading and textbooks in many diverse fields. The books, taped by expert readers, are circulated free of charge to blind students. Further, the organization will specially record books not already on tape for any blind student at no charge to the student.

The American Foundation for the Blind also provides many materials to blind people without charge.

Another aid is typing. Some blind students do know how to type. An asset for any college student, typing for blind students has special boons. Knowing how to type, you can listen to taped recordings of your textbooks and take your own notes, organized in your own way, while listening to the tape. When reviewing, your notes (rather than the text) can be read to you. This saves time: Having only certain portions of a text re-read obviously is swifter than replaying the entire tape. But in addition, even if you are only moderately skilled at typing, typing is faster than punching Braille.

F. LEARNING BY DAILY ACTIVITIES

While carrying on daily activities, you can practice and develop the skills of being educated. Some students do much of their learning at such unusual times, with beautiful results.

Consider talk sessions. In some, you idly chatter; in others, you practice the skills of attentive listening and critical thinking.

Critical thinking consists partly in seeing what is wrong about certain arguments. This is the part usually recognized, but it is a small part. Far more important, skill in critical thinking consists also in seeing what is "right" about the argument, in seeing the logical consistencies, the valid implications that can be drawn from the ideas presented, the new syntheses which can be made with the ideas, the new clues afforded for solving various problems. Skilled "critical thinking" is a highly constructive, creative enterprise. You greatly increase those skills by practicing them during conversations and discussions.

Practice the arts of an open mind: Sustain a tentative attitude with regard to the validity of other people's conclusions, and your own! Watch for new ideas and new ways of looking at things. Explore the meanings of beliefs, ideas, and hypotheses of all kinds. These activities are part of and contribute toward skillful thinking and creativity.[51] Conversing in such ways is wonderful fun and also wondrously effective for becoming more nearly an educated person.

In all your interactions with other human beings, you can be acquiring deeper understanding and sympathy, a new compassion. Every complex skill requires practice, and all require practice in the kinds of situations where you wish to use them. To gain greater understanding of people, you must practice reacting to people in new ways: You must learn not only that different people have different goals, different value systems, but also learn to recognize clues to these value systems. Learn what expressions and behavior patterns reflect various emotional states. Listen awake and alert for signals of an individual's needs and hopes. You must practice responding to more dimensions of the external world, in order to develop habits of being more perceptive. All these you can practice during any of your social interactions, becoming thereby more truly sympathetic and more alive.

Understanding is diluted by misconceptions. Singularly pathetic is the notion that people agree with each other mainly to curry favor or save face. Even college and university students fall for this fallacy, overestimating grossly the degree to which verbal agreement stems from fear of disagreement.[35, 66] Thereby they misunderstand each other and fail to profit from each other's support.

In daily reading, conversation, public forums, you will come across much new information which can obliterate varied misconceptions. You will meet thousands of new facts which, if reflected upon and acted upon, greatly enhance understanding of your world and its people.

During concerts, you can practice being alert to the various musical forms, hearing more keenly the contrapuntal themes, appreciating more acutely the development of the piece. Through using what you have learned in your music courses and elsewhere, you can learn to respond with fresh appreciations, and music will gain new richness.

In everything you do, you can practice the habits which comprise being educated. Thus, through the way you meet daily experiences, you become increasingly educated.

Being educated does not consist merely in possessing masses of information. It also consists in acting in certain ways, thereby developing certain skills. Being educated is a way of responding to the world.

This means we can become more educated while not formally studying. But further, only if we live in ways like those just sketched can we become educated. No one becomes educated through classroom activities and formal study periods alone — even when managing those parts with consummate skill. We also must live outside classes and study rooms in ways consonant with habits we want for part of ourselves. Being educated is not the outgrowth solely of studying. Being educated is a way of living, and the result of living in certain ways.

BIBLIOGRAPHY FOR CHAPTER 3

1. Allen, G. J.; and Cherney, R. J. Locus of control, test anxiety, and student performance in a personalized instruction course. J. Educ. Psychol., 66, 968–973, 1974.
2. Anderson, Richard C.; Faust, Gerald W.; and Roderick, Marianne C. "Over-prompting" in programmed instruction. J. Educ. Psychol., 59, 88–93, 1968.
3. Arendt, Jermaine D. Predicting success in foreign language study: A study made in selected Minneapolis schools from 1963 to 1964. Diss. Abstr., 28 (12A), 4869–4870, 1968.
4. Asher, James J. Vision and audition in language learning. Percept. Mot. Skills, 19, 255–300, 1964.
5. Asher, James J. Toward a neo-field theory of behavior. J. Humanistic Psychol., 4, 85–94, 1964.
6. Asher, James J. The strategy of the total physical response: An application to learning Russian. International Rev. Appl. Linguistics, 3, 291–300, 1965.
7. Asher, James J. The learning strategy of the total physical response: A review. Mod. Lang. J., 50, 79–84, 1966.
8. Asher, James J.; and Price, Ben S. The learning strategy of the total physical response: Some age differences. Child Dev., 38, 1219–1227, 1967.
9. Aström, Björn; and Nilsson, Lars-Goran. Overt repetition as a means of controlling rehearsal. Scand. J. Psychol., 18, 53–58, 1977.
10. Barlow, John A. Note: Student cheating in studying programmed material. Psychol. Rec., 17, 515–516, 1967.
11. Berlyne, D. E.; Carey, S. T.; Lazare, S. A.; Parlow, J.; and Tiberius, R. Effects of prior guessing on intentional and incidental paired-associate learning. J. Verbal Learning Verbal Behav., 7, 750–759, 1968.
12. Birkmaier, Emma; and Lange, Dale. Foreign language instruction. Rev. Educ. Res., 37, 186–199, 1967.
13. Blank, Stanley S. Teaching machines: What have studies in the classroom shown? Calif. J. Educ. Res., 12, 99–115, 1961.
14. Boeding, C. H.; and Vattano, F. J. Undergraduates as teaching assistants: a comparison of two discussion methods. Teaching Psychol., 3, 55–59, 1976.
15. Brilhart, Barbara L. The relationship between some aspects of communicative speaking and communicative listening. J. Communication, 15, 35–46, 1965.
16. Bryan, Quentin R. Experimental use of the University of Michigan Audio-lingual Self-instructional Course in Spoken Spanish. Inglewood, Calif.: Inglewood Unified School District, 1965.
17. Bugelski, B. R. Presentation time, total time, and mediation in paired-associate learning. J. Exper. Psychol., 63, 409–412, 1962.
18. Buiten, Roger; and Lane, Harlan. A self-instructional device for conditioning accurate prosody. International Rev. Appl. Ling. in Lang. Teaching, 3, 205–219, 1965.
19. Buschke, Herman; and Hinrichs, James V. Controlled rehearsal and recall order in serial list retention. J. Exper. Psychol., 78, 502–509, 1968.
20. Caldwell, E. C.; Bissonnettee, K.; Klishis, M. J.; Ripley, M.; Farudi, P. P.; Hochstetter, G. T.; and Radiker, J. E. Mastery: The essential essential is PSI. Teaching Psychol., 5, 59–65, 1978.
21. Calfee, Robert C.; and Peterson, Richard E. Effect of list organization on short-term probe recall. J. Exper. Psychol., 78, 468–474, 1968.
22. Calhoun, J. F. The relation of student characteristics to performance in a personalized course. Educ. Tech., 15, 16–18, 1975.
23. Carlson, J. G.; and Minke, K. A. The effects of student tutors in learning by unit mastery instructional methods. Psychol. Record, 24, 533–543, 1974.
24. Carpenter, C. R.; and Greenhill, L. P. Instructional television research: I and II. An investigation of closed-circuit television for teaching university courses. University Park, Pa.: Penn. State Univ., 1955 and 1958.
25. Carroll, John B. A primer of programmed instruction in foreign language teaching. International Rev. Appl. Ling. in Lang. Teaching, 1, 115–141, 1963.
26. Carroll, John B.; and Burke, Mary Long. Parameters of paired-associate verbal learning: Length of list, meaningfulness, rate of presentation, and ability. J. Exper. Psychol., 69, 543–553, 1965.
27. Cassel, R. N.; and Ullom, W. L. A preliminary evaluation of programmed instruction with students of high ability. Psychol. Rep., 10, 223–228, 1962.

28. Chastain, Kenneth D. A comparison of the audio-lingual habit theory and the cognitive code-learning theory to the teaching of Introductory College Spanish. Diss. Abstr., 29 (3A), 830–831, 1968.

29. Corbett, Albert T. Retrieval dynamics for rote and visual image mnemonics. J. Verbal Learning Verbal Beh., 16, 233–246, 1977.

30. Cross, K. P. Accent of Learning. San Francisco: Jossey-Bass, 1976.

31. Culbert, Sidney S. The principal languages of the world. In Delury, George E. (Ed.) The World Almanac and Book of Facts. New York: Newspaper Enterprise Assoc., 1978, p. 186.

32. Cutler, R. L.; McKeachie, W. J.; and McNeil, E. B. Teaching psychology by telephone. Amer. Psychologist, 13, 551–552, 1958.

33. Deese, James. Associative structure and the serial reproduction experiment. J. Abnorm. Soc. Psychol., 63, 95–100, 1961.

34. Deno, Stanley L. Effects of words and pictures as stimuli in learning language equivalents. J. Educ. Psychol., 59, 202–206, 1968.

35. Deutsch, M. The pathetic fallacy: An observer error in social perception. J. Personality, 28, 317–333, 1960.

36. Diamond, M. J. Improving the undergraduate lecture class by use of student-led discussion groups. Amer. Psychologist, 27, 978–981, 1972.

37. Dizney, Henry F.; and Gromen, Lauren. Predictive validity and differential achievement on three MLA-Cooperative Foreign Language Tests. Educ. and Psychol. Meas., 27, 1127–1130, 1967.

38. Dong, Tim; and Kintsch, Walter. Subjective retrieval cues in free recall. J. Verbal Learning Verbal Behav., 7, 813–816, 1968.

39. Dwyer, Francis M., Jr., The effectiveness of visual illustrations used to complement programmed instructions. J. Psychol, 70, 157–162, 1968.

40. Ebbinghaus, Hermann. Über das Gedachtnis Leipzig: Duncker and Humblot, 1885. (Translated by Ruger, Henry A.; and Bussenius, Clara E., as Memory: A Contribution to Experimental Psychology, with a new introduction by E. R. Hilgard. New York: Dover Publications, 1964.)

41. Edwards, A. L. Political frames of reference as a factor influencing recognition. J. Abnorm. Soc. Psychol., 36, 34–50, 1941.

41a. Epstein, Michael L.; and Phillips, W. Daniel. Effects of semantic and non-semantic orienting tasks on the free recall of words. J. Gen. Psychol., 96, 281–290, 1977.

42. Erickson, C. G.; and Chausow, H. M. Chicago's TV College: Final Report of a Three-Year Experiment. Chicago, Ill.: Chicago City Junior College, 1960.

43. Fawcett, Annabel Elizabeth. The effect of training in listening upon the skills of intermediate grade children. Diss. Abstr., 25 (12), 7108–7109, 1965.

44. Fernald, P. S.; Chiseri, M. J.; Lawson, D. W.; Scroggs, G. F.; and Ridell, J. C. Systematic manipulation of student pacing, the perfection requirement and contact with a teaching assistant. Teaching Psychol., 2, 147–151, 1975.

45. Frincke, Gerald. Word characteristics, associative-relatedness, and the free-recall of nouns. J. Verbal Learning Verbal Behav., 7, 366–372, 1968.

46. Furbay, Albert L. The influence of scattered versus compact seating on audience response. Speech Monogr., 32, 144–148, 1965.

47. Gadzella, Bernadette M.; and Goldston, John. Effects of study guides and classroom discussions on students' perceptions of study habits. Percep. Motor Skills, 44, 901–902, 1977.

48. Gardner, E. Fundamentals of Neurology. Philadelphia: W. B. Saunders Company, 1963.

49. Gay, Lorraine R.; and Gallagher, Paul D. The comparative effectiveness of tests versus written exercises. J. Educ. Res., 70, 59–61, 1976.

50. Gerber, L. A. Coping, not craziness: Psychology's contribution to teaching psychopathology to medical students. JSAS Cat. Selected Documents Psychol., 1, 13–14, 1971.

51. Gibson, James W.; Kibler, Robert J.; and Barker, Larry L. Some relationships between selected creativity and critical thinking measures. Psychol. Rep., 23, 707–714, 1968.

52. Gladis, Michael; and Abbey, Osborne. Relationship between whole and part methods of learning and degree of meaningfulness of serial lists. J. Exper. Psychol., 81, 194–196, 1969.

53. Goggin, Judith; and Stokes, Charles. Whole and part learning as a function of approximation to English. J. Exper. Psychol., 81, 67–71, 1969.

54. Goldbeck, R. A.; and Campbell, V. N. The effects of response mode and response difficulty on programmed learning. J. Educ. Psychol., 53, 110–118, 1962.
55. Griffith, C. R. A comment upon the psychology of the audience. In Bentley, M. (Ed.) Critical and Experimental Studies in Psychology. Psychol. Monogr., 30, No. 136, 36–47, 1921.
56. Hilgard, E. R. Teaching machines and learning theory. In Sutherland, R. L.; Holtzman, W. H.; Koile, E. A.; and Smith, B. K. (Eds.) Personality Factors on the College Campus: Review of a Symposium. Austin, Texas: Hogg Foundation for Mental Health, 1962.
57. Hollingsworth, Paul M. Can training in listening improve reading? Reading Teacher, 18, 121–123, 1964.
58. Hollingsworth, Paul M. So they listened: The effects of a listening program. J. Communication, 15, 14–16, 1965.
59. Hollingsworth, P. M. Effectiveness of a course in listening improvement for adults. J. Communication, 16, 189–191, 1966.
60. Horowitz, Milton W.; and Berkowitz, Alan. Listening and reading, speaking and writing: An experimental investigation of differential acquisition and reproduction of memory. Percept. Mot. Skills, 24, 207–215, 1967.
61. Jain, Sharat K.; and Jain, Surendra K. Study of habits and academic attainments. Psychol. Res., 2, 13–20, 1967.
62. Janssen, P. With a little help from their friends. Change Mag., 8, 50–53, March, 1976.
63. Jarman, Betty Jane. The effect of parental messages on the career patterns of professional women. Diss. Abstr., 37 (7-B), 3580, 1976.
64. Jenkins, Joseph R.; and Bausell, R. Barker. Cognitive structure variables in prose learning. J. Reading Beh., 8, 47–66, 1976.
65. Johnson, Ronald C.; and Watson, Nancy. Individual meaning production as related to amount of verbal learning. J. Gen. Psychol., 67, 117–120, 1962.
66. Jones, E. E.; Jones, R. G.; and Gergen, K. J. Some conditions affecting the evaluation of a conformist. J. Personality, 31, 270–288, 1963.
67. Katz, Albert N.; and Denny, J. Peter. Memory-load and concreteness in the order of dominance effect for verbal concepts. J. Verbal Learning Verbal Beh., 16, 13–20, 1977.
68. Kaufman, Maurice. The effect of instruction in reading Spanish on reading ability in English of Spanish-speaking retarded readers. Diss. Abstr., 28 (4-A), 1299, 1967.
69. Kausler, Donald H.; and Olson, Richard D. Homonyms as items in verbal discrimination learning and transfer. J. Exper. Psychol., 82, 136–142, 1969.
70. Keislar, Evan R.; and Mace, Larry L. Sequence of speaking and listening training in Beginning French. In Krumboltz, John D. (Ed.) Learning and the Educational Process. Chicago: Rand McNally and Co., 163–191, 1965.
71. Keislar, Evan R.; Stern, Carolyn; and Mace, L. Sequence of speaking and listening training in Beginning French: A replication experiment. Amer. Educ. Res. J., 3, 169–178, 1966.
72. Kelly, Charles M. Listening: Complex of activities — and a unitary skill? Speech Monogr., 34, 455–466, 1967.
73. Kintsch, Walter, Recognition and free recall of organized lists. J. Exper. Psychol., 78, 481–487, 1968.
74. Krumboltz, J. D.; and Weisman, R. G. The effect of overt versus covert responding to programmed instruction on immediate and delayed retention. J. Educ. Psychol., 53, 89–92, 1962.
75. Kulik, J. A.; Kulik, C.; and Carmichael, K. The Keller Plan in science teaching. Science, 183, 379–383, 1974.
76. Kunihira, S.; and Asher, J. J. The strategy of the total physical response: An application to learning Japanese. International Rev. Appl. Ling. 3, 277–289, 1965.
77. La Gaipa, John J. Programmed instruction, teacher ability, and subject matter difficulty. J. Psychol., 68, 257–260, 1968.
78. Lappin, Joseph S.; and Lowe, Charles A. Meaningfulness and pronounceability in the coding of visually presented verbal materials. J. Exper. Psychol., 81, 22–28, 1969.
79. Levinger, G.; and Clark, J. Emotional factors in the forgetting of word associations. J. Abnorm. Soc. Psychol., 62, 99–105, 1961.

80. Lorge, Sarah W. Language laboratory research studies in New York City high schools: A discussion of the program and the findings. Mod. Lang. J., 48, 409–419, 1964.

81. Lyon, D. O. The relation of length of material to time taken for learning, and the optimum distribution of time. Part II. J. Educ. Psychol., 5, 85–91, 1914.

82. McGeoch, John A.; and Irion, A. L. The Psychology of Human Learning. New York: Longmans, Green, 1952.

83. McGinnies, E.; and Adornetto, J. Perceptual defense in normal and in schizophrenic observers. J. Abnorm. Soc. Psychol., 47, 833–837, 1952.

84. Mackey, W. F.; and Savard, J. G. The indices of coverage: A new dimension in lexicometrics. IRAL: International Rev. Appl. Ling. Lang. Teaching, 5, 71–122, 1967.

85. Macomber, F. G.; and Siegel, L. Final report of the experimental study in instructional procedures. Oxford, Ohio: Miami University, 1960.

86. Mandler, George. Association and organization: Facts, fancies, and theories. In Dixon, Theodore R.; and Horton, D. L. (Eds.) Verbal Behavior and General Behavior Theory. Englewood Cliffs, N. J.: Prentice-Hall, 1968.

87. Murray, D. J. Repeated recall in short-term memory. J. Verbal Learning Verbal Behav., 7, 358–365, 1968.

88. Myers, Ruth L.; and Gates, Louise W. Effective Listening and Cognitive Learning at the College Level. Muncie, Ind.: Ball State Univ., 1966.

89. Nakazima, S.; and Saheki, O. A study on an English teaching method in Japan based on a comparative study of Japanese and English. Jap. J. Educ. Psychol., 15, 39–54, 1967.

90. Neale, J. G.; Toye, M. H.; and Belbin, E. Adult training: The use of programmed instruction. Occupational Psychol., 42, 23–31, 1968.

91. Nelson, Thomas O. Repetition and depth of processing. J. Verbal Learning Verbal Beh., 16, 151–171, 1977.

92. Newman, E. B. Forgetting of meaningful material during sleep and waking. Amer. J. Psychol., 52, 65–71, 1939.

93. Norberg, Robert B. Teaching machines — six dangers and one advantage. In Roucek, Joseph S. (Ed.) Programmed Teaching. New York: Philosophical Library, 1965.

94. Petrie, Charles R.; and Carrel, Susan D. The relationship of motivation, listening capability, initial information, and verbal organizational ability to lecture comprehension and retention. Communication Mono., 43, 187–194, 1976.

95. Pimsleur, Paul; and Bonkowski, R. J. Transfer of verbal material across sense modalities. J. Educ. Psychol., 52, 104–107, 1961.

96. Pimsleur, Paul; Sundland, D. M.; Bonkowski, R. J.; and Mosberg, L. Further study of the transfer of verbal materials across sense modalities. J. Educ. Psychol., 55, 96–102, 1964.

97. Postman, L.; Bruner, J. S.; and McGinnies, E. Personal values as selective factors in perception. J. Abnorm. Soc. Psychol., 43, 142–154, 1948.

98. Postman, L.; and Schneider, B. H. Personal values, visual recognition, and recall. Psychol. Rev., 58, 271–284, 1951.

99. Reeber, Arthur S. Transfer of syntactic structure in synthetic languages. J. Exper. Psychol., 81, 115–119, 1969.

100. Repin, V.; and Orlov, R. S. The use of sleep and relaxation in the study of foreign languages. Australian J. Psychol., 19, 203–207, 1967.

101. Roe, K. V.; Case, H. W.; and Roe, Anne. Scrambled versus ordered sequence in autoinstructional programs. J. Educ. Psychol., 53, 101–104, 1962.

102. Saltzman, Irving J. Programmed self-instruction and second-language learning. International Rev. Appl. Ling. Lang. Teaching, 1, 104–114, 1963.

103. Santogrossi, David A.; and Roberts, Michael C. Student variables related to rates of pacing in self-paced instruction. Teaching Psychol., 5, 30–33, 1978.

104. Scherer, George A. C.; and Wertheimer, Michael. A Psycholinguistic Experiment in Foreign-Language Teaching. New York: McGraw-Hill Book Company, 1964.

105. Schramm, Wilbur. What we know about learning from instructional television. In Stanford Institute for Communication Research. Educational Television the Next Ten Years. Stanford, Calif.: Stanford University, 1962.

106. Silverstein, Albert; and Marshall, Alice. Incidental vs. intentional paired associate learning. Amer. J. Psychol., 81, 415–424, 1968.

107. Skoff, Barry; and Chechile, Richard A. Storage and retrieval processes in the serial position effect. Bull. Psychonomic Soc., 9, 265–268, 1977.

108. Sones, A. M. A study in memory, with special reference to temporal distribution of reviews. Univ. of Iowa Studies, Aims & Progress in Research, No. 72, 65–72, 1943.
109. Southwestern Indiana Educational Television Council. Second Year Report, 1959–1960. Evansville, Ind., 1960.
110. Srivastava, S. S. Study in relationship between vocabulary and academic achievements. Indian J. Psychol., 41, 35–38, 1966.
111. Stabler, John R.; and Perry, Oliver B. Learning and retention as a function of instructional method and race. J. Psychol., 67, 271–276, 1967.
112. Stafford, K. R.; and Combs, C. F. Radical reductionism: A possible source of inadequacy in autoinstructional techniques. Amer. Psychologist, 22, 667–669, 1967.
113. Terman, Michael. Personalizing the large enrollment course. Teaching Psychol., 5, 72–75, 1978.
114. Traxler, A. E. (Ed.) Improving the Efficiency and Quality of Learning. Washington, D.C.: American Council on Education, 1962.
115. Trease, B. D. Personal communication to William McBlair. 1977.
116. Van Krevelen, Alice. The relationship between recall and meaningfulness of motive-related words. J. Gen. Psychol., 65, 229–233, 1961.
117. Wachtel, P. L. Anxiety, attention, and coping with threat. J. Abnorm. Psychol., 73, 137–143, 1968.
118. Walker, Clinton M.; and Bourne, Lyle. The identifications of concepts as a function of amount of relevant and irrelevant information. Amer. J. Psychol., 74, 410–417, 1961.
119. Weir, Morton W.; and Helgoe, Robert S. Vocalization during discrimination: Effects of a mixture of two types of verbalization patterns. J. Verbal Learning Verbal Behav., 7, 842–844, 1968.
120. White, Kathleen M.; and Kolber, Robert G. Undergraduate and graduate students as discussion section leaders. Teaching Psychol., 5, 6–8, 1978.
121. White, Kathleen M.; and Waranch, Larry. The undergraduate as professor. Teaching Psychol., 5, 88–91, 1978.
122. Wood, Gordon; and Terborg, Robert H. Learning strategy, list abstractness, and free-recall learning. Psychonomic Sci., 13, 113–114, 1968.

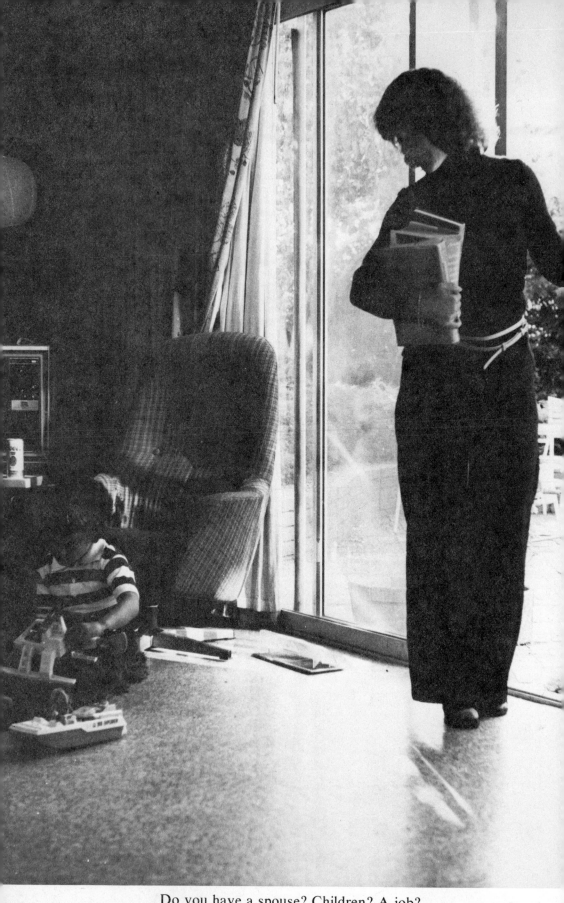

Do you have a spouse? Children? A job?

Chapter 4

Time Management

Suzie and Pete marvel at how much Lou manages to get done. They attribute Lou's success to being well-organized. But being well-organized is only part of the "secret." Part of the secret rests on not squandering time. Even ten or fifteen minutes frittered away mounts up. If this is done three or four times in the course of a day, one hour is lost and one hour is probably about 10 per cent of the total time you have for that day outside of sleep, eating, and classes.

Just as some people get a lot more for ten dollars than do other people, so also some people get a lot more out of ten hours than do others. A part of Lou's secret is spending time on the right activities. The rest of the secret is efficiency: knowing how to use time effectively in order to make the most of each hour available. Seniors usually have a lot of skills along these lines, but even they are still learning additional ways to get the most they can out of days and weeks which fly by.

This chapter deals with all three aspects of time management: organization of activities, avoiding losing hours, and most effective utilization of hours. We'll start with some aspects of the last phase — efficient use of study hours.

93

A. WHEN TO STUDY

1. Materials Reviewed Just Before Sleep Are Remembered Better.

Material learned just before sleep generally is remembered better than material learned at other times — provided it is learned.[4, 20, 24] The "provided" complicates matters, since we are apt to learn more slowly just before sleep[24] (or just after sleep[36]). This poses a dilemma.

You can, however, take advantage of both facts: Learn the material early in the day when you are fresh and wide awake. At such times you acquire new information and use complex skills efficiently. Review the material just before going to sleep.

Reviewing just before sleep is most effective for retaining details not previously integrated well.[28, 37] For instance, three stories were read and reported eight hours later.[28] In some cases, the eight hours were spent asleep; in other cases, awake. The amount retained after eight hours asleep versus eight hours awake was practically the same for aspects of the stories essential to the broad outline of the plot. (Eight-seven per cent was retained after eight hours asleep and 86 per cent after eight hours awake.) Very different results were obtained, however, for the details which few students would be apt to integrate either with the rest of the story or with anything else. For such fragmentary material, more than twice as much was retained, on an average, after eight hours asleep than after eight hours awake (47 per cent and 23 per cent respectively)

The superiority of retention during sleep may be even more pronounced for nonsense syllables than for details of stories.[20, 24] In one experiment, the students recalled about six times as many syllables after eight hours of sleep as after eight hours awake (56 per cent and 9 per cent respectively).[20] Incidentally, almost all of the forgetting that occurred during sleep took place in the first two hours. During a good night's sleep, you probably will forget no more than during a nap.

2. Review Immediately after Class to Consolidate Learning.

In a fascinating study,[34] half the students had no immediate review after the class meeting; half had a five-minute review test at the end of class. This difference in procedure seems trivial, but six weeks later the "immediate test review" group recalled one and a half times as much material as the no-review group — a significant difference in retention.

Other data likewise suggest the benefits of reviewing class notes either just after or just before the class meeting. If you have a class break and a free hour, you can use it effectively. But even the ten minutes between classes affords excellent opportunity for review or preview.

An efficient policy is to practice recall whenever and wherever you can, thus making future recall easier.[32, 38, 43]

3. Proper Spacing of Study Improves Learning.

In any learning situation you can bunch together your practice or learning trials. This procedure is called massed or undistributed practice. Or you can make each practice period shorter and spread the same total amount of study over a longer period of time. This is called spaced or distributed practice. Although the problems of massed versus distributed practice are extremely complex, some aspects are clear.

For rote memorizing and for acquisition of many motor skills, spaced practice is distinctly superior to massed practice.

For example, various individuals each were given two hours to learn a code.[35] They had the time distributed differently: The first group had twelve 10-minute periods; the second group, three 40-minute periods; and the third group, one 2-hour period. The efficiency with which they mastered the code varied greatly depending upon the way in which the study time was distributed: the longer the study period, the slower the learning of the code. Figure 2 clarifies this point and others as well.

Distributed practice has facilitated learning code substitutions,[14, 16] as well as learning mirrow-drawing and mirror-reading,[15] some other tasks involving new hand-eye coordinations,[1] and lists of numbers, words, and nonsense syllables.[26, 39, 41] This advantage of distributed trials over massed practice is greater for long lists of material than for shorter lists.[18, 25]

These facts have important applications when you are first learning a new sport or learning to play a musical in-

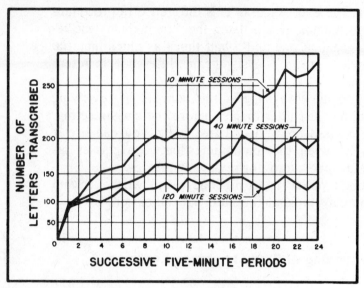

Figure 2. Advantage of short practice periods in learning to transcribe a code.[35]

strument. Apply them also for better learning of words in a new language; terms in anatomy and other sciences; atomic numbers, valences, equations in chemistry; and lists of all kinds. For each of these, break up your learning periods. Instead of one long learning session, try three or four short periods. You will be surprised by how quickly you can learn, and amazed by your fine memory.

Study periods as short as ten minutes can be extremely effective and even more effective than longer study periods. However, it is possible to make learning periods too short. This is what you would expect on logical grounds and this is what has been found experimentally. For example, ten minutes of practice once a day was superior to five minutes twice a day, for mastering problems similar to code-learning.[11]

So far we have examined the relative facility with which learning is achieved by distributed practice, as contrasted with massed practice. Let us look now at the degree of retention achieved.

For lists of numbers, words, and nonsense syllables, for codes, mazes, and some manual skills, distributed practice generally results in higher retention than does massed practice.[12, 27]

For example,[30] four groups of students tried to learn and remember a list of seven pairs of nonsense syllables. They were given 1, 2, 4, or 8 presentations of the list per practice period, until each student had been given a total of 16 presentations. Two weeks later they were tested for recall of the syllables. When study was jammed together into one or two sessions, retention was poorer.

Evidence of the same phenomenon from another experiement[6] is shown in Figure 3. Distributing the same amount of practice over more study periods resulted in better retention of nonsense lists.

Some of your studying is probably much like memorizing nonsense syllables. You have a bunch of nearly meaningless, isolated globs of information which you need to remember. For such work especially, do not drive yourself to study for long periods. Instead, study intensively for 10 or 15 minutes. You will be delighted to discover how much you can learn when you use a lot of short study periods rather than one long unbroken period for such assignments.

Let us summarize two implications of the above data: First, extremely short periods of time can be utilized effectively in study — e.g., the ten minutes between classes. Further, for rote memorization and for some other activi-

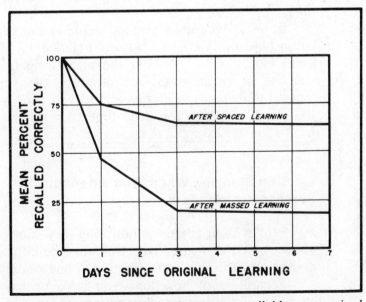

Figure 3. Retention of nonsense syllables memorized by spaced trials and by massed trials. Retention tests were given 1, 3, and 7 days after the original learning.[6]

ties, these short study periods actually are superior to long unbroken stretches — both in terms of speed of learning and extent of retention.

None of the foregoing means short study periods are the only effective way to study. When school work is to you not like memorizing nonsense syllables, when you enjoy the studying and are doing it eagerly because you want to and not as a slave who "has to," you can study extremely well for very long times. Nothing in the experimental literature suggests that short study periods are superior to long study periods for such a person.

In some situations, massed practice is superior to distributed practice.

Suppose you are writing a term paper or outlining a talk. For such activities a considerable massing of trials is desirable. Arrange your study so you have relatively large blocks of unbroken time. An hour or two is fine. Sometimes even longer stretches are needed if you are "in the middle of an idea."

Suppose you are deriving the implications of sets of data, or working up a laboratory report or a library research report. Or suppose you are synthesizing various facts, reconciling differences, organizing information. Or you are working out basic principles implicit in your readings. For all of these, you need relatively large blocks of unbroken time.

In brief: Whenever you are deriving and organizing relationships for yourself, massed practice is preferable to small bits of time.[7, 14] After the main insights and understanding of relationships are attained, the superiority of massed trials tends to disappear.[7, 9] Even here you can have too much massing; you need time to rest, and periods of incubation are essential in creative work.[13]

4. Stop Studying When Your Attention Persistently Wanders.

People differ greatly in how long they can work without getting bored or inattentive. This must be considered when determining the proper distribution of one's study time.

Regardless of how long you have or have not been studying, if you *repeatedly* come to the bottom of a page with little notion of what it said, you would be wise to stop studying.

Whenever you do not stop at those times, you are not merely *failing to learn* the information and habits you value; *you actually are learning* an inability to concentrate. While you are daydreaming at your desk, the sight of your textbook, the stimuli from sitting at your desk, all the other stimuli present at that time, are becoming cues not for study but for daydreaming.

Suppose you persist in "studying" when what you actually are doing is merely daydreaming or feeling bored. Soon you will not need to study for an hour or two, nor become fatigued, in order for those responses to be evoked. The stimuli from merely sitting down with a textbook (even though you now are refreshed) will elicit feelings of boredom and thoughts of other action. You may even reach the point where merely entering your study room evokes those responses. Some of you probably have had this happen to you — much to your consternation and despair.

In general,[2, 21, 40] whatever patterns of stimuli are present while some response is underway become cues for that response. Later, any of these stimuli will tend to elicit that reponse. The phenomena sketched above illustrate, rather poignantly, that highly important principle. You actually can learn to be unable to study! Sitting with a textbook before you while daydreaming or half-asleep is a fine way to learn that inability; and learned it will be under those circumstances — albeit you heartily dislike the habit.

Here is a system whereby you can avoid learning that habit. (1) When not concentrating, stop studying. (2) Review the sort of person you are trying to become, the particular habits and skills you are trying to learn. (3) Review also the various ways for better achieving your ends. (4) Select a few of them to practice during your next study session. (5) Then do something else for a few minutes — listen to a tape, wash a pair of socks, rearrange some furniture, do anything which requires five minutes or so and is different from the activities involved in studying. (6) Then return to your studies, and start out practicing a few of the suggestions you just reviewed. Throw yourself into the studying. Begin, at least, with all the enthusiasm and fire at your disposal.

No matter how low you rate your abilities to concentrate, even you believe you can concentrate for five minutes. Do so. If you cannot concentrate longer than that, stop at the end of five minutes — for a few minutes. Repeat the process sketched in the paragraph above, stopping whenever you find yourself daydreaming. Before long, if you are free from the disrupting emotional habits discussed later, you will be studying for 15 minutes (really studying); then 20, then 30, Eventually you will join the happy group who can study for several hours with verve and profit. And you will enjoy it. Studying will become one of the most exhilarating and exciting games you ever discovered. You may even wonder why concentration once was so difficult. The system is worth trying, don't you think?

5.   Cramming Often Is Counter-Productive.

Of all the times for study, the night before a test is one of the least efficient. If that is the time you do most of your studying, it is probably *the* least efficient time for you.

Several factors make this practice undesirable.

Studying the night before a test results in a massing of "trials" which is highly inefficient. (See pages 95–98.) Jamming too much into too short a time makes too many items to process all at once. This damages learning.[19]

Moreover, during marked anxiety or annoyance, complex mental processes such as thinking, information processing,[22] and reasoning are impaired.[8, 17, 33]

As you and I both know, many students are terribly anxious the night before a test, far more anxious than usual. This means that on that particular night, those students will think less clearly than usual. And yet at just that inauspicious time, they attempt to study. This is pathetically inefficient.

During anxiety-ridden states it is practically futile to try to ascertain fundamental principles, or acquire an ability to see the implications of various facts, or get new integrated pictures, or build skill in seeing what leads to what, or do anything else toward becoming an educated person. All of those activities demand a feeling of leisure, a sense of security, and an intellectual playfulness wholly incompatible with pre-examination haste and semi-panic. If learned at all, they must be learned at times other than the night before a test.

Even ability to memorize is impaired by marked anxiety. Studying the night before a big. exam (if you are seriously unprepared before beginning that session) costs far more time for poorer results than can be accomplished during other hours.

Anxiety is particularly great, of course, when you have done little studying prior to the eleventh hour. This means that the less you have done before the night preceding a test, the less you can accomplish on that evening. Nonetheless, we sometimes try to do the bulk of our studying at those unfavorable times. Small wonder we become discouraged and distrust our capabilities.

Another trouble: The skills of studying wholeheartedly and with concentration tend to be broken up by last-minute cramming, for worry is a potent distractor and wholly incompatible with enthusiastic enjoyment. After the test, therefore, you will have suffered setbacks in concentration and decreased study skills.

For some people, the mere *sight* of a textbook arouses anxiety. Have you wondered how this came about? Worried cramming is one way the habit is learned. Whenever you study with anxiety, all aspects of that study situation tend to become cues for anxiety. If you do most of your studying during pretest apprehension states, you will reach the point where test *or no test,* just picking up a text, just the sight of a text, even the thought of studying, will send you off into a state of apprehension or a sort of gloom.

Doing most of your studying just before a test has another grave drawback: It precludes learning to study independently of threats. It also precludes learning to study for intrinsic rewards such as the joy of discovering more about the nature of the world. Those delightful habits are developed only if you study in situations relatively devoid of threats.

In short, frantic last-minute cramming is ineffectual: It affords almost no opportunities for becoming educated. It furnishes relatively poor preparation for tests. It seriously impairs your skill in studying at other times. And ultimately it ruins what could have become an exciting, satisfying endeavor.

The foregoing does not mean that you should do no reviewing, or that you should never review the night before a test. Suppose you have studied well previously, and are free from undue emotional stress (which you may well be when you already have quite thoroughly mastered the material). No harm is inevitable then in studying the night before a test. Under those circumstances, it can be a benefit. Re-

viewing, when it is calm re-viewing, is known to be helpful.[42]

B. WARMING UP QUICKLY

Many students take a long time to get "warmed up."
Some even spend most of their study period simply trying
to get started. This is not due to any innate characteristic.
Though you may be like that now, nothing compels you to
remain that way. You need not go on wasting half your
time getting into the swing. You can learn how to sit down,
immediately become engrossed in what you intend to do,
and study effectively. Here are some hints to help you develop those skills.

1. Before Sitting Down at Your Desk, Decide Whether or Not You Are Going to Study.

Attempting two incompatible tasks at once impairs performance.[3, 5, 23] Most of us know this; yet we are prone to
ignore it. For example, we neglect to decide whether or not
we are going to study, what we are going to study and for
how long, and whether we are going to continue under various circumstances; we then undertake making these decisions simultaneously with endeavoring to study. This intro-
duces needless wear and tear.

Before trying to study, ideally before even getting out
your books, decide whether you are going to study or do
something else. Ask yourself: Am I going to telephone
someone? If anyone suggests going somewhere during the
next hour, am I going to accept the invitation? Or am I
going to study? Really decide these matters. Failing to do
this causes much difficulty in studying and prevents concentration.

Do you ever sit down at your desk and find something
like this happening? "I wonder if I should go to the movies
tonight with Charlie? No, I'd better study. . . . But Charlie
sure is a swell guy. . . . It's an awfully long time since I
saw him. . . . Need to study. . . . Maybe I ought to go and
pick him up and catch that show. . . . No, I'd better
not. . . . Gosh! I haven't got the gas yet for tomorrow. . . . Guess I'd better do that now. . . . No, I'll finish

this first. . . . Might forget it again, though. Better do it now, No! I *have* to study and I'm not getting anything done. . . . But still. . . ." And so it goes. During the time represented by the dots, you try to study. Simultaneously you try to decide *whether* to study. Those attempted responses are wholly incompatible.

Clearly one must make these decisions — or have them continue to hound one. Clearly too, it is simpler, and more efficient, to make these decisions *before* rather than *during* the studying.

In deciding whether to study, the crucial point is this: What do *you* prefer doing at this time — everything considered? Whether you study or not is up to you. To no one else does it matter nearly as much as to you. Studying is not an imposed task, but a privilege — a privilege you may or may not want to exercise at some particular time. There is a choice, and the choice is yours.

2. Before Beginning Study, Decide What You Are Going to Study and for How Long.

Your decision of how long to study may be made either in terms of time (e.g., studying mathematics one hour) or in terms of activities to be completed (e.g., solving twelve problems.). The second system frees you from having to watch a clock and generally results in less time being needed to accomplish the same amount of work.

Too often we neglect to make these decisions. We say in an off-hand fashion, "Guess I'll do some math now," and then keep wondering if maybe we ought to be studying something else instead. This is one reason we become so tired studying. We are in an almost constant state of conflict and indecision, tearing against ourselves.

Weariness and inefficiency can be reduced if you take a bit more time before beginning study to make the necessary decisions. Weigh at that time the various relevant considerations; reach a clear-cut decision as to what you are going to do; then make it a habit to adhere to your decision.

Postponing decisions does not reduce their number; it simply increases their difficulty. The number of decisions can be reduced, of course, by setting definite hours for study and by devising an order for studying subjects, studying them always in the same order except when unusual considerations make changes advisable.

3. Sit Down and Throw Yourself into the Project Energetically.

When you truly decide to study, sit down at your desk as if you meant business; open your books and begin. Throw yourself into studying heart and soul. If you cannot begin with genuine enthusiasm and wholehearted endeavor, begin anyway with as much earnestness and intentness as you can muster. To the best of your ability, act *as though* you felt wholeheartedly enthusiastic. Paradoxical though this sounds, simply going through the motions of intently studying facilitates intently studying.

4. If Necessary, Start with Some Particularly Easy or Interesting Aspect.

If you dread study or currently have to spend a long time "warming up," you especially should try arranging your studying so you start with easy or interesting parts.

For example, if you are working on a term paper, start with correcting spelling. If you are studying a text, start with a self-quiz over the earlier sections. You can learn to start studying with less dread, if you customarily stop where the task is particularly easy and seldom stop at an especially difficult stage. Then begin with that easy part the next time you study. You need not keep this up forever. When you become skilled at studying, you can start effectively with anything.

Some persons should start with the hardest parts. Getting the difficult completed and out of the way gives them such a lift they sail through the rest of their studies. For this system to work, though, you need to be quite persevering, not readily discouraged, and a skilled student requiring little or no warm up. Then the system works splendidly.

5. Prepare for the Next Study Period As You Finish Studying Each Subject.

As you finish studying each subject, write yourself a note of what you plan to do next on that subject. This note will enable you to begin smoothly when you later return to the subject. For best results, your note should be very definite. It should be more definite than "Start with page such and such," though that is better than nothing.

Try notes such as these: "Chapter 21 — See if remember underscored parts with section headings as clues." "Term paper — check spelling, punctuation, and grammar of parts completed; fill in outline for next parts to be written." Or for a text assignment, formulate the main questions you hope to partially answer from the next sections and make a written note of these questions.

Such analyses can be made in a few minutes, or even seconds, at the end of studying; whereas they may take half an hour or more at the beginning of the next study period. That half hour is squandered needlessly.

Notes help get you off to a fine start when you return to your study; you know exactly what you are going to do and can start doing it immediately. When you combine this technique with others in this section, you almost eliminate the "warming up" period.

C. STRETCHING A DAY

1. Do You Have Children? Another Job? A Spouse?

University or college work is a full-time job, and an exceedingly complicated job. If in addition you answer "yes" to the foregoing queries, clearly yours is a strenuous life. Even if your answer is "no" to some of them, you may be badly crowded for time. Any university or college student who is striving for quality is busy.

When leading a complex life, one must use time wisely, far more wisely than most of us even contemplated. No time can be squandered. When we were in high school, much time could be wasted without serious repercussions. At the university, there simply is not that much extra time: The courses are stiffer; standards are higher; the assignments, more difficult; library work, extensive; the presentations are more condensed in both lecture and textbook. Far more must be done on your own — in the realm of education and outside of it.

You have many more responsibilities. You have more people counting on you. You may have many hours on a job. There is no time to waste.

2. Pick Efficient Times to Study and Warm Up Quickly.

Acquiring these two sets of habits will save you hours every week and greatly reduce stress and fatigue. How to accomplish this is presented in Sections A and B above. Here, as with the other approaches offered in this chapter, slight improvements can be achieved almost instantly and even slight improvements bring valued results.

3. Typing Is Valuable.

To save precious hours, learn to type, and improve your typing if you already know the rudiments of the skill.

Many professors require that term papers and various reports be typed. Even when not required, you would be wise to type any report. No handwriting is as easy to read as neat typing. The added ease in reading enhances communication, and may well enhance also the perceived quality of the work. Messy things are apt to be perceived as inferior in other ways too.

Entirely apart from such considerations, typing is handy for your own private purposes. You can take notes on your texts more rapidly and read them more readily. This can save hours. Struggling to decipher poorly written notes or laboriously rechecking with the text to see what was truly said can consume hours.

You make lecture notes more useful by typing them. Especially when done soon after class, typing up lecture notes affords excellent review, and in other ways facilitates learning. For example, with typed material you see more facts at a glance, thereby making the material easier to comprehend and easier to remember. You can read your notes faster, thus freeing yourself to ponder meanings rather than having to use your time (and ingenuity) simply to decode scribbles.

Typed notes are easier to review. In fact, typed notes

sometimes are the only kind you can review. Every student probably has discovered that cold, untyped notes are sometimes barely decipherable, and sometimes wholly indecipherable. The discovery is jarring when made the night before a test.

Typing preliminary drafts of reports and papers saves you time. Typed material enables you to evaluate more swiftly your own work and greatly improve its quality: You more readily pick up ambiguities, repetitions, incomplete sentences, undeveloped thoughts. You see easily more appropriate organizations, smoother transitions, and other features of importance to your paper's overall worth. Instead of merely having a feeling something somewhere is radically wrong, you see precisely what is wrong and fix it. You also can see better what is right and leave it alone. Typing greatly aids effective study, review, and writing.

4. Learn While Not Studying Formally.

A professor conducted an entire university course via telephone.[10] Lectures, panel discussions, questions and answers, even role playing, were all conducted over a multiple hook-up telephone. This was an eminent success. The students learned a great deal — despite absence of the usual classroom setting.

Students often attempt something along those lines, talking assignments over with a friend, asking each other questions and answering them, clarifying matters for each other. Usually this is done during face-to-face get-togethers, but clearly it could be done as well over the telephone — saving each the time required for getting ready to go and transportation. Clearly too, that can be effective study, at least when the conversation includes a well-informed person.

But it is not only in that type of setting, still rather formal and structured, that you can learn. You can learn anywhere.

Standing in line at the supermart, waiting for class to begin, riding the bus to work, brushing your hair, cooking dinner, watering the lawn, these all are times for effective review and learning. During those times, find examples of whatever you were studying last. Ask yourself questions about your studies. And answer them. Practice giving yourself little quizzes. Rehearse new knowledge. Rehearse old knowledge. Overlearning improves retention.

5. Salvage Wasted Minutes to Learn.

Stray moments here and there can be salvaged and used. In the course of a week these become hours. Using these minutes for learning can reduce your formal study by several hours a week — making time for other activities. This becomes a valued mode of time management.

Suppose you are waiting for a bus which is late or for a dentist to keep an appointment. Do you gnash your teeth and bite your nails? Try instead mulling over the material you learned that day in class. Integrate whatever you observe in daily living with what you have discovered from your textbooks and lectures.

Every course has tie-ins with daily life; look for them. Any principle, concept, or fact you so illustrate, you are apt to remember.

If you take a bus or subway or trolley to work, you may be able to read during travel. Even if much reading is impossible, you can still study and rehearse lists of facts or vocabularies you need to master. Prepare the lists in advance.

A simple system is to list important details for each course on 3 × 5 file cards. For example, make cards with dates of key events for history, names of bones for anatomy, classification of animals for zoology, technical terms and their definitions for science courses, foreign language vocabularies, conjugation of verbs, muscles' insertions and origins, atomic numbers and valences, basic chemical equations, equations for physics; the applications are endless. You can carry these cards in your pocket or purse, and whip them out for perusal whenever you have to wait for anyone, or just sit. Use them for learning and review and testing yourself. Thus stray moments are captured and transformed.

6. Devise a Time Schedule.

When assignments are heavy, or housework piles up, or things go badly on the job, we may become a little frantic. When the children get sick and term papers are due and the doctor's appointment takes three hours instead of one, we become downright panicky. How to get everything done? Can we get everything done?

Even with conditions not so crowded, you might worry and fret over how to accomplish everything necessary.

An excellent way to reduce anxieties is to devise a schedule and stick to it. Schedules eliminate some anxieties before they arise, and lessen others. Schedules also save a great deal of time, since you can move more smoothly from one kind of activity to the next, and need make fewer decisions per day about what to do that hour and what to do later.

Devising a schedule is not as simple as it sounds — especially if you have many commitments.

The best place to start is to consider what activities you want to include in a week. Make one list of all the activities you must include in a week: eating, sleeping, studying each course, attending class, getting to class, and all the other necessary actions. Make another list of activities you enjoy and wish to include in your week.

Then make a chart of all the hours in a week, day by day. It is best to make one chart for each day, because days will have to be different from each other in order to get into a week the variety of activities you wish to include. Days will differ even though some activities do occur every day at the same time.

If you are exceedingly busy, make your chart by half-hour intervals. Even quarter-hour intervals in some parts of the day can help you work everything in. This is a good system, too, if you are forgetful or poorly organized. Making small intervals helps you remember the many small things you need to do and helps you organize them.

Before trying to fit your activities into your chart, see if it is possible to do so. Beside each of your items put an estimate of the amount of time needed for that item; then total them. A week has only 168 hours. You probably will find your lists tally more than 168 hours.

Four possibilities are available: Drop some items. Combine some items — arrange to do two or three at once. Reduce some items — do them less often, less thoroughly, for a shorter time, or do fewer of them. Schedule some items for alternate weeks.

You may be able to gain an extra hour or two by reducing sleep. Getting six or seven hours of sleep probably will work out all right if you are in good health.[29]

When cutting things out, do not delete all play. And be

sure to schedule some free time. Chapter 6, Section D–3, discusses these matters.

After you have your schedule completed, try it out and see how it goes. Regard this first schedule as simply a trial. Some items will take far less time than you expected, whereas other items will require more time than you had supposed. Adjust your schedule accordingly, and try it out again.

When you have a fairly promising schedule devised, stick to it earnestly. If sometimes some aspect seems abominable, make a note of it. As you go along through the days, jot down what about your schedule is great and what about it is unpleasant or not wholly satisfactory. After a month or so, devise a new schedule (if you wish) taking these added considerations into account.

You need to persist and stick by your schedule for a sustained period of time because some aspects which at first seem flaws will turn out to be altogether tolerable or even advantageous when you get accustomed to the schedule. You need to persist also because most of the benefits of a schedule becomes apparent only after you have used the system for quite a while. Little by little, you learn how to benefit. As you use the system you learn more and more about its possible assets.

7. You Can Develop Concentration.

How many hours have you spent daydreaming when you intended to study? How many hours were lost searching for the right place to study uninterruptedly? How many times have you started study only to become distracted? Concentration is a key factor in successful time management.

Having excellent power here is handy throughout life, bestowing freedom in what can be tackled, where, and when. For a busy college or university student, excellent concentration is absolutely indispensable. Quality education with a limited time budget, hinges on quality concentration.

Clearly you already have considerable ability to concentrate or you could not have come this far. This ability can be extended.

How to concentrate well and easily is set forth in Chapters 6 and 7. Those chapters identify sources of disruption and show you many ways to free yourself and heighten concentration.

8. Minimize Fatigue, Where Possible.

Fatigue steals time. As you almost certainly have noticed, fatigue impairs effectiveness. Simple jobs take longer.
Complex jobs take longer yet; they may even become impossible. Errors pile up, costing more precious time. Concentration becomes more difficult, so we work longer and longer to
get the same amount done. Coordination is shot, so we have
to concentrate harder in order to avoid piles of errors, and still
the job is apt to take longer than if we were fresh. The next
day we spend correcting errors.

"Time management" programs are all but worthless until
we tackle the matter of fatigue.

Fatigue is inevitable when we fill many functions at once.
You have your complex job as a student and you may have
another job to make needed money. Already things are complicated and weariness likely. In addition, you are part of a
family with desires and responsibilities there; you are a son or
daughter, and probably a brother or sister, and a member of a
larger family as well. You are also a friend to lots of persons; a
citizen of some country; perhaps a husband or wife, perhaps
a parent; probably a homemaker — be it only of a room in a
dormitory. You are an inhabitant of a beleaguered planet, a
neighbor, a member of various clubs and organizations. You
are also an individual with private interests. Have you wondered why you were tired? With so many roles and the
actions they entail, fatigue surely will occur. But it can be
lessened.

Here is a list of possibilities for lessening fatigue, so that
each moment yields more of quality.

Develop better concentration; Chapter 6 presents a
wealth of ways to do this. Lie down for a few minutes with
your feet up. Make use of the exercises given in the Addendum for relaxation training.

Get sufficient sleep. If you usually get only 5 or 6 hours'
sleep, are irritable or worried, are tired much of the time and
nervous, increase your amounts of sleep. Even an hour more
might be enough.

Eat sensibly. The busier we are, the more apt we are to
eat hurriedly and skimpily. Just when we most need an abun-
dance of energy, we tend to skip breakfast or lunch or both
and try to make up for it with a big dinner. This is unwise.
Energy levels will stay higher on three moderate meals than

on one large meal. And higher on three balanced meals than on junk food.

Are you drinking seven or eight cups of coffee a day just to keep going? Or lots of tea? Or large amounts of other caffeinated drinks, such as Coke or Pepsi? If you are, you are doing too much. Delete some activities.

Snacks can give you a lift. Try an apple, banana, orange, graham crackers, fruit juice, milk. These take no time to fix and furnish quick energy.

Instead of candy bars and soft drinks, try fruit, celery, or carrots. Fatigue sometimes is due to mineral and vitamin deficiencies.

Intersperse five- or ten-minute rest periods in long evenings or days of study. Ten minutes of playing with the children or taking a brisk walk, even 5 minutes spent watching a sunset, can do wonders for bedraggled spirits.

Take your rest periods before you become frazzled. A little rest can make a lot of difference if it comes soon enough. If rest comes too late, extra hours or days or weeks must be consumed to repair the damage.

When you play, play. When you rest, rest. For some people this is easier said than done, but at least we know what to aim for. Set your work aside for the time being and get yourself repaired.

Naps can save time. Can you get a short nap and wake up refreshed? If you can, that probably will be more efficient than adding the same number of minutes to night-time sleep. Obtaining rest before becoming too tired will save time in the long run. If, on the other hand, you wake up slowly and feel groggy and dull after a nap, you would do better by increasing your night-time sleep.

Reduce physical stress where feasible. Procure good lighting and ventilation, moderate temperatures, adequate food and rest, freedom from pain and undue discomfort.

Reduce emotional stress when feasible. Chapter 7 helps in this. Reducing physical stress also reduces emotional stress. A recent book for college students contains guides on handling money, easing financial problems, getting a job, and solving various other stressful difficulties.[31]

If nearing exhaustion or extremely tired, do whatever you can to reduce stress. All thresholds are lower, leaving the sufferer vulnerable. Under these circumstances, even small noises may be a burden and any added pressure a serious drain. At these times, reduce all possible stresses as much as you can. And get rest as soon as possible.

9. Make More Efficient Use of Study Time.

When you are exceedingly busy with many interests, desires, and commitments, you cannot spend endless hours studying. For you it is imperative to use effectively what study time is available. For any activity, the best way to enhance efficiency is to increase your skill. Increasing skill always increases efficiency.

How to increase your skill in studying and learning is the subject of this entire book.

For example, the next chapter deals with effective use of books. Parts 8 to 14 obviously are ways to save time and effort when reading or studying; but parts 1 to 7 are just as handy for saving time and effort. So also with the rest of the book. Every part of this book is intended to help you increase your efficiency, thereby reaping more per hour invested and gaining, too, the opportunity for life with more variety.

BIBLIOGRAPHY FOR CHAPTER 4

1. Adler, Alon; Strasser, Helmut; and Muller-Limmroth, Wolf. Effects of massed and distributed practice, additional monetary and placebo incentives. Percep. Motor Skills, 42, 1335–1338, 1976.
2. Allen, Max M. Cueing and retrieval in free recall. J. Exper. Psychol., 81, 29–35, 1969.
3. Baddeley, A. D.; Scott, Denise; Drynan, Rosemary; and Smith, Janet C. Short-term memory and the limited capacity hypothesis. Brit. J. Psychol., 60, 51–55, 1969.
4. Benson, Kathleen Louise. The effect of sleep on long-term verbal memory. Diss. Abst., 37 (2B), 999–B, 1976. Also, with Feinberg, I. The beneficial effect of sleep in an extended Jenkins and Dallenback paradigm. Psychophysiology, 14, 375–384, 1977.
5. Boggs, David H.; and Simon, J. Richard. Differential effect of noise on tasks of varying complexity. J. Appl. Psychol., 52, 148–153, 1968.
6. Cain, L. F.; and Willey, R. The effect of spaced learning on the curve of retention. J. Exper. Psychol., 25, 209–214, 1939.
7. Cook, T. W. Massed and distributed practice in puzzle solving. Psychol. Rev., 41, 330–355, 1934.
8. Costa, Paul T.; Fozard, James L.; McCrae, Robert R.; and Bosse, Raymond. Relations of age and personality dimensions to cognitive ability factors. J. Gerontology, 31, 663–669, 1976.
9. Cummins, R. A. Improvement and the distribution of practice. Teachers Coll., Columbia Univ., Contr. Education, No. 1, pp. vi + 72, 1919.
10. Cutler, R. L.; McKeachie, W. J.; and McNeil, E. B. Teaching psychology by telephone. Amer. Psychologist, 13, 551–552, 1958.
11. Dearborn, W. F. Experiments in learning. J. Educ. Psychol., 1, 373–388, 1910.

12. Frost, Robert R.; and Jahnke, John C. Proactive effects in short-term memory. J. Verbal Learning Verbal Behav., 7, 785–789, 1968.
13. Fulgosi, A.; and Guilford, J. P. Short-term incubation in divergent production. Amer. J. Psychol., 81, 241–246, 1968.
14. Garms, Joe D. Predicting scholastic achievement with nonintellectual variables. Diss. Abstr., 28 (8B), 3460, 1968.
15. Gentry, J. R. Immediate effects of interpolated rest periods on learning performance. Teachers Coll., Columbia Univ., Contr. Educ., No. 799, pp. vi + 57, 1940.
16. Henry, L. K.; and Wasson, R. The repetition of classical experiments: I. Starch's distribution of practice. J. Appl. Psychol., 23, 503–507, 1939.
17. Higginbotham, Timothy E. Irrationality in college students. Rational Liv., 11, 34, 1976.
18. Hovland, C. I. Experimental studies in rote-learning theory. VII. Distribution of practice with varying lengths of list. J. Exper. Psychol., 27, 271–284, 1940.
19. Imhoff, David L.; Horton, David L.; Weldon, Linda J.; and Phillips, Robert V. Rehearsal and processing capacity as factors in memory. J. Exper. Psychol.: Human Learning and Memory, 3, 551–559, 1977.
20. Jenkins, J. G.; and Dallenbach, K. M. Obliviscence during sleep and waking. Amer. J. Psychol., 35, 605–612, 1924.
21. Johnson, Ronald E. Rehearsal activities to a paired-associate task. J. Verbal Learning Verbal Behav., 7, 439–445, 1968.
22. Kanekar, Suresh. Academic performance in relation to anxiety and intelligence. J. Soc. Psychol., 10, 153–154, 1977.
23. Logan, Gordon D. Attention in character-classification tasks. J. Exper. Psychol.: Gen., 107, 32–37, 1978.
24. Lovatt, D. J.; and Warr, P. B. Recall after sleep. Amer. J. Psychol., 81, 253–257, 1968.
25. Lyon, D. O. The relation of length of material to time taken for learning, and the optimum distribution of time. Parts II and III. J. Educ. Psychol., 5, 85–91, and 155–163, 1914.
26. Maskarinec, Ann S.: and Thompson, Charles P. The within-list distributed practice effect. Memory Cognition, 41, 741–746, 1976.
27. Melton, Arthur W.; and Shulman, Harvey G. Further studies of a distributed practice effect on probability of recall in free recall. Psychonomic Bull., 1, 13–14, 1967.
28. Newman, E. B. Forgetting of meaningful material during sleep and waking. Amer. J. Psychol., 52, 65–71, 1939.
29. Noles, Keith O.; Epstein, Leonard H.; and Jones, H. Tate. Instructional control of sleep reduction. Percep. Motor Skills, 43, 669–670, 1976.
30. Perkins, N. L. The value of distributed repetitions in rote learning. Brit. J. Psychol., 7, 253–261, 1914.
31. Pivar, William H. The Whole Earth Textbook: A Survival Manual for Students. Philadelphia: W. B. Saunders Company, 1978.
32. Rosner, S. R. The effects of presentation and recall trials on organization in multitrial free recall. J. Verbal Learning Verbal Beh., 9, 69–74, 1970.
33. Sarason, Irwin G. Test anxiety and the intellectual performance of college students. J. Educ. Psychol., 52, 201–206, 1961. And with Palola, Ernest G. The relationships of test and general anxiety, difficulty of task, and experimental instructions to performance. J. Exper. Psychol., 59, 185–191, 1960.
34. Sones, A. M. A study in memory, with special reference to temporal distribution of reviews. Univ. of Iowa Studies, Aims and Progress in Research, No. 72, 65–72, 1943.
35. Starch, D. Periods of work in learning. J. Educ. Psychol., 3, 209–213, 1912.
36. Stones, M. J. Memory performance after arousal from different sleep stages. Brit. J. Psychol. 68. 177–181. 1977.
37. Sullivan, Michael John. The effect of wakefulness and sleep on the memory for complex linguistic ideas. Diss. Abstr., 37 (B4), 1949B–1950B, 1976.
38. Thompson, Charles P.; Wenger, Steven K.; and Bartling, Carl A. How recall facilitates subsequent recall. J. Exper. Psychol., 4, 210–221, 1978.
39. Underwood, Benton, J.; Kapelak, Susan M.; and Malmi, Robert A. The spacing effect. Memory Cognition, 4, 391–400, 1976.

40. Voeks, Virginia W. Gradual strengthening of S-R connections or increasing number of S-R connections? J. Psychol., 39, 289–299, 1955.
41. Watts, Doyle; and Chatfield, Douglas. Response availability as a function of massed and distributed practice and list differentiation. Psychol. Record, 26, 487–493, 1976.
42. Wittmaier, Bruce C. Low test anxiety as a potential indicator of underachievement. Meas. Evaluation Guid., 9, 146–151, 1976.
43. Yuille, J. C. A detailed examination of meditation in PA learning. Memory Cognition, 1, 333–342, 1973.

Typed notes facilitate review . . .

Chapter 5

Becoming an Expert at Exams

A. PERVASIVENESS OF TESTS

Throughout life we are confronted by examinations: aptitude tests, intelligence tests, achievement tests, tests of knowledge, of vocabulary, or of our skills, examinations for entering college, for continuing college, for getting various jobs in industry, business, the civil service, tests for the Army, Navy, or Marine Corps, tests for entering the practice of law or medicine or other professions, tests for licensing, promotion, or reclassification, tests for driving.... These are some of the obvious ones. In addition, we take many many tests not so obvious — try-outs for plays, or symphonies, or teams; interviews for new jobs, transfers, or promotions; on-job ratings; review by critics; casual-appearing conversations which nonetheless are evaluative of us and influential of trends for our future life. The list is far longer than this. As is apparent on reflection, we take tests of one kind or another throughout our lives — no matter what line of work we undertake.

Much of our life hinges upon how we do on various tests. And the tests go on for as long as we live.

We need, therefore, to develop skill in facing and taking examinations — both because they themselves are a sizable chunk of life and because they influence greatly other aspects of our present and future. College is as good a time as ever for developing the skills and healthy outlooks which will enable you to do more gracefully and effectively those portions of human life. Certainly you will have a lot of opportunities to practice. No day goes by, probably, that you are not taking *some* kind of test.

Practice can make perfect. Practice also can make us a mess. The latter happens if we practice sloppy ways, and errors, and disruptive patterns. We get more and more habits of an adverse sort, and can reach the point at which any examination (even a physical examination by an M.D.) plunges us into an apprehensive, poorly functioning state. The thought of an examination, the mere word "examination," can cue disorganizing thoughts and behavior.

You can practice, on the other hand, responses which make you increasingly adroit and cheerful. You can practice techniques, approaches, attitudes, and feelings which build into habits comprising amazing skill handling examinations. Grade school would have been a fine time to begin, but your college years are convenient times too.

B. FORMAL REVIEW AND OTHER PREPARATIONS

1. Practice Expert Preparation and Execution on Trivial Tests.

One advantage to university and college work is that we usually take a considerable number of rather unimportant tests. Compared with many tests one meets later in life, relatively little rides on some college quizzes. This furnishes an almost perfect chance to practice more sensible habits of preparing for and taking tests. During study for an unimportant test, it is easier to stay collected and serene. If you study for a small quiz with calmness and alertness, you thereby have a start on studying for other tests with calmness and alertness. Habits do generalize. If you do this a lot, the chances are high that these healthy emotional habits will generalize even to quite important tests, and from them to very important tests.

The same point holds for the intellectual skills of studying and taking examinations, and also for the mechanics of studying and taking examinations. If you practice these on unimportant matters, you can practice more serenely and thereby facilitate the acquisition of complex skills and increase the likelihood of transfer to exceedingly important tasks. Building new skills in thinking, studying, writing, and building other complex chains, discriminations, and organizations, is easier when you are relatively calm than when it is utterly imperative that you establish new habits and get the hang of the new skills with alacrity and almost no errors.

2. Studying as Already Sketched Is Excellent Preparation for Tests.

If you have studied in the way described so far, you will be well prepared for any test. When an examination is announced, you need do little more, except tie together a few loose odds and ends, and perhaps do some further reviewing.

Reviewing means, of course, re-viewing. It should not be restricted to your formal study periods. Rather, reviewing should be a continuous process, a part of your daily living. That type of reviewing we already have considered. Let us look now at more formal types.

Some students do their original study and also their formal review of the material at the same session, often with disastrous results. Other students study in advance, but then review by merely re-reading everything one or more times. This too can have miserable results, and at best is a flagrant waste of time. Little merit exists in devoting equal amounts of time to all aspects of the material. More profitable uses of time are available. Here are some of them.

3. In Formal Review, Try First to Recall the Chapter Subheadings.

If you are reviewing a textbook, look at the chapter title, then see if you can list the main ideas or headings of the chapter. If you are reviewing notes, try to write the main headings of your outline. Do this before looking at that material. Then carefully check the accuracy of your memory, visibly marking any omissions or errors.

Next try to recite the details under each heading. After doing that, read the section rapidly, marking anything you omitted in your rehearsal. The parts you remember correctly at this time probably need no further attention. The parts you forget are a different matter.

4. Tie Forgotten Parts More Adequately to Other Facts.

Memory is greatly helped by more active and deeper processing of details.[21, 35, 97] Integrate elusive data and concepts with your personal experience and other knowledge, so you do not again forget them. Many ways of making such integrations were presented in Section D of Chapter 2 (The Use of Books, pages 44–50). Especially if you have trouble on examinations, you will profit by re-reading that section.

When you derive implications and other inferences from the lecture material, mark these on your notes to distinguish them from the professor's statements. Otherwise you probably will treat your inferences and the instructor's statements as though they were the same, making no distinction in your recall between the two.[35] This can lead to various errors. Also, marking your inferences gives you an opportunity to later find them and check their accuracy and perhaps improve or extend them.

5. Group Together Similar Facts and Label the Categories.

Grouping similar things together and constructing other logical orderings help us to remember them.[14, 22, 27] Even lists of words are remembered better by organizing the words in some way.[12, 104] almost any way which occurs to the learner.[19, 63, 64, 103] So are facts and concepts,[12, 18, 38] and other materials.[4, 60, 88] Labeling the categories increases the efficacy of organizing.[54, 101]

In your study, when you have a great array of facts to remember, try arranging them so similar facts are together.[37] For example, in history and other courses, sort out important dates and make a list of them and the events occurring on each of them — preferably arranging the dates in order. For zoology and biology, list together animals or plants or other phenomena having certain characteristics in common. For any science, compile a glossary of technical terms and basic concepts (with their definitions), grouping together those which are related and labeling the categories. In all courses, collect the names of key persons and what they did, putting persons with similar achievements together.

This is a way of re-working your notes rather than merely copying them or re-reading them and is a way of enhancing memory. A precise memory for details is helpful on any examination, but especially helpful on essay tests[19, 52] where one needs to re-capture facts, not simply recognize them.

6. Ask Yourself Questions and Practice Answering Them.

The basic idea, here again, is to practice doing what you want to learn. If you want to use what you have been studying to answer questions, then practice doing that. Ask yourself questions and answer them, checking the answers against your notes and textbooks.

This method has an added merit: With practice, the questions which you ask yourself will often resemble the test items. There is, after all, only a limited number of questions one can sensibly ask on any specified material.

When you are preparing for a true-false examination, be sure to write yourself some false items. As long as we are in lecture or studying in ordinary ways, we are confronted with "trues" only — or at least what someone deems true. On the test, we suddenly are in a morass of trues and falses and partial truths — a jungle. This sudden change can be highly disconcerting and even terrifying. We are apt to be disrupted by this strange world, and become worried lest we learn the falses and forget the trues and get all mixed up. The confusion and anxiety can be reduced by familiarizing yourself in advance with tangles of trues, half-trues, quarter-trues, trues except for one word, and outright falses. In the quiet of your study, familiarize yourself with these messes and practice sorting trues from falses. You can become very adroit at such sorting. It is, of course, a handy skill to have in real life.

7. Study as if the Test Were an Essay Examination.

Some students once were told to study for an objective test and they did. Then they were given an essay test. You will not be astonished that their performance was inferior to that of students who had studied for an essay test.[68]

However, you may be somewhat astonished that the reverse was not true. Students who had prepared for an essay test and then were given a conventional objective test did just as well as those who had studied for the objective test. This has been found repeatedly.[33, 34, 68]

As you know, many of us study quite differently when preparing for objective tests than when preparing for essay tests.[14, 68] In studying for essay tests, we practice presenting in orderly fashion as many facts and ideas as we can with only a few cues being furnished. We look for implications and tie-ins; we practice applying the material; and in other ways too, we try to make the material meaningful. In studying for objective tests, on the other hand, we often merely reread the chapters and memorize some isolated facts. This is poor preparation for making the logical analyses, reconstructions, and integrations requisite for fine performance on essay tests.[33, 34, 68] It even is poor preparation for some kinds of objective tests.

Some true-false, short-answer, and multiple-choice tests measure substantially the same skills as do essay tests: e.g., the ability to reconstruct material, the ability to remember information with few cues, the ability to draw logical inferences from facts and principles, and the ability to see the pertinence of these facts to new problems. In taking such objective tests, people who studied in the usual way for an objective test would be handicapped gravely compared with ones who studied for an essay examination. And even when the objective test is of the recognition type, such persons have no advantage (you recall) over people who studied for an essay test.

These facts suggest that even in terms of grades a wise policy is this: Always study as if an essay test were scheduled, regardless of whether the test will be essay or objective. In terms of becoming educated, the policy also is wise, for the activities you engage in during that kind of study are far more similar to the habits you wish to make part of yourself and to the skills you need in the rest of life. With this approach to reviewing, you can prepare for any type of test and simultaneously prepare for living.

8. Review, and Then Go to Sleep.

Almost nothing is forgotten during sleep for material that is well-integrated or meaningful. This you know (see page 94). Further, even material that is lightly learned is apt to be remembered almost as well as much-practiced material, if the time between learning and testing is spent in sleep. For example, college students learned pairs of adjectives; some they learned to the point of one correct anticipation, some to two, some to three, four, five, six, or seven, and some to eight or more correct anticipations. The amount remembered after nine hours in sleep was very high (between 87 and 98 per cent), regardless of the amount of correct practice.[56]

9. On the Night Before the Test, Get Your Usual Amount of Sleep.

Review well in advance of the examination, sleep the night before the test. This is far superior to the more common practice of sleeping well in advance of the test and then reviewing madly on the last night.

During last-night cramming, you may pick up some miscellaneous bits of information. However, the odds are slim that the value of those facts will offset the losses in concentration, clear thinking, and perceptual organization which occur when you are badly fatigued.[5, 9, 57] Certainly these last-minute gains in information will not counterbalance other losses incurred by cramming (see pages 100–101 and 140).

Perhaps you are afraid to review well in advance of tests, lest you forget before the test many important facts and principles. Retention curves for some materials do drop rapidly for the first few hours and then level off; but this is true mainly for nonsense syllables. We hope that what you are learning bears little resemblance to nonsense syllables. We hope it is not a bunch of memorized, nearly meaningless globs. But even if it is, you cannot get the jump on this drop in retention. The sharp drop (for nonsense material) occurs too rapidly and ends too soon. To take the examina' tion before that retention drop occurs would require that the test be given only a few hours after your original learning and reviewing. You simply cannot do much learning nor efficient reviewing in that period of time.

Further, and this is worth noting well, material you have tied in with your life and made meaningful has no sharp quick drop in retention. For such material, very little is forgotten in a few days or even weeks. Using the methods of study we have been considering, you can finish your formal review long before the test and run no danger of forgetting much between then and the time of the test. A great deal of it you will remember for years. Rarely will you forget what you use.

C. TAKING EXAMINATIONS EXPERTLY AND FREE FROM TERROR

Skill in the mechanics of taking examinations has little to do with becoming educated, but it has much to do with grades. Skill in the mechanics of taking examinations also has much to do with obtaining certain jobs in the military and civilian life, with getting promoted, with entry into graduate schools, and with satisfactory achievement in other areas as well. These are probably among your objectives too, so let us look at ways you can take tests more skillfully.

1. How Should One Take Essay Examinations?

Read the entire set of questions before starting to write.

Start with the question on which you feel most qualified to write. Cogent arguments favor this approach, even when items have unequal weight: In the first place, that is the question you need least time to ponder. Second, you avoid the danger of losing your best ideas while struggling with the questions which are harder for you. Third, while writing on it, ideas concerning the other questions will occur to you.

One last advantage: while answering the question directed most along the lines of your previous thinking, you become calmer and more self-possessed. This calmness, in turn, facilitates clearer thinking on the other questions. You get in the "set" of thinking coherently, and the set carries over to other problems. It is pleasant to discover that "hard" questions look far easier when you return to them after doing the items simplest for you.

The set of coherently thinking cannot be created well when you start out with the questions most difficult for you. When you begin with them, the set you create is apt to be distraught apprehension and anxiety. This too can carry over and seriously impair your performance even on questions you understand thoroughly.

Suppose you have no clear ideas on any of the questions. Then what? Fold your tent and silently steal away? You can find wiser procedures. One is to start writing anyway. On a separate piece of paper (not to be turned in), write the number of each question, and then beside each number jot down any scattered, fragmentary thoughts that occur to you in connection with various questions. If you can get a few general headings for an outline, fine. Write them — even if you cannot recall immediately any of the facts necessary to support the points, nor many of the main points. Some of these additional facts will occur to you later.

If worst comes to worst, and absolutely no sensible, partial answers occur to you, start writing anyway. Write anything which is even remotely relevant to any of the questions. Never mind how remote the relevancy is. Start writing. Gradually your thoughts will become more germane to the topics involved. The approach sounds a bit idiotic, but it does work.

This procedure helps rescue you from the near trance-like state, or panic, into which you otherwise tend to subside. Using it, you gradually recall more nearly relevant facts; then, wholly relevant ones. (Do not turn in those first preliminary notes, of course. They served their purpose in getting you started.)

Use proper spelling and grammar. Unconventional spelling and grammar, poor handwriting, sloppy punctuation, and clumsy sentence construction are serious impediments to communication. At best, they distract the reader. At worst, they cause him to completely lose the thread of your ideas while attempting to decode the misspelled words, translate the misused terms, cipher some peculiar script, and straighten out garbled phrases and sentences.

During a test it is difficult to write well, but use as lucid and graceful a style of composition as you can under those rather trying circumstances. Be concise and precise in your wording. Write legibly, using accurate spelling, grammar, and punctuation. Attending to these details can enormously enhance communication and greatly enhance also the perceived quality of your answer.

If your spelling and punctuation are standing in your way, a little book by Anderson, Straub, and Gibson could help you considerably.[3] The book gives a very clear, and short, set of rules for spelling and for effective punctuation. It notes words commonly interchanged by college students and briefly defines them.

Trying to achieve proper, clear spelling is a bugaboo to some students; but English is not the horrendous mess you might fancy. Approximately 90 per cent of its syllables are phonetic, enabling one thereby to spell correctly a great many words. Of 17,000 words analyzed,[32, 43-45] almost half could be perfectly spelled phonetically, and more than two thirds of the remaining words could be spelled with one error only. That leaves only 14 per cent which are rather tricky.

In trying to achieve greater accuracy in spelling, watch for words which sound alike but are spelled differently and for misspellings in which the letters have the same sound as the correct spelling but are not appropriate (e.g., "work" spelled as "werk"). Such errors are easy to overlook.[58]

The foregoing procedures will improve your test results vastly. To aid you further, here are a couple of dozen additional tips — very briefly presented.

For full credit, you must answer the question asked, and not one of your own creation. Therefore, before beginning to write, re-read the question carefully. Make certain you understand exactly what is being asked.

Make at least a sketchy outline of your answer before starting to write your full answer.

Be as specific *and also as complete* in your answer as you can in the time available. Give all general points which are relevant, but do not stop there. Also give some examples, substantiating facts, and correlated details. (You need not give *all* that occur to you, nor would there be time.) Always write to the point.

While writing on one question, you will get ideas pertinent to other questions. Jot down some clue to these ideas on a separate sheet, in order that you neither forget them nor have to remember them while writing on another topic. This procedure increases the coherency and completeness of your answers. It also helps reduce your tension and anxiety.

Leave space for additions to your answers. One practicable method is to write on only one side of bluebook pages. Then you can draw arrows from any sentence to the back of the preceding page, and there make any additions which later occur to you.

Budget your time, checking frequently. When you first

receive the test, figure out how much time to allow for each question. Save some time to go over the test, checking and filling in parts, or to take care of emergencies (such as some part requring longer than you had thought, or for going blank for a while).

An incomplete answer to all items is better than no answer to some questions and a too long answer to some others, so be certain to keep track of the time. If you fail to check on your time, or fail to budget it, you may find yourself in the miserable predicament of knowing an answer but having no time to write it. Few things are more disheartening than to know the answer to a question, or to several questions, and to get a zero on that section simply because of poor planning of time.

Allow time to re-read your answer and to make any changes necessary for clarity and completeness. This practice always is sound; for some people, it is indispensable for achieving a truly coherent answer.

Use the terminology of the lecturer and of the subject under consideration. In spite of our lament that we said the same thing as someone given more credit, but said it in different words, the tacit accusation often is unjustified. Different words do not have the same meaning; therefore, they may not be "just as good."

Try all questions. On *every* question, turn in the best answer you can devise — even though you feel your best is miserable. Never wholly omit a question, unless you are certain your answer would be faking. Seldom is there a question about which you know absolutely nothing. Although you can give only a fragmentary, poorly developed answer, write that! Then develop it the best you can. "Never decline a challenge" is a motto with much in its favor.

2. How Should One Take Objective Examinations?

Most multiple-choice tests in essence are true-false examinations arranged in a somewhat different format. If one choice only is correct, the two styles of test are identical except for form. Consider a multiple-choice item with five choices. That really is a block of five true-false items on the same subject — whatever subject is stated in the "lead." (The lead is the part of the item which precedes the first choice.) Regarding multiple-choice tests this way can make your job a lot easier and less nervewracking.

In answering a multiple-choice item, read the lead and the first choice. If it is correct, mark it. If it is false, leave it out. Then do the next choice.

If several choices seem correct and you are to put down one answer only, re-read the lead and each seemingly correct choice. Make sure you are reading all parts of the item correctly and check on your thinking. Make sure the lead *plus* the choice is correct, not merely the choice alone. No matter how excellent the choice alone, unless the combination of it and the lead makes a true statement, the choice must be rejected. Suppose a lead states: "We eat at tables because" and two of the choices say "it is our custom," and "some tables are painted green." Both choices are correct in themselves, but only the first choice is acceptable. Only the first choice when added to the lead makes a true statement.

Always be sure the choice, when actually following the lead, makes a true statement before putting in that choice.

If more than one choice really is correct and you are to put down only the one best choice, a discrimination element is added. From the two or three correct choices, pick the choice which is most inclusive, the most precise, the least ambiguous, the more important, and less trivial.

With multiple-choice tests and true-false tests, read all items carefully. This is excellent policy for any kind of test. Many mistakes are from sloppiness. Do not read into the question. For example, do not add an "always," "all," or "every" that is not there, and then say the item (or choice) is false. This happens with dismal frequency.

Suppose an item states: "A great deal of bickering occurs among brothers and sisters." This is true. Some students will miss it, however, by adding "all." Their mental item reads: "A great deal of bickering occurs among all brothers and sisters." The revised item is false (a few brothers and sisters fight very little), but it is *not* the same item as the one on the test.

Similarly, refrain from adding a qualifying phrase and then saying "true" to this new item you just composed. For example, suppose an item is this: "Hunger generally leads to decreased activity and increased apathy." This is false. Suppose we add a phrase: *Extremely intense and prolonged hunger generally leads to decreased activity and increased apathy.* This new item is true. Some students will add that italicized phrase, unwittingly, and thus put down the wrong answer.

Likewise, if the question says, "If X, then Y," do not change it mentally to "If and only if X, then Y." That is a different question from the one asked and may well have a different answer. "If a person boasts a lot, he probably has intense feelings of inadequacy." "Only if a person boasts a lot does he probably have intense feelings of inadequacy." The first statement is true; the second is false.

Perhaps we should warn you: Many students are utterly unaware they do these things. This complicates their problem. However, if you watch closely for such tendencies in yourself, you will become better able to detect them and thus better able to avoid them.

Another important policy: Guard against reading out of the question — e.g., dropping qualifying phrases which are in the statement, ignoring a "generally" or a "to some extent." Answer the question asked, not some alternative question you make up during the test. You can guard against this danger by underlining "generally," "not," "sometimes," "in part," and other similar modifying words or phrases. For example, suppose an item on a true-false test is this: "Hostile aggression is caused in part by frustration." That statement is true. However, some students will mark it false because they will forget the "in part" and will remember that frustration is not the entire cause. If you underline "in part," this will help you avoid making that mistake.

Watch carefully the meaning of double negatives. "No one is always incorrect" does not mean "someone is always correct."

Watch for systematic errors. By a systematic error we mean making the same kind of mistake over and over, and making that kind of mistake much more often than other kinds. For example, some students make the majority of their errors by marking false items "true"; some others make the majority of *their* errors by marking true items "false."

On multiple-choice tests, many more students change wrong to right than vice versa.[16, 20, 48, 76] However, this is not the case for everyone. Some students, when they change their answers, consistently change more correct answers to incorrect than they change incorrect answers to correct. They are more apt to spoil good answers than fix incorrect ones. Check on yourself to ascertain what your own tendencies are and what, if any, kinds of systematic errors you make.

Look for various kinds of systematic errors in yourself. Another common error is to assume that because some statement or choice looks familiar it is probably true. Even university students make this mistake: They tend to assume a statement is true merely because they have read it a couple of times before. For instance, some university students read a list of statements, marking whether they were "true" or "false." The writer was anonymous, wholly unidentified, and did not even say the statements were true, nor were there any additional grounds for believing the statements to be true.[36] Even so, having seen a statement once or twice significantly increased the students' tendency to mark that statement "true."

Avoid also the reverse error: Do not assume that because a proposition looks unfamiliar, it is probably false. Although a proposition may not have been in the textbook or lectures, quite possibly it can be derived logically from that material and therefore is an acceptable choice or a "true" item.

If at first the answer to some question is obscure, take a few minutes to try to figure out the answer. Use your store of relevant facts and principles; see if you can deduce from them an answer.

If the answer still is not clear, mark the item and skip it temporarily. You can learn during tests, gaining new insights and new understandings. You also can get free of the set with which you first reviewed these questions. Quite often, therefore, when you return to these items, you will find the answer now clear in light of your new information and new internal organization.

Under no circumstances stay on some question until you become anxious and apprehensive. Doing so merely impairs your ability to answer other questions which would have been easy for you.

When you receive the test, glance over the test to ascertain whether all parts are about the same. Then plan your time (pages 126–127).

Know before you begin the test whether guessing will be penalized, whether wrong items will be subtracted from right, etc. Procedures vary from professor to professor, and also from test to test. If the answers to these questions are known before the test begins, full attention can be devoted to the test without needlessly cluttering your mind with such simple, but important, questions.

One last tip: Of all occasions for attempting to educate your professor, during an objective test is least suitable. On an objective test, you have no opportunity to develop your view. You have no opportunity to state why you think your answer is more sound than the one you suspect the professor deems "right." You have no chance, even, to show that you know which answer he considers right — unless you put that answer down.

If you value being a free spirit, a test is no time to declare your independence. Far better times are an office hour, class-time, or over a cup of coffee, for then you can present your ideas more adequately and discuss with your professor the evidence you think is inconsistent with his views.

3. Anxiety Is Lessened by Studying in Ways Outlined Above.

How one has studied throughout the term is a large part of skill in taking examinations. This takes only a sentence to say, but probably it is the most important single pointer you can be given.

The techniques of study and preparing for examinations discussed in the preceding sections not only help one do a more creditable job on a test; they also help one stay calm. Let us now look into some of the other, deeper aspects of test-panic.

4. Are We Nervous Because the Questions May Be Unfair?

Often we say we are nervous because the test may be unfair. Sometimes we really are. More usually, however, when we say we fear the test will not be fair, we fear the opposite even more: We are deeply afraid the test will be fair, all too fair. We are terrified lest our real or imagined weaknesses be displayed. When unprepared or when deeply unsure of ourself, no prospect is more terrible than that of a *fair* test. Only rarely is the possibility of illegitimate questions a major cause of anxiety.

5. Often We Worry and Do Poorly Because We Feel We Deserve to Fail.

Bizarre though this idea at first appears, it is true. Often we feel incompetent, inadequate, and as though we simply do not deserve to succeed. We feel unworthy of high success. As a common consequence, we become panic-stricken and do poorly.[25, 67, 95]

Guilt feelings, as they technically are called, often are rooted deeply and stem from basic conflicts or from imagined sins. Experts can help you alleviate such difficulties. Other times, guilt feelings arise from relatively superficial causes. For example, we may have feelings of guilt because we studied only a little when we feel we morally were obliged to study more.

D. MORE CAUSES OF FEAR AND WAYS TO GET FREE

1. Studying a Tremendous Amount Causes Anxiety, If Done Mainly for Grades.

With such a procedure, too much is at stake during the test. Too much depends upon "success" on the test to be able to stay calm. *If* you feel you have made heavy sacrifices in order to study, and *if* the main point of that studying was to make a high grade, then you feel you *must* make a high grade in order to justify the expenses already incurred. You simply must do well on the test, in order to keep your sacrifices from having been in vain. The possibility that all those sacrifices may have been for nought can lead to real terror.

So we see that studying very little can lead to anxiety and also studying a great deal can lead to anxiety (under the particular circumstances specified above).

This dilemma can be resolved neatly: Instead of studying for grades primarily, study for intrinsic values. For example, if you value becoming more skilled in thinking, practice thinking while studying; then the study process itself is valuable to you. If you care about having a wide fund of information, be increasing your store of facts while studying. In short, study in such a way that the studying itself is worthwhile, and is worthwhile *regardless* of grades or any other extrinsic reward which may or may not accrue subsequently. That method can greatly reduce your anxiety on examinations. You can take tests with new nonchalance, for no matter how the test goes, you cannot possibly lose everything. You *know* that not all can be lost — no matter what the grade you get, for your studying will already have been profoundly worth doing.

In life in general, much anxiety, many disappointments, considerable bitterness can be avoided by following this policy: In all your activities, do them in ways such that the "doing" itself is of worth. In other words, strive largely for intrinsic values rather than extrinsic rewards (such as grades, higher pay, or people's applause). This approach to life can free you from many deep, unverbalized fears, and give you new peace, new exuberance in living.

The feeling that "all will be lost unless I do well on this test" can be alleviated in other ways too. One is this: Ask yourself, "If I should fail to do well on this test, just what will be lost?" Then determine whether that is everything to you. Is it even what you value most in life?

To face these questions requires courage. Much courage always is needed for looking at ourselves, or for looking at anything else — when we fear what we may discover. If, however, you can bring yourself to face these matters, you often will discover that not as much rests solely on the outcome of the test or other dreaded event as you originally felt. In a few rare instances, your fundamental values actually will be at stake. Even then, you often can create alternative ways of achieving those same values. A high grade on some examination or in some course is not, for example, the only conceivable route to your most fundamental goals.

2.   Loss of Anonymity May Cause Near-Terror.

We spend much of our lives immersed in groups. We sit in large lectures, a part of a sea of persons. We shop in supermarts, anonymously. We belong to committees and are one of several names at the bottom of the report. We go to concerts, talks, mass meetings, and are one of the many — unidentified, not sorted out. We speak of "our group." We may think of ourselves primarily in terms of our membership in some group — as a Gamma Delta, a hippie, a Young Republican, a teen-ager, a . . . . We are accustomed to living as part of a group, acting as a part of a team, working as a part of committees, a part of a choir, a part of some other group.

Probably nobody thinks of himself or herself only as a part of some group. Nor are anyone's actions ever wholly anonymous. And yet this is a large part of our accustomed life.

Examinations are quite different. Examinations can become very personal. One can feel that one is being scrutinized, sorted out, no longer just one of an amorphous class. This can be frightening. On examinations we are expected to act separately and independently, and are held responsible for whatever answers we put down. These are highly desirable skills to possess but they are not ones with which many students begin their college career, and this poses problems hard to handle.

Knowing what the problem is can help you some in coping with it. Some other aids are these: Know that rarely or never is your worth being judged; seldom are you yourself being evaluated, but only one fragment of you. (By the way, in some courses you will be as anonymous as ever on examinations.) Realize that very rarely are you on display, being singled out. Use examinations as a place to practice being an independent, self-reliant, self-contained unit of action. Take test situations as an opportunity to grow and to extend your skills and abilities to handle various situations.

In the last chapter of this book, suggestions are offered on ways to handle problems of dependency, self-debasement, fear of failure, and ridicule. These can aid you here, too.

3. Fear on Examinations Can Stem From Fear of Losing Friends.

Sometimes we hardly dare do well on an examination lest people no longer like us. Almost anyone, of course, is apt to dislike us if we belittle his efforts, make adverse remarks about his intelligence, or in other ways demean him.

But suppose you are not a braggart nor a bully, and do not flaunt your achievements nor debase those of others. There is no evidence, then, that high grades place you in jeopardy. In fact, there are many data suggesting the opposite (see pages 215–217).

High grades do not jeopardize friendship. This is what one would expect if one were thinking about the matter quietly. Friends, by definition, want you to develop your potentialities the very best you can — especially those potentialities you care most about (whether or not *they* value developing those same assets in themselves). If you do not ridicule their interests and talents, they are not apt to ridicule yours nor lament your successes.

4. Set Reasonable Goals for Yourself.

Demanding the nearly impossible as a prerequisite for self-respect is another major cause of anxiety on examinations. For that matter, it causes much of the deep anxiety which plagues our lives. We should, therefore, avoid demanding perfection of ourselves.

A procedure opposite to perfectionism that is hit upon by some very young, and some not so young, will not do either for civilized human living: viz., jettisoning all goals, junking all values. We cannot build any of the things which take time; we cannot pool resources; we cannot count on others, nor upon ourselves, without clear and definite standards. But we need not be perfectionists. Another way is open.

Make your self-respect rest upon *approaching* your ideals with increasing closeness, rather than upon *reaching* those ideals. Ideals should be something to steer by and work toward, not something to attain instantly or else to abandon.

5. Stop Scaring Yourself.

Some students try to motivate themselves on examinations by impassioned pep-talks on the importance of remembering everything. We have considerable reason to believe that being-motivated-to-remember while learning is a facilitator to learning.[6, 39] but being-motivated-to-remember only while taking a test is no help at all.

Therefore, if you are going to make speeches to yourself stressing how important it is to remember a great deal — do it while you are studying, not while taking tests. During tests, such injunctions are no help, and in fact are apt to frighten you and impair your chances of doing well.

Cindy Lou accidentally acquired an equally disruptive habit. When she comes to an item for which she does not remember the answer, she immediately thinks how stupid she is. "You stupid sap," she says to herself, "how could you forget something that simple?" "Anyone should know something that simple." "What's wrong with you anyway?" "Don't you know anything?" "Any idiot could do better than this!"

Greg is just as bad. On a math problem he doesn't know how to solve, he flips. "Come on now, you dummy," he tells himself sternly. "Any imbecile can solve this." "What's the matter with you anyhow?" "What a dunce!" He heaps other condemning labels on his own head.

Such remarks do not encourage us. Indeed they may be the final straw, causing us to panic and blank out totally.

And there is something else wrong here: Are these self-incriminations really justified? Are the statements even true? At some level, we know that many of our harsh statements are not true. Yet we go on making them. Quite unwittingly we are teaching ourself that we cannot rely upon our judgment nor accuracy, that we can not trust ourself. Thus we are damaging our faith in ourself. Thus we undermine our own self-confidence.

Tell yourself only true things about yourself. And try to encourage yourself.[74] You have difficult tasks to accomplish. You need yourself as a friend, not as an enemy who kicks you when you're down and berates you when you are stuck. So on tests tell yourself you are doing fine when you get several items in a row answered easily. Notice how smoothly some parts are going. Remind yourself that answers which are not immediately apparent nonetheless may be recalled later on in the test. Remind yourself how well you sometimes have figured out difficult problems; assume this may be another such time. When Dan gets a page finished, he thinks triumphantly: "That's the way, guy!" And goes happily on to the next page of the exam.

Cheer yourself on. You are a friend to others. Be a friend to yourself.

6. To Reduce Test Panic, Do Not Study the Night Before a Test – Unless You Can Study Serenely at That Time.

One way to reduce test anxiety is to study well in advance of any test. This proposition follows directly from our previous consideration of the effects of anxious cramming on anxious test-taking. (See pages 100–101.)

Note too that fatigue increases anxiety. With inadequate amounts of sleep, one worries more and is more apprehensive and anxiety-ridden. A part of the very intense anxiety students suffer during final examinations may well arise from the serious deficiencies in sleep they incur at that time. This again suggests that whether you do or do not study the night before a test, arrange life so you get sufficient sleep. Especially if you are prone to high anxiety, arrange your time to get adequate rest.

We should note here that a sudden increase in anxiety is as damaging to test performance as intense anxiety.[8] Suddenly increasing anxiety, even if only to a moderate level, has effects like those of intense anxiety. Tracy has noticed this.

As part of preparation for anything difficult, Tracy gets a good night's sleep and avoids frantic activities. The night before a big test and on the day of a big test, Tracy steers clear of those people apt to pounce upon one with disruptive, disconcerting questions, glum predictions, or sudden disturbing demands. Tracy tries to show the same needed consideration to other classmates, skipping anything disconcerting or in other ways anxiety-engendering. On test days, especially, loving friends aim to be cheerful and tranquil with each other, encouraging each other, saying happy things to each other, nothing harsh or worrisome. Black tidings can wait. Now is the time to be supportive.

E. STILL MORE WAYS TO REDUCE TEST PANIC

1. Allow Time to Get to the Test Leisurely.

We have watched our friends rushing about the house and campus, madly collecting things, frantically finishing last-minute details, dashing to class at something approaching a wild gallop, arriving with pounding heart as the bell rang and the papers were being passed out. Yet they wonder why they are tense when the test begins, and why they need half an hour to get calm enough to think. This is no occasion for wonder, really. Those students had made themselves appallingly tense and anxious before ever getting to the test.

On the day of a big test we are apt to be especially disorganized, running back and forth half a dozen times for stuff we ordinarily get all at once. We even start off for class two or three times, each time dashing back for something else we simply must have and just remembered and have absent-mindedly left at home. And the clock ticks on.

Kelly handles this by setting his alarm ten minutes earlier than usual, so he can get ready knowing he has enough time.

Thereby he has one less worry. Linda checks out her car a day or two in advance, making sure it has plenty of gas. Sam schedules nothing extra on days of exams, and thus cuts down on confusion and stress. The night before a test, Sandy lays out her clothes and books and other items needed for the coming day. This enables her to make a smoother start on test day, with some anxieties disbanded. She knows the articles she needs are ready to go and all collected so nothing will be forgotten. This calms Sandy; she knows she will not have to dash back home in pursuit of some crucial item left behind in the scramble, nor spend precious minutes before the exam frantically hunting for something hopelessly misplaced.

These little devices help more than you might guess. If you are apprehensive enough, any reduction in anxiety is welcome. Actually these simple procedures help greatly to soothe and relax.

2.   Sit Where You Usually Sit.

The chair you have used during lectures and discussions has decided advantages over other spots. In that spot you have done some clear thinking, have considered in detail the subject matter of this course, have answered aloud or to yourself some questions, and have been relatively calm. You also feel at home there. This means that when you sit there, you have at least some of the now-present stimuli already nicely established as cues for being relaxed and calm, for thinking clearly, for verbalizing pertinently and coherently. These supports will not guarantee that on the examination you will think well, remember everything you have heard there, and stay serenely calm, but they do stack the cards in your favor. The test situation will be less jarringly different from the learning situation. Further, it will contain many cues for the responses you want.

3.   Build a More Realistic View of the Uses of Tests

Our conception of tests shrinks, oftentimes, until finally we see one function only of tests and that their most wretched: We see them as a rather harsh way of grading our work, and possibly ourselves.

We become panicky lest our inner weaknesses be exposed. This fear of tests is much the same as our fear in other situations. We become jittery when forced to play a new game.

Will we make fools of ourselves? Will we be shown up? We are suddenly apprehensive about meeting the renowned scholar. Will she, or he, think us stupid? Or shallow? Or poorly informed? We dread parties. Will we make blunders, say the wrong thing, do the wrong thing, be disgraced in front of all those people? We shrink from doctors and from dentists too. They might discover something wrong with us. At a sudden question, we quake.

These fears are largely unwarranted. Certainly in examinations, your professors are not looking for anything very deep. Seldom do they draw any sweeping conclusion about you or your nature, no matter what you do on a test.

Tests are not a way of grading *you*. They are one way of partially grading your work. You can make them far more than that. You can make tests into things of horror, or you can make them into something immensely valuable. Let us see how.

4. Make Tests Serve You and Your Purposes.

Instead of being merely a recipient taking tests for four years, be an active user of the test situation.

You can use tests to further many of your purposes. So start with the obvious: Use tests to evaluate your present study techniques, their adequacy or inadequacy. In addition, use tests to ascertain where your information and thinking are strong, and where they are weak . . . as a clue to areas you might strive to improve . . . as a way to discover where you have been making mistakes, and where you are sound . . . as an opportunity to learn how to adjust to "failure" (skill indispensable for becoming a mature and happy person) . . . as one basis to help you select a major and an appropriate vocation . . . as a place to practice your skills in thinking and solving problems alone . . . as opportunities to practice courage while facing challenges . . . as occasions to pick up skill in adult living. You can make tests into valued tools. Utilizing such possibilities lessens your fear and improves your performance.[26]

Examinations are not designed as instruments of torment; you need not let them function as such.

5. Mild Anxiety Can Be Tolerated.

Some days are too warm. Some days are too cold. And some days are anxious ones. Much can be said for learning to tolerate such inconveniences, when not extreme, and for learning to carry on creditably in the face of them.

You can reduce anxiety in many ways. Almost certainly, however, you cannot reduce anxiety to zero; nor is there any compelling reason that you should. Mild amounts of anxiety are not particularly harmful[59, 92] and can be helpful.

Mild anxiety ("concern" may be a more appropriate term) can have diverse utility — dispelling apathy, arousing action, motivating sustained endeavor.[82, 91] It can improve academic performance if the individual is functioning far below his potential,[78, 105] and sometimes under other circumstances too.[59, 96] This contrasts sharply with intense anxiety.

Too much anxiety interferes with all kinds of skilled behaviors. Intense anxiety impairs accuracy,[17, 93] is disruptive to problem-solving,[40, 94] to performance on various kinds of achievement tests[10, 83] and college aptitude tests,[83, 87] to appropriate generalizing of concepts,[50] and to solving anagrams[82] and intellectual functioning in other respects.[2, 40, 84–87] It is also deleterious in other ways,[15, 73, 100] even affecting how much one can see at a glance,[31] especially if one is working against time[72] or feels trapped and unable to cope with the situation.[102]

We become anxious in the face of impending examinations, and still might do all right; then we worry, and become anxious about being anxious — thereby setting up a dangerous cycle and pushing anxiety to a damagingly high level. The data suggest that we should try to prevent anxiety from reaching high levels, but that small amounts of anxiety are no cause for alarm.

6. Relaxation Training Can Control Anxiety.

Personal control of one's own emotional reactions, especially the negative ones, has long been a dream of those working to improve the human condition. Imagine how much more successful and satisfied many of us would be if each of us could control our anger and anxiety. We have not reached that point, but remarkable developments in the last two decades have brought self-control within reach.

Recent advances in biofeedback training and behavior therapy, particularly relaxation training, have demonstrated that subconscious emotional responses can be brought within an individual's conscious control.[7] There have been amazing demonstrations of personal control: Many individuals have demonstrated an ability to control the electrical activity of their brain;[49] others have been enabled to change their heart rate and blood pressure in different directions at the same time;[89, 90] and others have learned to direct the flow of their blood to designated parts of their extremities, changing their skin temperatures by as much as 10 degrees.[61, 98] One of the earliest self-control procedures, relaxation training, was developed to cope with anxiety.

Relaxation training rests on the fact that no one can be anxious and relaxed simultaneously. When you learn to bring relaxation responses under your personal control, you gain a powerful tool to counter destructive effects of high anxiety.

Various techniques help you learn how to relax. An easy, highly effective way uses a method called tension/release cycles.[106] You focus on what it feels like to relax by first tensing up muscles and then releasing quickly, letting the tension go. As you practice relaxing, and actively concentrate on that feeling, you increase your skill in controlling that ability to relax.

This procedure has proved effective with thousands of people much like you.[7, 106] Its beauty is that although you practice and concentrate on relaxing in a somewhat artificial situation, your ability to actually relax in real-life anxious situations is improved. After you begin practicing relaxing, you will find yourself calmer and more controlled in situations that formerly left you churning.

Your ability to relax is increased further by repeating a word ("calm"), or image (sitting in your favorite armchair), or special stimulus (taking a deep breath) each time you practice relaxing. You associate your own special cue with relaxing, during practice, and then use that cue when you are in an anxious situation, thereby providing yourself a little extra help and support in tight situations.

The purpose of relaxation training is not, of course, to put you to sleep during a job interview; rather it is to take away the paralyzing fear so that you can perform at your best. You will still feel anxious and somewhat hesitant in new and unusual situations; we all do; but you will be more in control of that anxiety and, therefore, a freer person to do what you want to do. Also, you will be able to perform in situations heretofore closed to you, thus opening varied and interesting alternatives for you to explore and grow with.

Like all personal skills, control of relaxation doesn't occur immediately or automatically; it requires practice and diligence. Most students, however, report definite changes in their ability to handle anxiety-producing situations in as few as ten practice sessions.

For those of you who would like to bring your relaxation response under personal control, a training exercise is reproduced at the end of the book in the Addendum. The training exercise is flexible and harmless; almost everyone will benefit. All that is required is a quiet place where you won't be disturbed for a half hour or so, some provision to have the instructions read to you (a friend or a cassette tape recorder), and a willingness to participate wholeheartedly in the exercises. Some students practice each day, others report success when practicing once every four or five days; you can fit the sessions to your schedule.

To get the most from your training sessions, you must actively practice relaxing in anxiety-producing situations. An effective approach is to begin practicing relaxation (using your cue words or relaxation images) in situations that are only minimally stressful. For example, you might begin practicing while standing in a line that seems to be going too slowly or while stopped for a traffic light that seems to be broken. A slightly more stressful level of situation in which you might try out your newly learned skills could be while waiting for a medical or dental appointment, or while studying for an exam. After you find yourself becoming more relaxed in those situations, you might then try relaxing in stressful situations such as sitting in the dentist's chair, meeting someone important, giving a public speech or presentation, or taking a final examination. Patience is a virtue of the educated person. Do not try to do too much too quickly and you will be surprised pleasantly at the potential you have for controlling your own negative reactions.

7. The Foregoing Is a Foundation, But Not Complete.

Through understanding these causes of anxiety and fear, you can devise additional ways to reduce panic and despondency.

Suppose even with patience and practice of your new techniques, panic still persists. In such instances some complex difficulties may underlie your fear. You can work out such problems more easily with a partner who is an expert in the area of personality formation. Some social agencies, pastoral services, clinical psychologists, and psychiatrists can offer you effective assistance. These men and women have studied intensively what sorts of things make people happy and what sorts of things make them miserable. They understand many complicated difficulties and their causes. Through their training and experience, they often can help you find the roots of various troubles and can help you devise ways to reduce or eliminate them.

Sometimes counseling or psychotherapy makes no significant difference in one's academic performance,[41] although it may have other significant effects,[75] and sometimes the improvement is only temporary;[29] but sometimes the changes are quite dramatic, including significant improvement in one's course grades,[23, 80] as well as significant changes in one's self-concept, including heightened self-respect and increased joyousness and peace in one's interactions with others.[28, 30, 62] Such changes are especially pronounced when the style of counseling or psychotherapy is appropriate to the particular individual seeking aid,[11, 29] and at least sometimes the changes are known to persist.[13, 66, 80]

Various books by psychologists, psychiatrists, and psychoanalysts afford at least a glimpse of what these people can help one achieve. Such books also can aid you in gaining a more complete understanding of yourself. At the end of the chapter are listed some by Frank, Freud, Horney, Maslow, Menninger, and Rogers, which you might find of special aid.

8. What Should You Do When You Fail?

What constitutes failure depends upon the individual. For some students, anything less than an A is failing; for other students, flunking a major exam is failing. In this discussion, "failing" means whatever you construe as failing.

When we try for something and fail, we tend to become depressed and set lower standards for the future.[81] Our expectancy of success on other tasks decreases.[1, 69] We learn to feel helpless,[42, 51, 79] feeling we are doomed to fail no matter what we do.[53, 70] Feeling helpless impairs our performance,[53, 71, 79] and we have the start of a debilitating circle. These are quite natural reactions, but other courses are open to us which work out better.

Since failing is something we all are going to do a lot of, we would do well to learn how to cope with the phenomenon.

Let us note first: Failure tells us we went astray. Unfortunately it does not tell us where. And that is the heart of our problem.

When we do badly on an exam, we suppose we studied the wrong things. That may not be the trouble. The real trouble may be that we did not study enough things. Our failing was caused not by learning the wrong sample but from learning far too small a sample. Any test is intended to be a sample of the material, a sample of the facts, concepts, skills, principles, applications, and all else we need to know in that area, a sample of whatever we were to learn. When we fail, our failure quite often arises from having learned such a tiny proportion of the material assigned that we are bound to fail any extensive sampling.

This gives us our first clue to improvement: Learn more! Our problem is not usually that we need to learn different things from what we did learn. We need to learn what we did learn and a great deal more.

To combat depression and helplessness after a failure, do something at which you can succeed.[51, 53, 55] This need not be related to the area in which you were just tested. Succeeding in one task helps you succeed in subsequent tasks even when the tasks differ.[82] Simply recalling prior successes can help you, too.[99] After you re-discover there are things you do well and can still do well, tackle again the area in which you did poorly. Go at things differently from the way you did before. Here are some suggestions.

Set higher standards if your standards have been very low. (As is discussed in another section, standards too low can cause failure.) Go over the test and look for systematic errors. Look also for any kind of error, and learn now whatever you missed.

Save more time for study, and use it. If need be, drop temporarily some aspect of your previously planned activities so you will have more time available for your education. Attend class regularly; attend all class meetings.

Get some new study techniques. One way to do this: Apply more of the suggestions offered here. Go back over the suggestions in this book and pick out two or three you have not been following and add them to your study procedures. After you have them well under control, pick out two or three more and add them.

Implement more fully whatever effective techniques you already are following. Use them more conscientiously.

After you have done the above, or are doing them, confer with your instructor. Conferring with the instructor is helpful as a supplement, but not as a substitute for the above. Although we rely heavily on conferences, conferences do little good unless you also adopt procedures such as the foregoing.

F. GRADES VERSUS EDUCATION?

Most students value high grades. Grades make some difference in obtaining certain jobs and in being admitted to graduate school, though grades alone make less difference than is commonly believed. Most students also value the attributes we call "being highly educated." Valuing both grades and education poses a problem.

As is well recognized, one can get very high grades without becoming educated. The activities practiced by people working primarily for grades seldom facilitate becoming educated. In fact, working primarily for grades almost eliminates our chances for becoming educated.

This does not mean grades and education do not mix! It means they do not mix that way.

Working for grades usually prevents getting an education. But *working for a fine education* does not prevent getting high grades. This last proposition is scarcely debatable, for many people have done just that. They strove skillfully and consistently to become highly educated, and ceased working for grades. As a result they developed those skills and habits which constitute being highly educated; as a sort of by-product, they made top-flight grades.

There are, you see, two alternative methods of making a high grade-point-average. One is to work for grades; the second is to strive to become educated. The second is probably a more effective way to achieve a high grade-point-average and the *only* way to become highly educated.

These two ways of approaching learning have other radically different results. Persons who primarily work for grades usually find studying a tiresome series of chores, an onerous burden imposed by someone else. When they graduate, the results of their studying seldom seem worth the effort. They wonder why they worked so hard and so long. They feel let down, betrayed.

Persons who, on the other hand, set out to become educated, generally enjoy the process. They make classwork and studying a stimulating series of experiences, fascinating and fun. When schooling is finished, they are not disillusioned nor in doubt about the worth of their work. The results of their study seem even more precious and satisfying than anticipated.

Getting grades and getting an education are incompatible if (perhaps *only* if) one works primarily for grades. They are highly compatible when one forgets grades and endeavors to become educated. One achieves, thereby, much of lasting pleasure.

G. POINTERS ON USE OF THESE SUGGESTIONS

As we were noticing, the same skills and habits that facilitate becoming educated also facilitate getting high grades. Each technique in these chapters does double duty — working toward both ends.

However, developing these modes of response requires practice. Even to remember the techniques takes practice.

When first starting, do not try to use all of these new methods simultaneously. Be satisfied with working on only a few. Practice a few one week, add some more the next week, and so on. They will become habitual, taking no more time and effort than commoner methods of study and with more gratifying results.

The prospect of trying to build new skill frightens some people. It takes so much time and effort. But are these such fearsome drawbacks?

Many of you play tennis beautifully. How many tips, informal coachings, and lessons did you receive from friends, partners, or professionals? How many times have you practiced your serve? Your backhand? How many hours have you studied an expert making drives, underspins, placements? Probably you cannot recall. And in addition to all those hours, each time you played tennis, you were practicing more. Some of us have devoted a sizable chunk of life to perfecting such skills, and they are worth it to us.

Are other skills in living worth as much time and whole-hearted effort? Is becoming educated worth as much? Your entire life is colored by how well you develop those skills and outlooks. So also are the lives of your friends and associates and the nature of the world of which you are a part. No time is better suited to their creation and development than these years at college and university.

We should observe that expending considerable time and effort on a project does not make it drudgery. Having spent uncounted hours on becoming more skilled at tennis in no way ruined the sport for us, nor made it burdensome work.

Whether something is work or play depends very little upon the nature of that activity, or the amount of time and effort it entails. Rather, whether something is work or play depends primarily upon us — and how we approach the activity. When we tackle a project enthusiastically, because we are eager to learn and not because we feel obliged to do so, it is play. When we do not, it is work.

Becoming skilled in tennis or any hobby was fun— despite the patience required, the slow progress made at first, the many mistakes to be corrected, and the huge energy and time still required. Becoming an educated person can be fun also.

BIBLIOGRAPHY FOR CHAPTER 5

1. Abramson, Lyn Y.; Garber, Judy; Edwards, Neil B.; and Seligman, Martin E. P. Expectancy changes in depression and schizophrenia. J. Abnorm. Psychol., 87, 102–109, 1978.
2. Amoroso, Donald M.; and Walters, Richard H. Effects of anxiety and socially mediated anxiety reduction on paired associate learning. J. Personality Soc. Psychol., 11, 388–396, 1969.
3. Anderson, Ruth I.; Straub, Lura Lynn; and Gibson, E. Dana. Word Finder. Englewood Cliffs, N.J.: Prentice-Hall, Inc., 1960.
4. Bahrick, Harry P. Discriminative and associative aspects of pictorial paired-associate learning: Acquisition and retention. J. Exper. Psychol., 80, 113–119, 1969.
5. Bartley, S. H.; and Chute, E. Fatigue and Impairment in Man. New York: McGraw-Hill Co., 1947.
6. Berlyne, D. E.; and Carey, S. T. Incidental learning and the timing of arousal. Psychonomic Sci., 13, 103–104, 1968.
7. Bernstein, Douglas A.; and Borkovec, Thomas D. Progressive Relaxation Training. Champaign, Ill.: Research Press, 1973.
8. Bond, J. B. Change in anxiety level as a factor in test performance. Alberta J. Educ. Res., 23, 97–102, 1977.
9. Broadbent, D. E. Neglect of the surroundings in relation to fatigue decrements in output. In Floyd, W. F.; and Welford, A. T. Symposium on Fatigue. London: H. K. Lewis and Co., 1953.
10. Bronzaft, Arline L. Test anxiety, social mobility, and academic achievement. J. Soc. Psychol., 75, 217–222, 1968.
11. Brown, Robert D. Effects of structure and unstructured group counseling with high- and low-anxious college underachievers. J. Couns. Psychol., 16, 209–214, 1969.
12. Calfee, Robert C. Recall and recognition memory in concept identification. J. Exper. Psychol., 81, 436–440, 1969.
13. Chestnut, William J. The effects of structured and unstructured group counseling on male college students' underachievement. J. Couns. Psychol., 12, 388–394, 1965.
14. Connor, Jane M. Effects of organization and expectancy on recall and recognition. Memory Cognition, 5, 315–318, 1977.
15. Costa, Paul T.; Fozard, James L.; McCrae, Robert R.; and Bosse, Raymond. Relations of age and personality dimensions to cognitive ability factors. J. Gerontology, 31, 663–669, 1976.
16. Davis, R. E. Changing examination answers: An educational myth? J. Med. Educ., 50, 685–687, 1975.
17. Davis, William E. Effect of prior failure on subjects' WAIS Arithmetic subtest scores. J. Clin. Psychol., 25, 72–73, 1969.
18. Dominowski, Roger L. Concept attainment as a function of instance contiguity and number of irrelevant dimensions. Proceedings 76th Annual Conv. Amer. Psychological Assoc., 3, 41–42, 1968.
19. Dong, Tim; and Kintsch, Walter. Subjective retrieval cues in free recall. J. Verbal Learning Verbal Behav., 7, 813–816, 1968.
20. Edwards, Anthony K.; and Marshall, Carol. First impressions on tests: Some new findings. Teaching Psychol., 4, 193–195, 1977.

21. Erdelyi, Matt; Buschke, Herman; and Finkelstein, Shira. Hypermnesia for Socratic stimuli. Memory Cognition, 5, 283–286, 1977.
22. Fischler, Ira. Semantic facilitation without association in a lexical decision task. Memory Cognition, 5, 335–339, 1977.
23. Flook, Alfred J. M.; and Saggar, Usha. Academic performance with and without knowledge of scores on tests of intelligence, aptitude, and personality. J. Educ. Psychol., 59, 395–401, 1968.
24. Frank, Jerome, D. Persuasion and Healing: A Comparative Study of Psychotherapy. Baltimore: Johns Hopkins Press, 1961.
25. Freud, Sigmund. Five Lectures on Psychoanalysis. (Translated and edited by James Strachey.) New York: W. W. Norton, 1977.
26. Geen, Russell G. Effects of anticipation of positive and negative outcomes on audience anxiety. J. Consult. Clin. Psychol., 45, 715–716, 1977.
27. Geiselman, Ralph, E.; and Riehle, Jonathan P. The fate of to-be-forgotten sentences in semantic positive forgetting. Bull. Psychonomic Soc., 6, 19–21, 1975.
28. Gilbreath, Stuart H. Group counseling with male underachieving college volunteers. Personnel Guid. J., 45, 469–476, 1967.
29. Gilbreath, Stuart H. Appropriate and inappropriate group counseling with academic underachievers. J. Couns. Psychol., 15, 506–511, 1968.
30. Goldman, Ruth K.; and Mendelsohn, Gerald A. Psychotherapeutic change and social adjustment: A report of a national survey of psychotherapists. J. Abnorm. Psychol., 74, 164–172, 1969.
31. Granger, G. W. Personality and visual perception: A review. J. Ment. Sci., 99: 8–43, 1953.
32. Hanna, Paul R.; Hanna, Jean S.; Berquist, Sidney R.; Hodges, Richard E.; and Rudorf, E. Hugh. Needed research in spelling. Elem. English, 43, 60–66 and 89, 1966.
33. Harari, H.; and McDavid, J. W. Cultural influences on retention of logical and symbolic material. J. Educ. Psychol., 57, 18–22, 1966.
34. Harkness, D. R. A surgical approach to large classes. J. Gen. Educ., 17, 179–185, 1965.
35. Harris, J.; and Monaco, Gregory E. Psychology of pragmatic implication. J. Exper. Psychol.: Gen., 107, 1–24, 1978.
36. Hasher, Lynn; Goldstein, David; and Toppino, Thomas. Frequency and the conference of referential validity. J. Verbal Learning Verbal Beh., 16, 107–112, 1977.
37. Hayes-Roth, Barbara; and Hayes-Roth, Frederick. Concept learning and the recognition and classification of exemplars. J. Verbal Learning Verbal Beh., 16, 321–338, 1977.
38. Haygood, Robert C.; Sandlin, J.; Yoder, D. J.; and Dodd, D. H. Instance contiguity in disjunctive concept learning. J. Exper. Psychol., 81, 605–607, 1969.
39. Heinrich, Barbara A. Motivation and long-term memory. Psychonomic Sci., 12, 149–150, 1968.
40. Higginbotham, Timothy E. Irrationality in college students. Rational Liv., 11, 34, 1976.
41. Hill, A. H.; and Grieneeks, L. An evaluation of academic counseling of under- and over-achievers. J. Couns. Psychol., 13, 325–328, 1966.
42. Hiroto, D. S.; and Seligman, M. E. P. Generality of learned helplessness in man. J. Personality Psychol., 31, 311–327, 1975.
43. Hodges, Richard Edwin. An analysis of the phonological structure of American-English orthography. Doctoral thesis. Stanford, Calif.: Stanford Univ., 1964, 635 pp. Diss. Abstr., 25, No. 10, 5788–5789, 1965.
44. Hodges, Richard Edwin; and Rudorf, E. Hugh. Searching linguistics for cues for the teaching of spelling. Elem. English, 42, 527–533, 1965.
45. Horn, Thomas D. (Ed.). Research on Handwriting and Spelling. Champaign, Illinois: National Council of Teachers of English, 79 pp. 1966.
46. Horney, Karen. Collected Works. New York: W. W. Norton, 1963.
47. Johnston, James J. Sticking with first responses on multiple-choice exams: For better or for worse? Teaching Psychol., 2, 178–179, 1975.
48. Johnston, James J. Answer changing behavior and grades. Teaching Psychol., 5, 44–45, 1978.
49. Kamiya, J.; DiCara, L. V.; Barber, T. X.; Miller, N. E.; Shapiro, D.; and Stoyva, J. (Eds.) Biofeedback and Self-Control. Chicago: Aldine, 1976/1977.

50. Katahn, Martin; and Branham, Lee. Effects of manifest anxiety on the acquisition and generalization of concepts from Hullian theory. Amer. J. Psychol., 81, 575–580, 1968.
51. Kilpatrick-Tabak, Blair; and Roth, Susan. An attempt to reverse performance deficits associated with depression and experimentally induced helplessness. J. Abnorm. Psychol., 87, 141–154, 1978.
52. Kintsch, Walter. Recognition and free recall of organized lists. J. Exper. Psychol., 78, 481–487, 1968.
53. Klein, D. C.; and Seligman, M. E. P. Reversal of performance deficits and perceptual deficits in learned helplessness and depression. J. Abnorm. Psychol., 85, 11–26, 1976.
54. Kozminsky, Ely. Altering comprehension: The effect of biasing titles on text comprehension. Memory Cognition, 5, 482–490, 1977.
55. Loeb, A.; Beck, A. T.; and Diggory, J. Differential effects of success and failure on depressed and nondepressed patients. J. Nerv. Ment. Dis., 152, 106–114, 1971.
56. Lovatt, D. J.; and Warr, P. B. Recall after sleep. Amer. J. Psychol., 81, 253–257, 1968.
57. Lybrand, W. A.; Andrews, T. G.; and Ross, S. Systematic fatigue and perceptual organization. Amer. J. Psychol., 67, 704–707, 1954.
58. MacKay, Donald G. Phonetic factors in the perception and recall of spelling errors. Neuropsychologia, 6, 321–325, 1968.
59. McKeachie, W. J. Interaction of achievement cues and facilitating anxiety in the achievement of women. J. Appl. Psychol., 53, 147–148, 1969.
60. Mager, Robert F.; and McCann, J. Learner-controlled Instruction. Palo Alto, Calif.: Varian Associates, 1961.
61. Malasch, C.; Marshall, G.; and Zimbardo, P. Hypnotic control of peripheral skin temperature. Psychophysiol., 9, 600–605, 1972.
62. Mandel, Harvey P.; Roth, Robert M.; and Berenbaum, Harris L. Relationship between personality change and achievement change as a function of psychodiagnosis. J. Couns. Psychol., 15, 500–505, 1968.
63. Mandler, George. Organized recall: Individual functions. Psychonomic Sci., 13, 235–236, 1968.
64. Marshall, George R. Stimulus characteristics contributing to organization in free recall. J. Verbal Learning Verbal Behav., 6, 364–374, 1967.
65. Maslow, Abraham H. Toward a Psychology of Being. Princeton: D. Van Nostrand Co., Inc., 1962.
66. Mendelsohn, Gerald A.; and Rankin, Neil O. Client-counselor compatibility and the outcome of counseling. J. Abnorm. Psychol., 74, 157–163, 1969.
67. Menninger, Karl Augustus. Sparks. New York: Thomas Y. Crowell Co., 1973.
68. Meyer, G. An experimental study of the old and new types of examination. I. The effect of the examination set on memory. J. Educ. Psychol., 25, 641–661, 1934.
69. Miller, W. R.; and Seligman, M. E. P. Depression and learned helplessness in man. J. Abnorm. Psychol., 84, 228–238, 1975.
70. Miller, W. R.; and Seligman, M. E. P. Learned helplessness, depression and the perception of reinforcement. Behav. Res. Therapy, 14, 7–17, 1976.
71. Miller, W. R.; Seligman, M. E. P.; and Kurlander, H. Learned helplessness, depression, and anxiety. J. Nerv. Mental Disease, 161, 347–357, 1975.
72. Morris, Larry W.; and Liebert, Robert M. Effects of anxiety on timed and untimed intelligence tests: Another look. J. Consulting Clin. Psychol., 33, 240–244, 1969.
73. Moses, Michael; and Marcia, James E. Performance decrement as a function of positive feedback: Self-defeating behavior. J. Social Psychol., 77, 259–267, 1969.
74. O'Donnell, William J. Test anxiety related to self-esteem in neutral and examination conditions. Bull. North Carolina Psychol. Assoc., Spr., 18–20, 1976.
75. Padgett, Harry G. Effects of group guidance and group counseling on the self concept and professional attitudes of prospective teachers. Diss. Abstr., 28 (10-A), 3976–3977, 1968.
76. Reiling E.; and Taylor, R. A new approach to the problem of changing initial responses to multiple choice questions. J. Educ. Meas., 9, 67–70, 1972.
77. Rogers, Carl R. Toward becoming a fully functioning person. In Combs, A. W.

(Ed.). 1962 Yearbook, Amer. Soc. for Curriculum Development. Washington, D.C.; National Education Assoc., 1962.

78. Rosmarin, Martin S. Reaction to stress and anxiety in chronically underachieving high-ability students. Diss. Abstr., 27 (5-B), 1630, 1966.

79. Roth, Susan; and Kubal, L. The effects of noncontingent reinforcement on tasks of differing importance: Facilitation and learned helplessness effects. J. Personality Soc. Psychol., 32, 680–691, 1975.

80. Roth, Robert M.; Mauksch, Hans O.; and Peiser, Kenneth. The nonachievement syndrome, group therapy, and achievement change. Personnel Guid. J., 46, 393–398, 1967.

81. Sacco, William P.; and Hokanson, Jack E. Expectations of success and anagram performance of depressives in a public and private setting. J. Abnorm. Psychol., 87, 122–130, 1978.

82. Samuel, William; Baynes, Keith; and Sabeh, Charlotte. Effects of initial success or failure in a stressful or relaxed environment on subsequent task performance. J. Exper. Soc. Psychol., 14, 205–216, 1978.

83. Sarason, Irwin G. Test anxiety and the intellectual performance of college students. J. Educ. Psychol., 52, 201–206, 1961.

84. Sarason, I. G.; and Minard, J. Test anxiety, experimental instructions, and the Wechsler Adult Intelligence Scale. J. Educ. Psychol., 53, 299–302, 1962.

85. Sarason, Irwin G.; and Palola, Ernest G. The relationships of test and general anxiety, difficulty of task, and experimental instructions to performance. J. Exper. Psychol., 59, 185–191, 1960.

86. Sarason, S. B.; Hill, K. T.; and Zimbardo, P. G. A longitudinal study of the relation of test anxiety to performance on intelligence and achievement tests. Monogr. Soc. for Res. in Child Devel., 29, #98, 1964.

87. Sassenrath, J. M. Anxiety, aptitude, attitude, and achievement. Psychol. in the Schools, 4, 341–346, 1967.

88. Schulz, R. W.; Miller, R. L.; and Radtke, R. C. The role of instance contiguity and dominance in concept attainment. J. Verbal Learning Verbal Behav., 1, 432–435, 1963.

89. Schwartz, G. E. Voluntary control of human cardiovascular integration and differentiation through feedback and reward. Science, 175, 90–93, 1972.

90. Schwartz, G. E. Biofeedback as therapy. Amer. Psychologist, 28, 666–673, 1973.

91. Sem-Jacobson, C. W. Anxiety and stress, stimulation to achievement, satisfaction, well-being, and pathological behavior. In Spielberger, C. D.; and Sarason, I. G. (Eds.) Stress and Anxiety: IV. Washington, D.C.: Hemisphere, 1977.

92. Sinha, Durganand. A psychological analysis of some factors associated with success and failure in university education. Psychological Studies, 11, 69–88, 1966.

93. Sinha, S. P. A study of the relationship between speed and accuracy of performance on the simple task in high and low anxiety subjects. Indian Psychol. Rev., 13, 15–17, 1976.

94. Solso, Robert L. The effect of anxiety on cue selection in the A-Br paradigm. Psychonomic Sci., 13, 105–106, 1968.

95. Sperry, Bessie; Staver, Nancy; Reiner, Beatrice S.; and Ulrich, David. Renunciation and denial in learning difficulties. Amer. J. Orthopsychiat., 28, 98–111, 1958.

96. Spielberger, Charles D. The effects of manifest anxiety on the academic achievement of college students. Ment. Hyg., 46, 420–426, 1962.

97. Sullivan, Michael John. The effect of wakefulness and sleep on the memory for complex linguistic ideas. Diss. Abstr., 37 (B4), 1949B–1950B, 1976.

98. Taub, E.; and Emurian, C. S. Self-regulation of skin temperature using a variable intensity feedback light. In Shapiro, D.; Barber, T. X.: DiCara, L. V.; Kamiya, J.; Miller, N. E.; and Stoyva, J. (Eds.) Biofeedback and Self-Control. Chicago: Aldine, 1973.

99. Teasdale, John D. Effects of real and recalled success on learned helplessness and depression. J. Abnorm. Psychol., 87, 155–164, 1978.

100. Tedeschi, James; Burrill, Dwight; and Gahagan, James. Social desirability, manifest anxiety, and social power. J. Social Psychol., 77, 231–239, 1969.

101. Tulving, Endel; and Pearlstone, Z. Availability versus accessibility of information in memory for words. J. Verbal Learning Verbal Behav., 4, 381–391, 1966.

102. Wachtel, P. L. Anxiety, attention, and coping with threat. J. Abnormal Psychol., 73, 137–143, 1968.

103. Wallace, William P. Influence of test trials on the development of subjective organization in free recall. J. Exper. Psychol., 81, 527–535, 1969.

104. Watts, Graeme H.; and Anderson, Richard C. Retroactive inhibition in free recall as a function of first- and second-list organization. J. Exper. Psychol., 81, 595–597, 1969.

105. Wittmaier, Bruce C. Low test anxiety as a potential indicator of underachievement. Meas. Eval. Guid., 9, 146–151, 1976.

106. Wolpe, J. Psychotherapy by Reciprocal Inhibition. Stanford: Stanford University Press, 1958.

Any place can be a good place . . .

Chapter 6

Improving Concentration; Reducing Fatigue

A. DISTRACTION: ITS FREQUENCY AND REPERCUSSIONS

Your memory is a spectacular asset. So is your capacity to learn. Sometimes, though, when efforts to learn and remember seem to get nowhere, we wonder whether we have any abilities whatsoever along these lines.

Of the difficulties interfering with our efforts to learn and remember, poor concentration is outstanding.[4, 36] Sometimes poor concentration is mentioned more often than any other difficulty, surpassing even lack of interest and insufficient time.

Distressing enough in itself, inability to concentrate is rendered yet more distressing by the fatigue which accompanies it. Almost always, poor concentration and fatigue go hand in hand, accentuating each other.[35] Poor concentration leads to fatigue. Fatigue leads to poor concentration.

Both poor concentration and fatigue are caused in large part by conflict. We try to study, but simultaneously we are half set to abandon the whole business and do something else. We are inclined to jump up and tell someone to make less noise. We debate going out for the evening. We try to figure out some personal problem. We do all these things and simultaneously we try to study. We attempt to make incompatible reactions at the same time. This is what conflict means.

As a consequence we become tired. Studying, or anything else done with much conflict, is highly fatiguing. Even an hour of such studying leaves us weary, more weary by far than an hour of tennis. This is small wonder. Fatigue always results when we tear against ourselves.

What can be done about this? How can we reduce conflict, thus becoming better able to concentrate and less subject to fatigue? The problem can be tackled in many ways.

B. SOURCES OF DISTRACTION AND WAYS TO REDUCE THEM

1. Quiet Is Neither Necessary Nor Sufficient for Concentration.

Have you debated the merits of playing the radio while studying? If so, some information uncovered by Fendrick[25] might interest you. He had several groups of students study in quiet rooms. Others studied in rooms where lively music was played. On the average, comprehension and retention of reading were decreased when exciting music was played. The decrease occurred for students of all levels of academic aptitude. However, speed of reading was not affected adversely, on the average; this could lure you into falsely believing you are doing as well with the music present as with it absent. Similar results have been found repeatedly: Speed of reading is not impaired but comprehension and retention are decreased by playing music during study.[63, 85] Rock music with words is more disruptive than music without words.[8]

Many students are also distracted in the presence of talking, noise, and other extraneous stimuli. Distraction is more likely when the task is very tedious,[89] complex,[18, 74] detailed or difficult,[17, 22] or the material is relatively unorganized.[13, 33] Distraction also is more likely when the extraneous stimuli are erratic[28, 90] or in the same sense modality as the information being processed.[11, 86] Also, intense noise superimposed on stress can increase anxiety or anger[19, 21] and have other adverse effects on mood.[54, '60, 86] A quiet place for study can help. However, quiet definitely is not essential for avoiding distractions.

You can learn to not be distracted.[33, 39, 84] If you develop skill in an activity under relatively quiet circumstances, before the distraction sets in, you can carry your skill over better to distracting circumstances than if you try to start under the distracting circumstances.[12]

The data above and others[18, 31, 41, 45] suggest a second way to become impervious to potential distractors: Practice easy but engrossing tasks under potentially distracting circumstances; then when you are adept at ignoring extraneous stimuli, shift to more difficult or less intriguing tasks.

You can become free from distractions even in noisy rooms; and you can be mightily torn by distractions even in quiet rooms. Quietness is neither necessary nor sufficient for concentration and freedom from distraction.

This fact is nicely illustrated by the experience of a friend. This girl lived in a sorority, not the quietest place in the world. Complicating matters further, her room became a gathering place. On many of the occasions when she found studying desirable, her room was filled with her friends, playing bridge, chatting, and laughing. She seldom sent them away. She simply excused herself from the conversation, curled up in a chair, and studied. Other people would stop by. She greeted them, invited them in, and then went on with her work. She said this racket in no way distracted her, and probably it did not. She rarely was tired or cross. She made high grades — better than Phi Beta Kappa quality. Her concentration seemed in no way impaired.

Many other experiments show the same thing: One can work efficiently in noisy surroundings, even on complex tasks.[3, 15, 23, 59]

In a particularly enlightening experiment,[40] 171 people took two forms of an intelligence test; considerable speed and concentration were imperative for fine performance. The first form was taken in a quiet room, the second in a room equipped with many "distractors": seven bells, five buzzers, a 550-watt spotlight, a 90,000-volt rotary spark gap, a phonograph, two organ pipes of varying pitches, three metal whistles, a 55-pound circular saw mounted on a wooden frame, a well-known photographer taking pictures, and four students doing acrobatics. Sometimes there was quiet; sometimes one or two of these "distractors" were operating; sometimes several of them were going simultaneously. This is somewhat less peaceful than the typical library. But even with this horrendous welter of extraneous stimulation, the group did as well as when the room was continuously quiet. In fact, they showed some improvement on the second test, although a trifle less than that of a control group who performed both times in a quiet room.

Results of another experiment are possibly even more spectacular.[3] The students were doing addition problems. Two groups of students actually did *better* work in noisy surroundings than in quiet rooms. They solved the problems both more rapidly and more accurately in the noisy room. These students had been shown a graph, reputedly the results of a previous experiment, showing that fast work is facilitated by noise.

Two other groups were shown a graph supposedly demonstrating opposite results, that noisy surroundings retard mental work. These students did significantly worse in noisy surroundings than in quiet ones. Another group, shown no graphs, had no consistent differences in their performance under quiet and noisy conditions.

The behavior of these groups show that distractedness depends upon much more than the presence or absence of noise. *The same external pattern can act as either a distractor or a facilitator,*[7, 9, 38, 46] *or as neither.* Whether something acts as a distractor or not depends largely upon our expectations, upon our own internal organization.

To gain additional insight into the nature of distraction and its causes, let us look at a few more experiments.

In one of the earliest,[53] individuals translated numbers into letters and letters into numbers according to a code system, under conditions alternatingly quiet and noisy. The noise was furnished by a variety of bells, buzzers, and phonograph records. Accuracy of the work was not affected in any significant way. Speed was somewhat impaired with onset of either noise or quiet, but even this impairment did not persist. The poorest workers were most disrupted by these changes; the best workers were affected little.

In another experiment the subjects engaged in different kinds of activities (addition and number-perception tasks) and had different kinds of "distractors" (blasts of a Klaxon horn and reputedly humorous stories told in a loud voice). Results were essentially the same. The onset of either noise or quiet acted as a temporary distractor, but recovery was rapid.[26]

Thus we see that one can rapidly learn not to be distracted, and can work as well under what generally are assumed to be distracting conditions as under quiet conditions.

Moreover, concentration in the presence of many extraneous stimuli does not necessarily tax one's system. The onset of the "distractor" sometimes is[53] and sometimes is not[26] accompanied by an increase in energy expenditure. Sometimes, in fact, good work takes even *less* energy after the "distractor" has been present for a time than it took before the "distractor" began.[26, 53] However, even if energy expenditure were increased by 60 per cent (the most reported by these investigators), this would have no great effect on the general bodily economy of a student — because only trifling amounts of energy are needed for reading, thinking, and other mental activities.

One other study would probably interest you. Engineers of the United States Signal Corps tested precision instruments, working singly in well-soundproofed rooms. These rooms were specially constructed to eliminate all noise from outside the room and practically all noise too from the person within the room. The conditions seemed almost perfect for effortless concentration. However, after about half an hour, the men suffered acutely from "nervous exhaustion" and could not continue work. The apparently peaceful set-up, singularly free of all noise and all other external distractions, was acutely distracting. Men could not work in it for long.

College students are similar.[10] Working conditions again were arranged to be unusually free of varying external stimuli. Again these conditions were not conducive to high-quality intellectual endeavor. In fact, the students did considerably poorer intellectual work than usual.

The experiments we have just discussed, and others,[57, 78] eloquently demonstrate that the intensity, the number, and the nature of the external stimuli do not alone determine whether one is distracted. Whether you are distracted or not depends largely upon your nature — your own internal stimuli and personal habits.[2, 30, 66, 87]

You, not the external stimuli, determine whether you will be distracted. *Distractions, it appears, are basically from inside ourselves, not from outside.*

The most efficacious way, then, to eliminate distractions is this: Instead of attempting to change the external world, change yourself.

Let us try to analyze more clearly what it is about ourselves which makes us distracted, and how we can change. Since the inner distractions differ from person to person, you must make most of the analyses for yourself. However, here are the kinds of things to look for and some approaches useful in combating the difficulties.

2. Our Resentments Distract Us and Sensitize Us to Other Distractors; We Can Dispel These.

When people talk near our study room, many of us are disturbed. Why? The noise from talking is not great; and even if it were very great, not everybody would be distracted. Clearly we are not distracted by the noise *per se*; rather we are distracted by some of our reactions to the talking.

Often we feel the talking is inconsiderate. We feel abused and resentful. Why, we wonder, don't people treat us with more consideration? We are trying to work; therefore, they should keep quiet.

This is the way we often feel; and when we do, these feelings disrupt and distract us. What can we do about this? Tell the talkers to be quiet? You may *feel* that is a good plan. But do you *think* so? Probably you care about those people. Do you really want them to abandon activities they value? Or be obliged to go somewhere else — just because you happen to be studying? Sometimes, yes. But always? We may have a starry-eyed notion of what you are like, but we doubt that you often would want people to reshuffle their lives merely for your convenience. What do you think?

Let us consider this matter a little further. Do you like having those you love be happy? Do you want them to be as happy as possible? Do you want to accord them as much freedom as possible? Remember, these questions do not involve the relative importance of your studying versus their activities; for, with practice, you can learn to study well even while they are making some noise or talking. Do you really want them to drop whatever they are doing and keep still? Are you pleased by forcing people whom you cherish to drop pursuit of their interests? Or have to rearrange their lives because of you? Whenever you study well or pursue your other interests while permitting other people to continue their own activities, you increase their freedom and your own. Is this something you value?

Really think about these questions. If you do, you will become far less distracted in the presence of talking and laughing. Much of your annoyance will be broken up; much of your inclination to subdue people will be gone too. With these changes, distraction evaporates. You will have a new ability to study with concentration.

The same sorts of feelings often are aroused by interruptions, making them notoriously distracting. When we see an interruption as a call for help, we are less annoyed.[5, 61, 75] All too often, though, we see interruptions as intrusions. Someone calls to you or comes barging into your room while you are trying to study. You are annoyed. Without thinking, you make flash emotional responses. You are irritated at "the gross lack of consideration." And you are hurt — "People just don't care at all! They don't care about me and they don't care about what I am doing. At least, they sure don't show it." But wait! That impression cannot be accurate. That person must care about you, or he would not be there. He would not have interrupted you unless he wanted to be with *you*. He must want to communicate with *you*. Is that such a crime? From some standpoints, it would have been better had he chosen a different moment. There is much in favor of good manners. However, you can eliminate most of the losses from other people's inept timing. What moment a person arrives will usually not matter much, for it will not be very disturbing *if* you learn to avoid resentment at the "intrusion." When he leaves, you can return to work and become engrossed without any additional lost time — unless you go on feeling annoyed.

To become better able to concentrate, we need not change other people nor their behavior. We need to change ourselves. To do this, try out the ideas offered above. They can give you, and your friends, new freedoms.

3. Wistfulness Leads to Distraction.

The sound of people laughing, chatting, having a good time together, may arouse civil war within you. You become torn between continuing to study and going to join them. Wistfulness creeps in. Conflict storms. Here again, it is the stimuli from these internal responses (not the talking itself) which distract you. In this instance, your conflict and wistfulness are the distractors, and it is these feelings you need to reduce in order to concentrate.

How can you reduce this conflict and wistfulness? For one thing, remember that this is an instance when you can have your cake and eat it too. You can study at that particular hour and have the joy of others' companionship at some other times. You are not committing yourself to a life of solitude and eternal studying merely because you devote this particular time to study. We should remember this. Unfortunately we forget it and as a consequence are caused needless worry and misery.

Many students have greatly reduced their conflict by another system: They earmark definite hours for study and other hours for recreation. This frees them from the almost perpetual conflict of trying to decide whether to study or whether to play. It also enables them to really believe that they too are going to have fun later on.

Still another way to combat internal distraction is this: Whenever you decide to study or decide to do anything else, practice sticking to your decision until your self-appointed job is completed. Establishing this as a habit greatly reduces the conflict now elicited by conversation and other trivial stimuli; thus it eliminates much of the distraction.

4. Fear of Rejection and Other Conflict-Arousers Are Potent Disrupters; They Need Not Continue.

Sometimes the real distractor is fear of rejection.[73, 74] A nagging, almost unverbalized fear sets in: Unless I stop studying and join other people, I may lose their friendship. Perhaps they will think I'm stuffy.

This raises some questions. Would *you* consider a person stuffy just because he studied during some of the times you felt sociable? Do you withdraw *your* friendship and respect that easily? Is there any reason to believe others care less about you, or are so much less civilized than yourself? No sound basis exists, really, for thinking other people will drop you or withdraw their friendship on such slight provocation. A few may, but not many. Friendship is not that superficial, and you *know* this if, for a moment, you can stop feeling only and start thinking too.

Many students cannot study when company is present, and company is "always" present. Are you like that? If you are, you may suffer from the fear sketched above, a fear of losing friends. Or you may unwittingly feel obligated to drop whatever you are doing and join people who come to visit, albeit their presence was unexpected.

A part of the essence of friendship is this: One deeply wants his friend, or anyone else whom he esteems, to have as extensive freedom as possible for living his own life in his own way. Try giving your friends a chance to show this. If you have many things which need doing soon and few opportunities in which to do them, generally you can chat for a few minutes and then excuse yourself, making arrangements to meet at some other time. Such behavior is not only forgivable; it is deeply understandable. Further, such behavior is highly desirable — in the eyes of friends. To a great extent, friends want you to do whatever you think is best.

5.   The Threat of Devastation Disrupts Us.

For several decades now students have been trying to study and start their adult life under the continuing threat or actuality of extensive devastation. This is difficult. Today more workable tools for peace and abundant living exist than ever before; more tools for massive destruction or even obliteration of any life also exist.

If you are troubled by the specter of a thermonuclear disaster, as almost any sane, compassionate human being would be, the following books and article may prove especially worth looking into: Osgood's "An Alternative to War or Surrender," Hocking's "The Freedom to Hope," and Russell's "New Hopes for a Changing World." Particularly sustaining, they are suggestive of possible creative solutions to our new human dilemma.

6.   Your Responses to a Roommate's Mannerisms Can Distract You.

Is your roommate perfect? Most of us when asked this question could give plenty of reasons why our roommate is terribly annoying. He drums on the desk, or snaps his fingernails, or cracks his knuckles. Or maybe she hums, or sighs, or taps a pencil. Sometimes we are aroused to near-frenzy by such behavior. We go all to pieces and cannot study at all while such noises are going on.

Why are these trivial sounds so highly distracting? Here again it is not our roommate's behavior, but our own response, which shatters concentration.

A major source of our trouble is this: We are annoyed with ourself for being annoyed by him and his behavior. Then, naturally, we become annoyed with him for making us annoyed with ourself. (In many such cases, we notice only our annoyance with him.) Annoyance creates a great flood of internal stimuli which overwhelm and woefully disrupt us.

We sometimes become annoyed too because we feel our roommate's behavior is silly and thoughtless. His behavior *is* thoughtless — in the sense that it occurs without thinking. However, his behavior is not thoughtless in the more usual sense: Such behavior does not mean the person values your welfare lightly. As a matter of fact, unless your roommate expended great effort and unless he also possessed extraordinary skill in making and breaking habits, he could not possibly eliminate pencil-tapping and other such mannerisms — no matter how deeply he cared about you and longed to please you! He cannot eliminate those habits any better than you can cease twisting a lock of hair, or stop stammering occasionally, or quit blushing slightly. The reactions are made unconsciously. The person is not aware of making the reaction nor of the exact conditions which evoke it. He is aware only that he has made the reaction after it is done.

In a charming parody, Lewis Carroll pointed up the essential absurdity of irritation over these automatic reactions.

"Speak roughly to your little boy,
   And beat him when he sneezes;
He only does it to annoy,
   Because he knows it teases."[14]

That, of course, is ridiculous. Sneezing is not done to annoy us. Neither are the other reactions about which we have spoken. They do not mean that someone is indifferent to our wishes. What, then, do they mean?

These mannerisms signify tension. You are often tense, especially when working under pressure. Well, so is your roommate. Perhaps you "let off steam" by twisting a lock of hair; he "lets off steam" by drumming his fingers, or tapping his pencil, or acting in other similar ways. Such behavior merely shows that your colleague is overwrought. He is, for example, working very rapidly, or thinking hard, or worried.

The next time a pencil starts tapping or knuckles start

cracking, try to remember these things. Say to yourself, "Poor guy! He sure is tense tonight." If you can do this, life will run more smoothly for you, and also for your associates. Your world will be freer of annoyances and freer too, therefore, from distraction.

7. To Summarize — Distraction Often Is Caused by Some Emotional Response We Can Modify or Eliminate.

Here is a résumé of the potentially revolutionizing ideas we have been examining. Whether or not we are distracted depends rather more upon us, our own internal stimuli and learned reactions, than upon external stimuli *per se*. The real distractions are not from without, but from within ourselves. More specifically, our distractions spring from such responses as these: a feeling that someone is being thoughtless and inconsiderate; a conflict between two action tendencies; an unspoken fear of losing the respect of others, or their friendship; a misinterpretation of situations with resultant irritation. These are only examples. Other reactions may be more characteristic of you. You must figure out for yourself what *you* are like, for many other emotional reactions also are distracting.

This, in turn, means: To greatly reduce or eliminate distractions, we need to change ourself. We need to break up the sorts of emotional response sketched above and learn different patterns of response.

How? The general approach is this: First, try to analyze the situations in which you cannot concentrate. Examine your feelings. Determine what really is distracting you. Next, reinterpret the situation as rationally as you can, more rationally than usual. Often you then will perceive the external stimuli differently. Almost immediately these stimuli will be less potent distractors. Third, set out to build new responses to these "distracting" stimuli. Let your brain have a voice here too, rather than permitting your life to be tyrannized by flash emotional responses.

If you can have patience with yourself and persevere in your attempts, you can learn these arts.

Other means too are available for enhancing your ability to concentrate. We turn now to them.

C. MORE WAYS TO IMPROVE CONCENTRATION

1. When Potential Distractions Are Present, Launch Yourself Particularly Energetically into Your Work.

For example, try at those times especially to actively search for new implications and new applications of what you read. Actively sort what you already know from what you did not, rather than passively wait for facts to sink in and ideas to occur to you. Various other ways whereby you can get started energetically studying were presented on pages 38–42 and 43–55 of Chapter 2 (Starting Study and The Use of Books) and pages 102–105, Chapter 4 (Warming Up Quickly).

With these approaches, you sometimes will succeed in working effectively while former distractions are present. Each time you succeed, you are getting more stimuli established as cues for effective studying. You are making formerly distracting stimuli become cues for what you want to do. In the future, their presence actually will facilitate rather than hinder your studying. You will be developing increasingly great abilities to concentrate.

2. Keep a Pad of Paper on Your Desk; Jot Down Certain Ones of Your Distracting Thoughts.

Somehow it is just when we try to study that suddenly we recall dozens of things we should have done. We remember the button not sewn on our coat. The button has been loose for days, but we forget it until we start to study. We remember letters which are not written and should be, questions we meant to ask a friend but forgot, phone calls to be made, a suit to be pressed, nails to be filed, books to be returned, a host of other neglected "duties." To make things still more complicated, it is when studying mathematics, for example, that ideas start popping for our English paper.

When thoughts of those kinds occur during study, write a brief note of them. This is a small thing to do, but it greatly increases your power to concentrate.

Without some such technique, you are attempting the impossible: You are trying to talk to yourself about your studies; simultaneously you are trying to talk to yourself about utterly unrelated matters, such as what you wish to do later. These are incompatible responses; doing both at once is a logical impossibility. Under such circumstances, concentration is impossible.

3. Divide Your Studies into Definite Sub-parts.

When starting to study, specify the particular skills you are going to acquire in this session or the units of material you are going to master. For example, specify a certain number of pages to be read . . . a definite number of math problems to be solved . . . a particular task to be accomplished in writing a term paper (e.g., outlining the paper, or arranging the bibliography, or polishing the phrases). You work until that part is done (regardless of time). This method of tackling your studies facilitates concentration.

Concentration is hindered, you recall, by specifying merely the number of minutes to study and failing to specify the job to be accomplished. Studying by the clock necessitates watching the clock while studying. Obviously this precludes becoming wholly absorbed in your studies. You cannot, under those conditions, build habits of studying wholeheartedly with real concentration.

Possibly you are so pressed for time you dare not do anything but allot a certain amount of time to each subject. One neat solution is to set an alarm or timer. This sounds a bit silly; but it helps. Setting an alarm gives you at least a chance of building habits of concentration. You can study without one eye and "half your mind" on the clock.

A useful variation is this: Set a goal for yourself of having completed a certain number of problems or pages or other parts in a certain amount of time. This can help appreciably when you are first learning to concentrate. Set a timer to go off when you should be half done (or have done a quarter, or some other fraction of your choosing). On various occasions you will be making your self-set goal; this heartens you. When you are not making it, this too can spur you on. When you note that you are a bit behind, try remembering your time-goal and throw yourself into your work with new fervor and interest; often (to your surprise) you will still manage to finish in the allotted time what you had hoped and intended. It becomes a game and a challenge.

If you have long lists to learn, divide them into shorter

lists. These are far easier to learn and better remembered. As you probably have noticed, items at the beginnings and items at the end of a list are remembered better than items in the middle.[80] You take advantage of that by making several short lists instead of one long list.

4. Set Reasonable Tasks for Yourself.

It is folly to try to do a week's assignments in one evening. The only results of such practices are apt to be a new crop of fears, intensified anxieties, and a berating of oneself for failing a self-assigned task. Such emotions further impair our ability to concentrate.

We must learn to distribute our study sessions, setting reasonable objectives, doing some study every work day, and avoiding piling everything on a few hectic days that are bound to be insufficient for our purposes. Chapter 4 should help you set more reasonable goals, as does section 3 above and section D following.

Avoid setting your goals too low. Especially if you did poorly on a recent test, expectancy of success is lowered.[1, 72] However, setting goals too low is a damaging practice, undercutting your morale and impairing performance.

Orient yourself toward achievement and success, not merely toward avoiding failure. This strengthens concentration and persistence.[56]

These are skills useful throughout life.

D. STILL MORE WAYS TO AID CONCENTRATION AND REDUCE FATIGUE

1. Arrange Each Study Period So Different Types of Study Follow One Another.

For example, suppose you have two somewhat similar courses, such as sociology and psychology, and a third course that is quite different, such as mathematics. First study sociology, then mathematics, then psychology; or else, psychology, mathematics, sociology.

Or suppose you wish to read two chapters and review another chapter during some study period. Do not do all the reading first and then all the reviewing. Instead, interweave those activities. If you read and review in ways like those sketched in Chapters 2, 3, and 5, reading and reviewing will be quite different activities and refreshing changes from each other.

You can devise many other interweaving systems of your own. The basic idea is to arrange your study period so you get variety *while* studying. Alternate many different sorts of activities. This enables you to study more easily for long periods of time, and need far fewer rest periods. In addition, interference effects are reduced — especially the kinds of interference in which learning one thing impairs retention of something previously learned[79, 88] or impedes subsequent learning and retention of something new.[24, 27, 47, 65]

2. Make the Most of Rest Periods.

The purpose of rest periods is to provide relief from doing the same thing for too long. Naturally, then, your activity during rest periods should be as different as possible from that involved in the studying you were doing. If you have been writing a term paper, "resting" by writing a letter will not be very refreshing. Better far would be washing dishes, telephoning a friend, walking around the block, playing with the children, or doing some gardening. You will think of other activities which also take only a little time, and are a change from studying.

Often you can do a couple of items from the list of neglected "duties" which occurred to you while studying. This has a twofold value: it relaxes you by being a different sort of activity; and it relaxes you by eliminating one more small, but pestering, worry. You will have completed one more thing you wanted to get done.

3. Devise a Schedule, Unless You Are Strenuously Opposed to the Idea.

If you find concentration difficult or are troubled by vague anxieties, a schedule can help considerably. Chapter 4 offered ways to start. Let us supplement those now. One of the best kinds is this: Parts of various days are reserved for social activities; other periods for taking care of various obligations; others for studying; and some parts of each day are left unscheduled.

Be sure to schedule time for social activities. To many people, having some time with friends is as important as study.[29] Take that into account when making your schedule. This way of arranging one's week decreases the fear that all of life is going to be spent poring over books, that never will one have any fun. Such fears haunt many a student while trying to study and are a potent distraction. The fears are no less intense because they are irrational. Having certain hours reserved for social activities can be deeply reassuring. While you are studying you *know* lighthearted times are coming; thus you can study with a greater enthusiasm and concentration.

Equally important is to leave a significant amount of time unscheduled. Many people, when first making a schedule, designate almost every waking hour for some particular activity. Consequently they feel enslaved — as indeed they are. Further, a student's life is chaotic. What we think will be the work of a moment turns out to take hours. Unforeseen things come up by the score — some of them urgent. A schedule must leave time free for attending to these.

Devising a schedule appropriate to you will take some trial and error. If your first schedule turns out to be impracticable and you cannot abide by it, revise it so you can.

Scheduling can work like a charm in cutting down on tensions, worries, and daydreams. Thus a schedule frees your ability to concentrate. But in order for the system to work, the earmarked periods must be held inviolate. They must be used for their designated purpose and other activities re-directed to the free times.

4. Cast Yourself for a Worthy Role. [6, 16]

The first reason for doing this is that we tend to become what we are labelled as being,[81] or are expected to be.[48, 52, 67] Other people tend to become what you label and expect them to be. Likewise you tend to become whatever you label yourself as being. Think of yourself as someone worthwhile, label yourself in those terms, live in ways appropriate to that concept, and you are more apt to become who you want to be.

The second reason is very direct: Greater self-respect and better grades frequently appear together.[42, 43, 82] You can increase your self-respect in many ways; some we have touched upon already; others are discussed later. Here is one more.

You are many things. For one: You are a student. Define "student" in a way worthy of you and your talents, and consistent with your most cherished goals. When you are discouraged or your "mind begins to wander," remind yourself of this role.

Many of you have been pummelled by strong forces leading you to see yourself as weak, or lazy, or stupid, or distraught. You need not cooperate on that project. Think of yourself in new ways worthy of your most wonderful capacities. "I *am* a potential doctor, by George!" "I *will* become a perceptive reader."

This is not suggesting self-hypnosis. The suggestion is this: Devise for yourself and live a role worthy of your best potentialities.

Do not define your role too narrowly! "We have artists with no scientific knowledge and scientists with no artistic knowledge and both with no spiritual sense of gravity at all, and the result is not just bad, it is ghastly. The time for real reunification of art and technology is really long overdue."[62]

You can be more than simply a laboratory technician, or chemist, or architect. You can be whole. You need not choose among the goals set forth in Chapter 1. They all can be worked for at the same time. You can achieve them all.

You can be an increasingly excellent student. You can learn to learn. Squirrel monkeys learn to learn;[68] so do macaque monkeys,[32, 77] chimpanzees, gorillas and orangutangs,[51, 69, 70] and even pigeons.[20] Members of all those species can get better and better at learning, making increasingly few errors on successive tasks, mastering new tasks and solving new problems increasingly swiftly. So can people.[44, 64] And so can you.

Never forget what you have excellent reason to believe: You can learn increasingly well. You can learn, and change, and grow. You can become more nearly the person you long to be.

5. Aim at Quality.

Benton intends to do the least he possibly can and still get by. Quite often he misjudges and does less than is necessary to get by. Benton gets a "D," or fails entirely. This is traumatic. When he succeeds, Benton has nothing of worth. When Benton gets what he aims at, it is a sleazy product, prized by nobody. Benton is disgusted with his "education;" so is everyone else. No wonder he can't concentrate.

Instead of intending to do the minimum possible, strive for something worth attaining. Strive for excellence.

Whatever you are doing, strive for quality. If you wholly succeed, you have something of great value. If you miss, you will still have something of worth. Falling somewhat short of quality goals, you still have a creditable performance and results of value. If you partially succeed, you have a product of merit. And job satisfaction is greater when the quality of your product is high.[34, 49, 76, 83]

When you aim for quality, there are additional boons: You utilize all your resources and talents. This is profoundly satisfying. You are developing and growing. This is satisfying. One more: All the while you are working, you know you have a chance for something really great; of a sudden the process itself glows with meaning.

The changes reach far. Pirsig describes a university English class where students found everything dreary. Writing themes, class work, reports, all were drudgery. Gradually the students changed. And then it happened; they started trying for quality! They had been plodding along, grinding out assignments, sloppy and dull. "Now that was over. . . . The vacuum was suddenly filled with the positive goal of Quality, and the whole thing fit together. Students, astonished, came by his office and said, 'I used to just hate English. Now I spend more time on it than anything else.' Not just one or two. Many. The whole Quality concept was beautiful. It worked. It was that mysterious, individual, internal goal of each creative person on the blackboard at last."[62]

Quality is what you should be striving for. If you work for something worth having, you work far more wholeheartedly — with less stress, less conflict, less fatigue — and less distraction. When you are accomplishing something worth accomplishing, you sail along with verve and concentration.

6. You Are on Scholarship.

Some of you realize that your attendance at a university or college is being made possible through a scholarship or fellowship you were awarded. However, in actuality all of you at any university or college are there on scholarships. Only a tiny part of the cost of your advanced education is borne by you or your family. Aside from meals and lodging, you pay only about one tenth or even a twentieth of the costs, sometimes far less, rarely as much as a fourth.

If you are a student at a state university or college, a major part of your expenses is covered by other citizens through taxes. If you are attending a private university or college, again most of the cost of your education is covered by other people through their endowments, trust funds, and other gifts to the university or college. These are almost incredible gifts.

Universities and colleges are incredible worlds. One such place anywhere would be worthy of wonder. Having hundreds and thousands in one country is a marvel. The remarkable libraries of books, and journals, and paintings, and films, and artifacts of other cultures; the lovely buildings and grounds — some spots truly beautiful; the projectors and screens and slides and microscopes and telescopes and other doorways to let you see worlds you have not seen before; the cafeterias and dormitories; the carefully designed rooms with special lighting for art and engineering and other studies; auditoriums with special acoustics and special seating, for drama, music, speech, seminars; special supplies for music, athletics, botany, physics demonstrations, and other courses; the many kinds of laboratory equipment for dozens of kinds of courses; all of these and much more are made available to you through the care and generosity of former students and other citizens — the individual giver and taxpayer alike. These gifts are immense.

My husband wrote about this to his students, in connection with the prosaic matter of laboratory supplies. He noted:[50]

"To carry on research requires considerable material and equipment. Even simple investigations of the kind you will be doing here require considerable material and equipment — some of which is very expensive. Most of what you will need will be furnished to you as a gift from people you probably never will meet. Regardless of whether you are at a private university or college or are at a state university or college, the major expense of your education is being borne by people who do not know you and will probably never meet you. But nonetheless they are investing their resources in you, to enable you to better develop your abilities and realize your potentialities. Remember this as you accept and use their gifts."

These people, strangers to you, make no gain directly from your life becoming enriched and happier — nor from your becoming educated in any other sense. They are playing it on faith, that somehow this will be a better world when you are better educated; they are offering their gifts on trust to you. We have a high responsibility to these individuals. If we accept their gifts, we must keep faith and not betray that trust. The gifts are inestimably valuable to millions of persons. To be a recipient of such a gift (directly or indirectly) is a privilege and a great honor. To be a student is a splendid thing.

When you are distraught and frantic, discouraged or filled with gloom, these facts are worth recalling. Many persons care tremendously about you, are backing you, and deem your undertaking as a student one of great merit.

E. A Forecast

For study to bring results of value, three questions must be answered: Where am I now? Where do I want to be? What is necessary to get there? Solving any problem depends upon answering these three questions.

Chapter 1 dealt mainly with the second question, "where you want to be," the kind of person you wish to become. Chapters 2 through 6 indicate routes for reaching those goals and steps aiding one to use those routes. "Where you now are" has been only lightly touched; Chapter 7 treats that aspect in more detail.

This step is vital. No matter where you are trying to get, you must start from where you are. It helps tremendously to note where that is! From failure to recognize this fact and impatience with its implications, we spend much time in futility. We try to brush our teeth in the fireplace — because the living room is where we happened to be when we desired clean teeth. Of course you will not do that, exactly. However, you do behave in similar fashions. You try to leap to some goal which simply cannot be reached directly from where you happen to be. That you are so behaving may not be clear to you. That the results are poor will be all too clear, however.

Let us consider together where you now are. Let us see which aspects of your current position hinder achieving your goals, and formulate then some additional steps for leaving there and moving to positions from which your goals can be achieved more readily.

BIBLIOGRAPHY FOR CHAPTER 6

1. Abramson, Lyn Y.; Garber, Judy; Edwards, Neil B.; and Seligman, Martin E. P. Expectancy changes in depression and schizophrenia. J. Abnorm. Psychol., 87, 102–109, 1978.
2. Amoroso, Donald M.; and Walters, Richard H. Effects of anxiety and socially mediated anxiety reduction on paired associate learning. J. Personality Soc. Psychol., 11, 388–396, 1969.
3. Baker, K. H. Pre-experimental set in distraction experiments. J. Gen. Psychol., 16, 471–488, 1937.
4. Baker, R. W.; and Madell, T. O. A continued investigation of susceptibility to distraction in academically underachieving and achieving male college students. J. Educ. Psychol., 56, 254–258, 1965.
5. Baron, Robert A. Invasions of personal space and helping. J. Exper. Soc. Psychol., 14, 304–312, 1978.

6. Battle, E. S. Motivational determinants of academic competence. J. Personality Soc. Psychol., 4, 634–642, 1966.
7. Bee, Helen L. Individual differences in susceptibility to distraction. Percept. Mot. Skills, 23, 821–822, 1966.
8. Belsham, Richard L.; and Harman, David W. Effect of vocal vs. non-vocal music on visual recall. Percep. Motor Skills, 44, 857–858, 1977.
9. Berlyne, D. E.; and Carey, S. T. Incidental learning and the timing of arousal. Psychonomic Sci., 13, 103–104, 1968.
10. Bexton, W. H.; Heron, W.; and Scott, T. H. Effects of decreased variation in the sensory environment. Canad. J. Psychol., 8, 70–76, 1954.
11. Boggs, David H.; and Simon, J. Richard. Differential effect of noise on tasks of varying complexity. J. Appl. Psychol., 52, 148–153, 1968.
12. Broadbent, D. E. Effects of noises of high and low frequency on behavior. Ergonomics, 1, 21–29, 1957. Also, Effect of noise on an "intellectual" task. J. Acoustical Soc. Amer., 30, 824–827, 1958.
13. Buschke, Herman. Verbal noise and linguistic constraints. Psychonomic Sci., 12, 391–392, 1968.
14. Carroll Lewis. Alice in Wonderland. New York: Grosset & Dunlap, Inc., 1946, p. 63.
15. Cofer, C. N.; and Dorfman, P. W. Free recall of trigrams in the presence of distractors: A replication. Psychonomic Sci., 14, 197, 1969.
16. Crandall, Virginia C.; and McGhee, Paul E. Expectancy of reinforcement and academic competence. J. Personality, 36, 635–648, 1968.
17. Daee, Safar; and Wilding, J. M. Effects of high intensity white noise on short-term memory for a position in a list and sequence. Brit. J. Psychol., 68, 335–349, 1977.
18. Davis, Gary A.; Train, Alice J.; and Manske, Mary E. Trial and error versus "insightful" problem solving. J. Exper. Psychol., 76, 337–340, 1968.
19. Donnerstein, Edward; and Wilson, David W. Effects of noise and perceived control on ongoing and subsequent aggressive behavior. J. Personality Soc. Psychol., 34, 774–781, 1976.
20. Eck, Kenneth O.; Noel, Richard C.; and Thomas, D. R. Discrimination learning as a function of prior discrimination and nondifferential training. J. Exper. Psychol. 82, 156–162, 1969 (pigeons).
21. Edsell, Richard D. Noise and social interaction as simultaneous stressors. Percep. Motor Skills, 42, 1123–1129, 1976.
22. Edsell, Richard D. Anxiety as a function of environmental noise and social interaction. J. Psychol., 92, 219–226, 1976.
23. Egeth, Howard. Selective attention. Psychol. Bull., 67, 41–57, 1967.
24. Eschenbrenner, A. John, Jr. Retroactive and proactive inhibition in verbal discrimination learning. J. Exper. Psychol., 81, 576–583, 1969.
25. Fendrick, P. The influence of music distraction upon reading efficiency. J. Educ. Res., 31, 264–271, 1937.
26. Ford, A. Attention-automatization: An investigation of the transitional nature of mind. Amer. J. Psychol., 41, 1–32, 1929.
27. Frost, Robert R.; and Jahnke, John C. Proactive effects in short-term memory. J. Verbal Learning Verbal Behav., 7, 785–789, 1968.
28. Glass, D. C.; and Singer, J. E. Urban Stress. New York: Academic Press, 1972.
29. Good, Lawrence R. Perceived value of personality characteristics. Percep. Motor Skills, 44, 590, 1977.
30. Grim, Paul F.; Kohlberg, Lawrence; and White, Sheldon H. Some relationships between conscience and attentional processes. J. Personality Soc. Psychol., 8, 239–252, 1968.
31. Grosjean, L.; Lodi, R.; and Rabinowitz, J. Noise and pedagogic efficiency in school activities. Experientia, 32, 575–576, 1976.
32. Harlow, Harry F. The development of learning in the rhesus monkey. American Scientist, 47, 459–479, 1959.
33. Harris, C. Stanley. Aftereffects of random and fixed intermittent sound on human performance. USAFAMRL Tech. Rep., No. 76–75, 9 p., 1976.
34. Heilbroner, R. L.; Mintz, M.; McCarthy, C.; Ungar, S. J.; Vandiver, K.; Friedman, S.; and Boyd, J. In the Name of Profit. New York: Warner, 1973.
35. Henley, W. E. Fatigue. New Zealand Med. J., 50, 212–221, 1951.
36. Hepner, Harry Walker. Psychology Applied to Life and Work. (Fifth ed., page 203.) Englewood Cliffs, N.J.: Prentice-Hall, Inc., 1973.
37. Hocking, William Ernest. The freedom to hope. Saturday Review, 46, 12–15 and 50, 1963.

38. Houston, B. Kent. Inhibition and facilitating effect of noise on interference tasks. Percept. Mot. Skills, 27, 947–950, 1968.
39. Houston, B. Kent; and Jones, Thomas M. Distraction and Stroop color-word performance. J. Exper. Psychol., 74, 54–56, 1967.
40. Hovey, H. B. Effects of general distraction on the higher thought processes. Amer. J. Psychol., 40, 585–591, 1928.
41. Jerison, Harry J. Performance on a simple vigilance task in noise and quiet. J. Acoustical Soc. Amer., 29, 1163–1165, 1957. Also, Effects of noise on human performance. J. Appl. Psychol., 43, 96–101, 1959.
42. Johnson, Edward G., Jr. A comparison of academically successful and unsuccessful college of education freshmen on two measures of "self." Diss. Abstr., 28, (4-A), 1298–1299, 1967.
43. Jones. John G. The relationship of self-perception measures and academic achievement among college seniors. J. Educ. Res., 63, 201–203, 1970.
44. Keppel, Geoffrey; Postman, Leo; and Zavortink, Bonnie. Studies of learning to learn. VIII, The influence of massive amounts of training upon the learning and retention of paired-associate lists. J. Verbal Learning Verbal Behav., 7, 790–796, 1968.
45. Kesselhaut, Ilene Malovany. The effect of noise conditions on performance of complex mental tasks in a classroom environment. Diss. Abst. 36(A 10), 6555 A-6556 A, 1976.
46. Kirk, R. E.; and Hecht, E. Maintenance of vigilance by programmed noise. Percept. Mot. Skills, 16, 553–560, 1963.
47. Kothurkar, V. K. Effect of similarity of interpolated materials on short-term recall. Quart. J. Exper. Psychol., 20, 405–408, 1968.
48. Kuhlman, D. M.; and Wimberley, D. L. Expectations of choice behavior held by cooperators, competitors, and individualists across four classes of experimental game. J. Personality Soc. Psychol., 34, 69–81, 1976.
49. Locke, E. A. The nature and causes of job satisfaction. In Dunnette, M. D. (Ed.). Handbook of Industrial and Organizational Psychology. Chicago: Rand McNally, 1976.
50. McBlair, William. Experiments in Physiology (Second Ed.). Palo Alto, California: National Press Books, 1968.
51. Miles, R. C. Discrimination-learning sets. In Schrier, Allen M.; Harlow, Harry F.; and Stollnitz, Fred (Eds.). Behavior of Nonhuman Primates. Vol. 1. New York: Academic Press, pp. 51–95, 1965.
52. Miller, D. T.; and Holmes, J. G. The role of situational restrictiveness on self-fulfilling hypothesis. J. Personality Soc. Pyschol., 31, 661–673, 1975.
53. Morgan, J. J. B. The overcoming of distraction and other resistances. Arch. Psychol., 5, No. 35, 84 pp., 1916.
54. Murdoff, Kenneth Harold. Performance and mood in the presence of noise and high density. Diss. Abstr. Index, 37 (2-B), 5671B-5672B, 1976.
55. Norman, Donald A. Memory and Attention. New York: John Wiley and Sons, Inc., 1969.
56. Nygard, Roald. Personality, Situation and Persistence: A Study with Emphasis on Achievement Motivation. Oslo, Norway: Universitetsforlaget, 1977.
57. O'Malley, John J.; and Gallas, John. Noise and attention span. Percept. Motor Skills, 44, 919–922, 1977.
58. Osgood, C. E. An Alternative to War or Surrender. Urbana: University of Illinois Press, 1962.
59. Ottman, Phillip K. Field dependence and arousal. Percept. Mot. Skills, 19, 441, 1964. Also, Activation and cue utilization. Diss. Abstr., 26, No. 8, 4800, 1965.
60. Page, Richard A. Noise and helping behavior. Environment Behav., 9, 311–334, 1977.
61. Patterson, M. L. An arousal model of interpersonal intimacy. Psychol. Rev., 83, 235–245, 1976.
62. Pirsig, Robert M. Zen and the Art of Motorcycle Maintenance (pages 294, 209). New York: William Morrow & Company, Inc., 1974.
63. Poock, Gary K.; and Wiener, Earl L. Music and other auditory backgrounds during visual monitoring. J. Indus. Engr., 17, 318–323, 1966.
64. Postman, Leo; Keppel, Geoffrey; and Zacks, Rose. Studies of learning to learn. VII, The effects of practice on response integration. J. Verbal Learning Verbal Behav., 7, 776–784, 1968.

65. Proctor, Robert W. Attention and modality-specific interference in visual short-term memory. J. Exper. Psychol., 4, 239–245, 1978.
66. Reese, H. W. Manifest anxiety and achievement test performance. J. Educ. Psychol., 52, 132–135, 1961.
67. Rosenthal, R. On the social psychology of the self-fulfilling prophecy: M. S. S. Modular Publ., 1974.
68. Rumbaugh, Duane M. The learning and sensory capacities of the squirrel monkey in phylogenetic perspective. In Rosenblum, Leonard A.; and Cooper, Robert W. (Eds.). The Squirrel Monkey. New York: Academic Press, pp. 256–317, 1968. With McQueeney, J. A. Learning-set formation and discrimination reversal. J. Comp. Physiol. Psychol., 56, 435–439, 1963.
69. Rumbaugh, Duane M.; and McCormack, Carol. The learning skills of primates: A comparative study of apes and monkeys. In Starck, D.; Schneider, R.; and Kuhn, H. J. (Eds.). Progress in Primatology. Stuttgart: Gustav Fischer, pp. 289–306, 1967.
70. Rumbaugh, Duane M.; and Rice, C. Learning-set formation in young great apes. J. Comp. Physiol. Psychol., 55, 886–868, 1962.
71. Russell, Bertrand. New Hopes for a Changing World. New York: Simon & Schuster, 1951.
72. Sacco, William P.; and Hokanson, Jack E. Expectations of success and anagram performance of depressives in a public and private setting. J. Abnorm. Psychol., 87, 122–130, 1978.
73. Sanders, Glenn S.; and Baron, R. S. The motivating effect of distraction on task performance. J. Pers. Soc. Psychol., 32, 956–963, 1975.
74. Sanders, Glenn S.; Baron, Robert Steven; and Moore, Danny L. Distraction and social comparison as mediators of social facilitation effects. J. Exper. Soc. Psychol., 14, 291–303, 1978.
75. Schiffenbauer, A.; and Schiavo, R. S. Physical distance and attraction. J. Exper. Soc. Psychol., 12, 274–282, 1976.
76. Schumacher, E. F. Small Is Beautiful: Economics As If People Mattered. New York: Perennial Library, 1973.
77. Schrier, A. M. Learning-set formation by three species of macaque monkeys. In Starck, D.; Schneider, R.; and Kuhn, H. J. (Eds.). Progress in Primatology. Stuttgart: Gustav Fischer, pp. 307–309, 1967.
78. Sherrod, Drury R.; Hage, Jaime N.; Halpern, Phillip L.; and Moore, Bert S. Effects of personal causation and perceived control on responses to an aversive environment. J. Exper. Social Psychol., 13, 14–27, 1977.
79. Shuell, T. J. Retroactive inhibition in free-recall learning of categorized lists. J. Verbal Learning Verbal Behav., 7, 797–805, 1968.
80. Skoff, Barry; and Chechile, Richard A. Storage and retrieval processes in the serial position effect. Bull. Psychonomic Soc. 9, 265–268, 1977.
81. Snyder, Mark; and Swann, William B., Jr. Behavioral confirmation in social interaction. J. Exper. Soc. Psychol., 14, 148–162, 1978.
82. Stillwell, Lois J. An investigation of the interrelationships among global self concept, role self concept and achievement. Diss. Abstr., 27 (3-A), 682, 1966.
83. Terkel, S. Working. New York: Avon Books, 1972.
84. Treisman, Anne M.; and Riley, Jenefer G. A. Is selective attention selective perception or selective response? A further test. J. Exper. Psychol., 79, 27–34, 1969.
85. Uhbrock, Richard S. Music on the job: Its influence on worker morale and production. Personnel Psychol., 14, 9–39, 1961.
86. Vanderhei, Sharon Lee. Annoyance and behavioral aftereffects following interfering and non-interfering aircraft noise. Diss. Abstr. 36 (B6), 3101–3102B, 1975.
87. Wagman, Morton. University achievement and daydreaming behavior. J. Couns. Psychol., 15, 196–198, 1968.
88. Watts, Graeme H.; and Anderson, Richard C. Retroactive inhibition in free recall as a function of first- and second-list organization. J. Exper. Psychol., 81, 595–597, 1969.
89. Weinstein, Neil D. Noise and intellectual performance. J. Applied Psychol., 62, 104–107, 1977.
90. Woodhead, M. M. The effect of bursts of noise on an arithmetic task. Amer. J. Psychol., 77, 627–633, 1964.

If your fears are many . . .

Chapter 7

Common Habits
You Don't Need

A. HABITS HINDERING US

The students left their lecture room, beaming, jubilant. They radiated a buoyancy seldom found. What was the occasion? An inspired lecture they had just heard? It might have been, for students sometimes look that way on such occasions. Or was there, perhaps, a marvelously stimulating class discussion in which they had been eager participants? Or a film in which they had lost themselves and found new understandings? It could have been any of these — and some of you will leave many classes in the manner described, fired with new ideas, aglow with new insights, inspired.

It could have been any of these; but as a matter of fact, it was not. The occasion for exuberance was a simple announcement: "Professor X is in the hospital. Class will not meet this week." That was the good news. Professor X, incidentally, was popular with his students, admired and liked with an uncommon devotion.

This incident spotlights some of the difficulties in becoming educated. Here are a few.

Were those students wholeheartedly eager to get an education? Are we?

What does such behavior signify? Does it reflect merely our natural liking of holidays? And what does a "natural liking of holidays" imply regarding our fondness for our chosen line of work — in this case, studying? If we deeply enjoy holidays and also deeply enjoy our work, we should be radiant and enthusiastic when holidays end, as well as when they begin. Were those students? Would you be?

Did the students perhaps feel somewhat like slaves, unexpectedly set free?

Was their reaction consistent with an unambivalent fondness for their professor? Or did it perhaps reflect some hostility and resentment?

From one incident it is foolhardy to draw many conclusions about anyone. But one incident does properly start a flow of questions worth pondering. What are those students like, deep inside? What is college like to them? What are they becoming as a consequence of their ways of going to college? More important, what are *you* like? How are you going to college? What will you be like in the future as a result of your current actions?

What any student is like depends partly upon his experiences in school. Put in other words, the nature of our personality is a *result* in part of how we go to school. But further, the nature of our personality is also a *cause* of how we go to school and college.[16, 21, 73]

This brings us to a fact of vital import: Some personality characteristics gravely limit our ability to get what we wish to attain and what we otherwise *could* attain from college and the university. We are handicapped by some of our own habits.

To get the most we can from our education, we must become able to recognize disadvantageous habits in ourselves, and then learn to do something about them.

These same characteristics which handicap us in college also hamper us in the rest of life.[23, 84, 106] They jeopardize or cause us to lose many things we cherish and otherwise could have — deeper friendships, better job opportunities, happier family relationships, more vivid enthusiasms, peace with ourselves, and more.

As one example, a study was made of persons earning a Master's degree in Business Administration. Persons making relatively high incomes five years after graduation were compared with those earning less. The high earners were self-starters, had a greater sense of responsibility, a willingness to make decisions, willingness to work longer hours, and more interest in helping people.[48] They also had greater job satisfaction.

Much of our unhappiness is caused not by the world but by ourselves and our own habits. These habits often are begun in childhood.

Most of us had parents who tried very hard to help us. They tried to start us off well in life, but they were woefully trained (or untrained, depending upon your viewpoint) for their difficult job. They lacked much information they should have had. They had much folklore, disguised as "information," without which they would have been wiser. They lacked the serenity and deep self-respect they sorely needed. They were racked by anxieties which led to sudden flashes of rage. With these handicaps, they did their best. They tried; but their attempts were almost doomed to partial failure. Our teachers often were in no happier a situation; nor were our friends.

As a result, we were subjected to many unfortunate experiences — experiences which caused us to develop some habits not healthy even in a child, and still more lamentable in adults. The personalities of most adults are peppered with these "infantile habits," as they are technically called. Even your personality probably is.

Unfortunately, getting older is no guarantee we will become more mature, nor more civilized — a sobering matter Overstreet discusses brilliantly. Infantile habits can persist a lifetime. Indeed, these modes of behavior often become stronger with passing years, despite the heartaches they engender both in possessors and in associates.

In a real sense, it is not your fault if you have many infantile habits; but it definitely is your responsibility if you *keep* them. You can break up those habits and build more satisfying ones.

Having infantile characteristics does not mean you are a weakling, or disgusting, or anything else remotely similar. You have many endearing qualities, too, and many remarkable skills. You might have all of these infantile characteristics and still be a truly wonderful person, although not *as* wonderful, nor as happy, as you otherwise could be.

Neither do these characteristics mean you are peculiar. These are extremely common habits: Their possession is normal, albeit highly unfortunate from many standpoints.

What does their possession mean? It simply means you have some unvanquished problems, the effects of which have long distressed you. That is all — but it is enough.

The object of this chapter is to make it easier for you to recognize these limiting characteristics and their effects, and to offer leads whereby you can better overcome them.

This chapter may be rather rough going. To look squarely at ourselves is difficult and takes great courage.

We fear what we may find, and we have little enough self-respect and confidence anyway. And yet we must scrutinize our own actions and learn to recognize inner hindrances in order to cope with them more adequately. The likelihood of solving any problem (including, of course, personality difficulties) is increased greatly by recognizing the nature of the problem.

Let us, then, plunge into an examination of these normal but unwanted characteristics which jeopardize our happiness and success in living.

B. GROWING AWAY FROM SLAVE ATTITUDES

1. Do You Have a Slave Attitude?

Slave attitudes seriously impair performance at college and the university[87] and on the job.[29, 40, 106] To do our best work and have a sense of satisfaction, we need to feel in control. Do you feel in charge of your life? Or do you feel a bit trapped or even enslaved, although no chains are visible?

Do you eagerly count the number of days to the next week-end? Or the number of weeks before the end of the term? Do you even count the number of terms left to go before you graduate? During vacations do you gleefully anticipate the beginning of school? Or do you regard its commencement ruefully? School, for many students, is piteously like a jail sentence — to be endured as best one can.

We feel abused and terribly sorry for ourselves: In class we listen casually, take as few notes as possible, do as little work as possible. We sometimes even reach the point of complaining because too many ideas and facts are presented. Assignments are resented. When we read the textbook, we feel we have done the *instructor* a gracious favor. When we turn in a paper, we feel positively noble. We may even react in ways like those sketched in the opening paragraphs of this chapter — feeling pleased by our instructor's illness. The slave driver is gone; for the moment we feel more free. Have you perchance had such experiences?

Probably you have, for apparently almost all of us possess at least some trace of this "slave attitude." Almost all of us also possess some buried antagonisms toward our professors.[72, 77]

To understand our problem, we should note that antagonisms are interlocked with slave attitudes,[47, 65,] self-debasement,[17, 76, 86] and apathy.[40, 41] They are an instance of reciprocal causation.

2. Hostility and Feeling Enslaved Increase Each Other.

In studying human behavior, you will find many such cases of reciprocal causation. In its simplest form, reciprocal causation consists of this: A causes an increase in B, and B in turn causes an increase in A. For example, Andy treats Tom in a hostile fashion. Andy's hostile behavior toward Tom increases Tom's hostile behavior toward Andy; and Tom's hostile behavior toward Andy, in turn, increases Andy's hostile behavior toward Tom. A vicious circle is set in motion, increments in either half of the circle bringing increments in the other half.

Similarly, our hostility and slave attitudes are reciprocally linked; each increases the other. In this case, however, the reciprocal pattern is more complicated than in the example of Tom and Andy. Between our hostility and slave attitudes is an intervening chain of events. The relationship is diagrammed in Figure 4, with each arrow signifying "leads to an increase in."

As is shown in the last step of the diagram, feeling abused by someone makes us more hostile toward him. You realize this, of course. But perhaps you have not realized that the reverse is also true: *Feeling hostile toward someone will cause us to feel abused by him.*

Strengthening any link in the chain above ultimately strengthens all of the links. It works this way: Feeling hostile toward professors (for example) leads to greater anxiety and guilt feelings. The anxiety is increased very greatly if the hostility does not seem "justified," for in our culture unprovoked hostility rarely is condoned and generally is condemned. This condemning attitude becomes part of our-

> → Hostility toward the professor
> ↓
> Anxiety and guilt feelings about this hostility
> ↓
> Need for rationalizing our hostility,
> attempting to justify it
> ↓
> Saying "He abuses me" and finding
> supporting "evidence" for the statement
> ↓
> Feeling deeply abused: i.e.,
> having a slave attitude.

Figure 4. Reciprocal relationship between hostility and slave attitudes.

selves, so we are anxious about our hostilities. Consequently, we set out to concoct excuses to justify our hostility. (Psychologists call this rationalizing.) We say to ourselves that the professor is mean, that he or she makes unreasonable assignments, gives unfair tests, and in other ways too abuses us; then we look for and find "evidence" supporting our accusations. The more we do this, the more deeply abused we come to feel. As a consequence, our hostility becomes even greater, which creates still more anxiety, and still more need for rationalizations, and so on and on, ad infinitum. Our hostility increases our feeling of being abused and enslaved. This in turn increases our hostility. Matters become ever worse and worse. We are caught in a spiralling circle of hostility and feeling enslaved.

As the diagram shows too, *being* abused is not necessary for *feeling* abused. We can, and often do, feel gravely mistreated without actually being mistreated at all. Deep hostilities toward someone are caused by many conditions other than being mistreated.

3. The Causes of Hostility for Someone Often Are Far Removed from That Person.

Let us consider, for example, some common causes of hostility toward professors. Such antagonism can arise from a great variety of conditions. The antagonism can arise from a general distrust of people with authority: We may have learned to view any powerful person with rancor and suspicion, and professors are powerful. Or hostility toward professors can grow from our own inner insecurities: We feel, for instance, that anyone with much intelligence will view us as stupid; we dislike that view and we dislike anyone we imagine to have it. The hostility can also stem from a generalized resentment of a world which often runs counter to our needs and cherished hopes. Hostility toward our professor can result too from antagonisms built up against some other individual and then transferred to the professor.

When we have the habit of making a particular emotional response to one pattern of stimuli, subsequently that emotional response can be evoked by other, rather different stimuli without our having had any experiences with these other stimuli. Psychologists call this phenomenon displacement, transference, or generalization. Displaced antagonisms occur frequently in life and have also been repeatedly demonstrated in the laboratory.

For example, white rats were trained to fight each

other whenever an electric shock was turned on in the floor of their cage. Then each rat was put into a cage with a celluloid doll, and no other rat. When the shock was turned on, half the rats attacked the doll, although they had had no previous experience with any doll. Rats not trained to fight each other almost never showed hostility toward the dolls, even when they were shocked.[78]

Transference of emotional responses likewise is found frequently in people. For example, a small boy was caused to have fear responses cued, through learning, to the sight of a small white rat.[118] As a result of this learning, fear also was evoked by (transferred to) the previously neutral stimuli from a rabbit, cotton wool, a fur coat, and the experimenter's hair, even though the child had had no adverse experiences with these objects.

Another child, previously fearful of a white rat, rabbit, fur coat, feather, and cotton wool, learned to have responses of interest and fondness cued to the rabbit. As a consequence, this new response of interest and fondness was evoked by each of the other stimuli mentioned — without any intervening experiences with them.[57]

Since these thought-provoking studies of emotion, numerous additional experiments and reports of transference have become available.[41, 62, 102]

Life is replete with instances in which stimuli have evoked some emotional response — not because of experiences the individual had had with those objects or persons, but because of the person having learned to make that emotional response to other, somewhat similar stimuli.[42, 77] Here is one other illustration.[89] A man had intense hostility toward his mother. The hostility engendered in him considerable uneasiness and feelings of guilt. One day a woman whom the man never before had seen, slipped and fell at quite some distance from him. In no way was he responsible nor was he accused of causing her fall. Nonetheless he protested, in a quite desperate way, that he had not pushed the woman and had not caused her to fall. Apparently the strange woman in an unhappy predicament aroused much the same feelings of uneasiness and guilt as were cued originally to his mother.

From these examples of transference, you can start building clearer notions of the significance of this widespread phenomenon. See if you can spot episodes when you transfer emotional responses evoked by one person, object, or event to another "innocent bystander." When you become able to see transference in your own behavior, many reactions which now seem strange will be more comprehensible. "Love at first sight," sudden immediate dislike for a person whom you have just met, over-responses to some rebuff, bewildering flare-ups, and many other confusing phenomena become more intelligible. You understand better, too, your partial antagonisms toward professors.

To the extent that this hostility for professors and its accompanying slave attitude are present, they spoil what could be wondrously joyous, edifying experiences. Even when present in small degrees only, they preclude studying with wholehearted delight. When present to a considerable extent, they make studying an onerous burden and ruin our university and college years.

Antagonisms toward professors and a slave attitude toward school predispose us toward similar responses elsewhere. They impair our ability to enjoy thoroughly our vocation; they dilute our delight in social affairs; and they contaminate many other aspects of life as well.

Are you doomed to that fate? Certainly not, for you can do much toward breaking up this pattern of "hostile slavishness."

Two major modes of attack are available: You can work on reducing your slave attitude, or you can work on reducing antagonism toward professors. Because reciprocally linked, partial success on either project alleviates the other condition too. Anything you do to reduce your hostility toward professors will reduce your slave attitude toward school and your feelings of abuse; this, in turn, further reduces your hostility. Likewise, any reduction in your slave attitude will reduce your hostility for professors (and other people also); this, in turn, further decreases your feelings of being abused. Any case of reciprocal causation can work in a vicious circle; but the circle can be reversed and it then will work in your favor. By tackling the problem with partial success at *either* end, you reverse the circle so it goes in the opposite, desired direction.

Let us tackle this circle at both ends. Here are several ways you can alleviate both your slave attitudes and your hostilities. You will think of other ways too.

4. Take Assignments for What They Are: Efforts to Help You Grow.

Often we feel that assignments are some low trick, perpetrated by professors to make life miserable. Actually the opposite is more nearly the case.

Assignments are intended to help us learn. They are offered to help us understand the confused and confusing world of which we are a part . . . to help us become equipped to deal with that world more skillfully than we otherwise could . . . to assist us in developing new technical competencies . . . to aid us in building the habits we need for interacting with our fellow inhabitants with greater mutual enjoyment. To facilitate achieving those goals, assignments are designed — often after hours of thought and study. Try to see them this way.

If we had no assignments, the hours we would spend searching for reliable authorities could be staggering. We could read dozens of books before finding an appropriate one. Then, finally successful, how would we know it?

5. Lectures Save You Time and Much Work.

Progress cannot be made if each of us must repeat, step by step, what other people have done. Somehow we must be enabled to pick up where they left off, and carry on from there.

Through lectures and discussions a gifted, educated person is trying to help you do that. He is trying to help you reach more quickly than did he the point where he now is, so that you may start near where he is finishing. In an hour, he passes on to your facts and ideas which he spent years accumulating and reworking into a more accessible form. This material you need not dig out and organize for yourself. He has done that; and he shares the results with you. He offers you concepts and principles, many of which he gained only after years of study and research, years of pondering and testing. He presents to you techniques he has found most satisfactory for tackling certain problems, and helps you master these techniques. He tells you of ideas which he has found illuminating. He shows you sources of information he has found helpful. All of these and more he gives you freely — in the hope that by so doing he can spare you at least some of the work he had to do, and leave you free to start from there.

Is it so very hard to remember that that is what lectures are? Probably not, if once you see them in that light.

6. Most Professors Care Deeply About You.

Is that surprising? It really should not be. You realize, of course, that for their services they often are paid far less per hour than, for example, the people who repair your plumbing or who help keep your car running or who build your roads. Many of your professors have been offered positions through which they could make considerably more money with their current skills than they make by teaching. But they continue to teach. They continue largely because, as you say, "they like their job." That, in large part, means they like you and your colleagues. They deeply value contact with you and helping you in your quests.

Most of your professors also have many interests apart from teaching. Many activities they find delightful and worthwhile. Yet hours they could spend playing chess, or engaging in sports, or dancing, hours they could be traveling, or reading, or talking with their friends, they spend instead preparing lectures for you. Hours far beyond what are needed to hold their job, they spend trying to make things more understandable to you. Unless they are badly confused as to what they most cherish, they must be deeply fond of you.

Some tips for brightening student-instructor relationships: Learn your instructor's name, its correct spelling and correct pronunciation. Maintain attentiveness in the classroom; be alive, warmly courteous to everyone, responsive. Clarify misconceptions when they occur instead of letting them continue. If a personal conflict occurs, discuss your feelings with someone whom you respect; attempt to identify the attitude that you are conveying to the instructor. Discuss the situation with the instructor when you feel able to do so calmly. Liking your professor can help you learn.[27, 43, 119]

7. Can You See Professors as Your Partners?

Can you see them as your partners in a cooperative enterprise? As colleagues working with you to achieve goals you both cherish? Professors can be marvelous partners with you in your effort to develop new skills and become more nearly the person you long to be.

No one, of course, can cooperate all alone. Cooperation always takes at least two. If cooperating with you is made impossible, what other forms of interaction are accessible? This is worth some thought. Suppose you regard your teachers as antagonists and act accordingly. Do you not thereby almost compel them to become antagonists?

Try to see your professors as partners. Learn to regard yourself as a collaborator (not as a receptacle nor yet as a slave). You will discover, then, that professors *are* your partners, working with you in a delightful, exciting game of discovery and building.

8. Textbooks Are Not Perfect.

Certainly a textbook has flaws, many of them. Having been created by human beings, it is bound to be noticeably less than perfect. It may, however, have many advantages too.

For any area of investigation there are dozens, even hundreds or thousands, of books available. From this great reservoir, your particular textbook was chosen as the one most apt to help you. It is the book which, in the opinion of your professor, can best help you discover the greatest amount about that area of investigation. It is the book thought especially apt to open new vistas to you, to answer soundly your questions, inform you accurately, incite you to further questions, and afford you exciting ideas. Terrible though this book may seem, your professor thinks it more apt to accomplish these goals than many other books.

No book, of course, can do all these things perfectly. But any book can do them better when you see these possibilities and view the book in this way.

9. Are You in College Mainly Because Somebody Else Thinks You Should Be?

Many students labor under that impression. Seldom, however, does a person attend college only because somebody else advocates it. How about you? Are you in college solely, or even primarily, because your parents or someone else desired it? Try examining this matter and see what you believe.

Suppose your primary reason for attending college actually is that someone else thinks you should do so. Suppose *you* do not share that opinion. If this is the case, you would be wise to withdraw. If, on the other hand, you too think college offers opportunities for a net gain by *your* standards, then you should keep that fact in mind.

Sometimes we feel (consciously or unconsciously) that we are doing someone a great favor by attending college, that we are forced to do this favor, and that that´is our main reason for attending college. These nagging impressions contribute much to our feeling enslaved, wretched, and rebellious. When weighted by such millstones, no one can enjoy school years nor profit as deeply as otherwise possible.

This furnishes another clue to how you can alleviate resentfulness and feelings of enslavement: Decide for yourself whether you should be in college. Is it worthwhile by your standards? If you decide to stay, remember that you are going to college primarily to attain goals of value to you by your standards and not merely to pacifiy or please somebody else.

10. Understand Better Your Spouse and Parents.

Do whatever you can to understand better your wife or husband and your parents. This may seem a miserably oblique attack on the problem of learning to study better; yet it is highly effective.[54, 113] Deeper understanding frees us from many slave attitudes and hostilities in general.

Many antagonisms toward professors (and toward other people in positions of authority) are caused in large part by early antagonisms toward our parents. These antagonisms are apt to be generalized, especially to our husband or wife and anyone else in a position similar to parents': that is, to anyone of key importance to us, anyone close, anyone vital to us, anyone who has considerable control or impact on our present and future life.

This transference of resentment illustrates the principle mentioned a few pages ago: When emotional responses are established to one class of stimuli, they tend to generalize to other, somewhat similar stimuli, and subsequently to be evoked by them. Displacement of resentment from our parents to our teachers is a particularly common reflection of that principle and also a particularly important contributor to difficulties in school.

Therefore, although it seems roundabout, we can markedly reduce hostility toward instructors and dispel feelings of helplessness and being enslaved, by reducing resentment and antagonism toward our parents.

You probably love your parents and are grateful to them for many things. You also have many antagonisms toward them. By stern injunction and awesome threats, you were compelled to follow courses far different from your choice. You did these things as you were ordered; but you did them feeling dreadfully abused and sorry for yourself. You were laughed at by them for awkward creative attempts, and sometimes patronizingly instructed to do things their way. You were ridiculed for mistakes in grammar, for mispronouncing words, for mistreating your sister, for ignoring folkways and mores, for breaking things they cherished, for reading books instead of playing outdoors, for playing outdoors instead of practicing. For a thousand actions which were ill-conceived or clumsily executed, you were shamed. Often your interests were scoffed at or simply ignored.

As a result of such psychological hardships, you have many habits of doing things reluctantly and with grave misgivings. As a result also, you have many buried antagonisms toward your parents. Your love for them became shot through with resentments.

Almost certainly you have many interests and values in common with your parents.[10] These can be shared and built upon to aid understanding. But even so, reducing resentments is difficult. It cannot be achieved in a day or a week, nor by firm resolutions alone. It can be achieved only through building new emotional responses. To help you on this difficult project, the next section is offered.

C. ALLEVIATING HOSTILITY TOWARD SPOUSES, PARENTS, AND OTHERS

Some of us had miraculous luck in the nature of our father and mother, drawing parents wondrously tender and skillful, adroit in helping us develop fine, healthy responses to them, to ourselves, and to other persons. Few, however, have such fortune.

More commonly, as we were just noting, resentments abound against much our parents did and still do. This is almost inevitable — but we need not go on forever being gnawed by these antagonisms. Resentments and antagonisms can be vanquished. It is exceedingly important that we do so — both for our parents' sakes and our own.

Suppose you are no longer living with your parents. Suppose you are an adult with children of your own. Even then your attitudes toward your parents color your view toward the rest of the world. In particular, how you see your father and mother colors deeply how you see your instructors, your wife or husband, your roommate, your employer, your closest friends, and yourself. And these outlooks greatly influence your success on any job, in marriage, and at the university or college.

1.　When Resentments Surge, Do Not Try to Shame Yourself Out of Them.

Such atttempts are depressing.[33] They also are futile. In fact, they are worse than futile, for being shamed increases rather than decreases hostile antagonisms.[41, 51, 107] Becoming *less* ashamed and *less* guilt-ridden will reduce hostility. This is not such a paradox.

Guilt-feelings, you recall, drive us to justify our hostility. The more ashamed we feel about something, the harder we work to justify it. The more ashamed we feel for partially hating someone, the harder we work to justify our hostility. We try to prove the person is despicable and therefore deserves our hostility. We search for, and find (!), additional "reasons" for feeling antagonistic.

Further, the more ashamed we feel, the less assurance we have of our own worth. The less inner respect we have for ourselves, the harder we try to show that other people are even worse. Thus we build greater and greater hostilities within ourselves.[37, 41, 95, 107]

This then would be a first step: Do not make your hostilities an occasion for treating yourself harshly, nor for feeling you or someone else is despicable. Accept your present hostilities as an almost inevitable reaction to the things which happened to you — to being hurt and ashamed and in many other ways sorely frustrated.

Although they were almost bound to occur, these hostilities need not haunt your life forever. Here is a second step toward reducing them.

2.　Try to Understand the Problems Your Spouse and Others Face.

We realize that we ourselves have numerous and complex worries, but we forget that other persons also do. Especially if the individual is someone we admire (like our wife, husband, or parent), we suppose all must be well. But strong and resourceful people have burdens and worry too.

Consider, for example, your parents. No matter how

large their income, they have financial difficulties. Everyone
has, but that does not lighten the burden. They worry too
about their status in the community — what other people
think of them and you. They are apprehensive about possibly
losing a job, or not getting a promotion, or missing a commis-
sion for which they have striven. They are distressed by the
specter of your being called to war, or in other ways killed or
damaged. They are worried about mistakes they made with
you. Almost certainly they are troubled deeply by signs that
youth is lost, forever, and old age irrevocably encroaching.

And those are but a few of the problems your parents
face. If you ask about these, you may be astounded by what
your folks confide. You are on your way to better understanding.

Your roommate, husband, wife, friends, clerks, all have
similar burdens and others too which make them apprehensive
and on edge. Explosions must be expected.

3. Regard Emotional Outbursts and
"Lack of Consideration" as Symptoms of
Anxiety and Other Inner Tensions.

One result of their many worries and anxieties is that
people make mistakes. They hurt you unwittingly.

How do *you* behave when apprehensive and worried? If
you are like most people, you become less able to behave with
the reasonableness and gentleness you desire. When worried
(or ill or fatigued), your voice has an edge not intended and
not often understood. The edge may be wholly unrelated to
rage or to the person you are addressing; but the hearer fails
to realize this and is hurt. Also when anxious or exhausted,
you are apt to be stubborn or curtly short in discussions. You
are prone to flare up "for no reason at all." You make harsh
remarks and behave inconsiderately, without even noticing
what you are doing.[93, 94, 100]

Parents, mates, and roommates are human too and probably respond to anxiety in these same ways. Such responses
mean the person is tense. Not necessarily is he tense from
rage at you nor from lack of love. He is tense, more usually,
from worry and feelings of failure, from conflict or anxiety.
Even the violent chest-beating of gorillas, so commonly construed as vicious rage, turns out to be merely a mode of
showing excitement — fight tendencies sometimes, but also
flight tendencies, or bewilderment, or general tension from
any of multifarious conflict situations.[103]

Understanding better the expression of tension and its various sources, we are less hurt by flare-ups, harsh voices, or "unreasonableness." We are more able to treat the person appropriately, with the consideration and kindness he deeply needs.

4. Rage and Contempt Are Not Necessarily Aimed at You, Nor Caused by You, Though Made in Your Direction.

Sometimes, of course, the person is angry when he "sounds" angry. He make genuinely angry responses, and in your direction. These angry responses may or may not be intended for you or caused by you.

The boss criticizes your dad unjustly, or your husband or wife or roommate. When they get home, they explode – more like a volcano than like a cannon. The lava is not aimed; it simply is there, scalding anyone near. Or the neighbors scoff. Or friends act cool. Or relatives make belittling remarks. Any of a thousand other events occur which hurt sorely your parents or mate. In their turmoil and pain, they do what people usually do when hurt: They lash out at anyone handy — often at their children, or husband, or wife. You might be amazed by how much that is cruel stems from the person's being hurt, and responding blindly. Quite possibly all cruelty is caused in part by the "cruel" person's being hurt.

Whether we caused the wound or not, we are be-hooved — in our own interests even — to do what we can to reduce the hurt and give the person peace and a sense of being valued. This is far more adequate protection than is counter-hostility.

Now, because of the key position held by your parents and your attitudes toward them, the next few sections aim to enhance understanding of them especially. Knowing what is happening can increase your nonchalance in the face of treatments which otherwise might be disruptive.

Although phrased in terms of parents primarily, you will find much of this bears on your other relationships, too.

5. Often Your Parents Feel They Are Partial Failures.

They may make a great deal of money. They may have a job with prestige. They may have a lavishly furnished home and many friends. And *still* they feel they are partial failures. There were so many things they wanted to do — and never did; so many things they wanted to be — and never were; so many attributes they wished to have — and never developed. And now it is too late. Life has more than half gone. Probably they do not feel complete failures, for there is much of which to be proud and much for which to be pleased. Yet, there is so much, so very much, that could have been — and wasn't.

Maybe, they hope fervently, you can do better. Maybe you can do and have and become what they did not. That is the great hope of most parents. But then again, perhaps you will be like them and have a life like theirs — no better. That is a deep fear. It is a fear mounting almost to terror in many parents, a terror nonetheless real because unverbalized, hidden from their own recognition except for disrupting flashes.

This fear leads them to watch anxiously your development and your actions. (Other factors do also, but this is a main one.) They apprehensively chivy you around and often quite unpredictably bawl you out. You, they feel, must not turn out as they did! In their great anxiety and yearning, they do all manner of things which make life rougher for you — while attempting, ironically, to make life smoother for you than it was for them.

To our amazement and dismay, a wife or husband or close friend can fall into this same dilemma and start putting astonishing pressure on us to succeed in their stead. This is an excellent time to highlight their successes and do whatever else communicates vividly their worth.

6. Many Mistakes Are Based on Popular Misconceptions.

None of us is immune to this misfortune — including parents. They try to secure for you a life better than that they had. But their attempts often are misguided, based largely on folklore and other common misconceptions.

Your parents may have the impression, for example, that unless they often "took you down a notch," you would become conceited, insufferably smug. But would you really have become conceited and smug? "Of course! Everybody knows this!" The phrase "everybody knows this" is a way of saying, "My associates all say so" or "All my friends are. . . ." And that, in turn, is a way of saying, "This is an embedded part of the folklore." To a highly sophisticated person, that means "Watch out! Folklore is often mistaken. Better look twice." Most people, however, are not highly sophisticated. They do not think of questioning the truth of what is popular with their peers. They blandly accept the folklore and have, as a consequence, all sorts of mistaken convictions. (This can happen also to you and me; our beliefs too can become an unsorted hodge-podge of fact and misconception — determined largely by what our friends believe.)

Some parents have the mistaken conviction that children are small savages, in the most unfavorable sense. Being small savages, they must be treated accordingly.

Or your parents may have the conviction and fear that unless they do everything possible for their offspring, follow his every whim, let him virtually rule the household, they will not be loved by him or will have caused their child's growth to be stunted forever.

Sadly enough, this list could be extended greatly, and still it would not exhaust the misinformation with which most parents take up their difficult profession.

Much information they really needed was not a part of their equipment.[122] Information concerning personality formation, the making and breaking of habits, what one can reasonably expect of a growing individual — much of this information they did not have.

Our parents' predicament (unless they are very unusual) is rather like that of a wanderer lost in a desert country, a desert country utterly unlike what he expected. In his quest for water and shade, he is given a map. But the map omits most of the crucial landmarks. Worse, it includes numerous directions for "right paths" which do not lead to the promised oasis. Instead they lead the weary stranger ever farther and farther from his objectives.

7. Your Parents Often Knew Their Methods Were Working Poorly. But What Else Was There to Do?

Contrary to what we expect from fairy tales and TV adventures, most of us have rather limited imaginations and resourcefulness. Many people cannot conceive what they *could* be doing other than what they *are* doing. Your parents probably never meant to make you feel left out, neglected, enslaved, or caged in. Without some training or some excellent model, they simply could not imagine what else they could do besides what they were doing.

Often your folks are acutely aware that *their* parents made terrible blunders, and they want desperately to do better by you. But just where did their parents err? They do not know, and (vaguely) they know they do not know. This too makes them apprehensive, while in no way making them more skillful.

They know they are poorly prepared for their intricate job; but this simply leads to more anxiety, and is often glossed over because of the pain involved in recognizing it. Squashing this recognition, in turn, precludes seeking help and leads to still more unresolved and unrecognized difficulties, to more problems, more anxieties, and more tensions — with their customary disquieting results.

Can you get some feeling for their predicament? The marvel becomes not that our parents made so many mistakes, but that they managed to do as well as they did.

If we can remember these things, we can understand our parents better and have less hostility.

8. Many Dreams Were Shattered.

What is it like to have bright dreams of some event, to work and struggle for that event, to have the event finally occur, and then to find out the reality is not at all as one had dreamed? Can you imagine what that is like? Probably you can, for at least in some way that has happened to you.

You maybe worked hard to get to college. And you had such bright, glorious hopes. What fun college would be ! What successes you would have! What wonderful things you would do! What exciting things you would learn! These played a part in your dreams, waking and sleeping. Then you got here, and you find it all quite different from your dreams. Such discrepancies are disconcerting and saddening. You can see how you are responding.

Our parents likewise had dreams for us, but their dreams were far more elaborate and of longer duration, and to make the dreams come true, they worked far harder. They dreamed of how cute we would be, of how much fun we would be, of the joy we would be to play with and talk with and watch, of how we would adore them and help them.

Finally we arrived. And we weren't particularly cute or fun. We interrupted their sleep — and we kept right on doing so. We broke things they cherished. We messed up our clothes. Even when we became older, we spilled stuff everywhere, tore clothes it took them long to make or earn, lost our sweaters and toys and books, made a shambles of rooms they had swept and dusted. This was not part of their dream. We often prevented their going out with companions they enjoyed. We gave them a mass of new responsibilities for which they were utterly unprepared. We were fairly stupid companions for a while. Then when we became capable of talking sensibly and associating with them in a companionable way, we left home for most of the day, or all of it, to spend our time with other people.

This is not the way we were supposed to be. And our parents are disappointed. So they cling to us when we want to have freedom; they try to force us into the mold of their dreams; they do the many other things we find deeply annoying.

9. Despite This They Brought You Much of Value.

Despite all the handicaps under which your parents worked, they did much to comfort you, to open new worlds of interest to you, to help you gain skills in living as an adult, to give you a place of refuge — with them or with one of your siblings. It is quite remarkable how much good your parents created, along with the psychological hardships on which we tend to dwell. These contributions are worth noticing too, and worth our gratitude and openly expressed appreciation.

10. Use Your Opportunities to Reassure Others of Their Worth.

As we were observing a bit ago, parents and the others close to us have almost numberless anxieties. They have made mistakes which trouble them greatly. They have a host of shattered dreams. They often feel their life has been more or less a failure. As a consequence, they have emotional outbursts, and do much which you (and they) regret. Remember that rages and contempt stem largely from these tensions and deep anxieties. Then do what you can to mitigate these anxieties, thus removing many of the sources of behavior you lament.

You cannot wholly undo what has happened to your folks. No one can. But you can give to your parents and to others the understanding all people need and crave.

You can show them the sympathy and love you feel. You

can notice their endearing qualities . . . respect their opinions
. . . listen attentively to their ideas . . . express appreciation
for the many little (and big) things they do for you in their
daily roles . . . accept their mistakes for what they usually
are — ineptitudes, blunders, misguided attempts to help you
grow . . . offer little services when they are desired. You can
show the courtesies all human beings deserve and need. In
these and many other ways, you can communicate to your
roommate, your spouse, your family that they are loved and
valued.

11. Treating Others Kindly Decreases
Your Hostility. [42, 76, 77]

Much of our hostility toward people is caused by our own
shabby treatment of them. We previously explored how this
comes about. We noticed that often we try to justify our abuse
of someone by "proving" he deserved such treatment. To
some extent we come to believe our "proof"; and thus we see
the mistreated person as more despicable, and dislike him
even more.

In addition, something else happens. When we feel
ashamed and rather sick inside because of our own poor actions, we tend both to hate ourselves and also to hate the other
person who partially occasioned such feelings. To make sad
matters worse, we fear retaliation from the mistreated person;
and most of us hate what we fear.

In all those ways, our shabby treatment of a person
increases our own hostility. We set up devastating circles.
Because we dislike someone, we mistreat him; and because
we mistreat him, we dislike him more. But this circle can be
reversed.

We can treat a person as kindly as we know how. We
become, as a consequence, more serene inside, enjoy that
person's company more, and like him more. With deepened
respect for ourselves and deepened liking of him, we become
able to treat him with still more consideration, and thus we
like him still more. A new sort of circle is set in motion. You
can do this with anyone. You can do it with your dad and
mother, with your professors, with roommates and classmates and friends.

While leading your own life as a free and self-reliant
individual, you need not be callous and indifferent to other
people. You still can heed their needs and wishes and do
much to brighten their worlds. In so doing, your buried antag-

onisms will melt, like ice-fields in spring, slowly. But melt
they will. A wistfulness may remain even when you are adept
in treating others well. A yearning for things-which-might-
have-been may still be present; but animosity will be largely
gone.

D. TAKING CHARGE OF YOUR OWN LIFE

1. Dependency, Projection, and Irresponsibility Limit You.

Habits of dependency, of projection, and of denying responsibility for our own life hinder our studying and hinder
our other attempts at growth. Such habits are more common
than we ordinarily realize.

Most of us tend to project our own inadequacies onto
other people. We blame incidental or external factors for
outcomes we ourselves largely caused. For example, when
we do not understand a lecture, "it's the professor's fault,"
"he doesn't explain things well." When we do poorly on a
test, often we say (and come to believe) that that is the
professor's fault too—"he didn't teach properly;" or it is the
examination's fault—"the test wasn't fair;" or the reader's
fault—"he doesn't grade fairly;" or the book's fault—"it
was confused;" or our parents' fault—"they interrupt too
much."

If you are like many people, doing poorly is regarded as
almost anyone's or anything's fault, except your own. Your
contribution to frustrating events is treated, quite generally,
as a factor of negligible importance.

Do you expect the professor to order your life for you?
To make detailed assignments, preferably daily ones? To see
to it that you do them? Do you ask him to analyze your errors
for you and tell you where to do things differently, and how to
do them differently? Do you do this even before you have
tried to figure these matters out for yourself? Many students
do. You would not be unusual if you even expect the professor to make everything clear, to *"give* you an education,"
while you do little more than be there.

We do better work and have more satisfaction when we
accept our responsibility, and thus gain some control over our
work situation and production.[29, 40, 61] When we have shallow
habits of responsibility, we limit ourselves, we put ourselves

in a psychological strait jacket and stunt our growth — a matter examined in Chapter 1, pages 25–27.

What can we do about this? How can we develop the skills of accepting responsibility? Here are some ways to get started.

2. Recognize Sooner Events Which Are Turning Out Poorly.

This is difficult, since most of us have learned to *not* recognize when events are going poorly. We have learned to pretend as long as possible that nothing is wrong — especially when we are partly responsible.

This partial blindness makes our task harder. By the time we finally notice that all is not well, so much has happened that we cannot ascertain where our mistake occurred. We decide we are stupid and have not much insight. We become more disheartened, and more afraid to accept responsibility, and more dependent.

How can we become able to recognize sooner when events are turning out poorly? Our first step should be to develop a willingness to be mistaken. Let us turn now to that.

3. Develop Willingness to Be Mistaken, to Admit Imperfection. [15, 51]

This is essential for recognizing well our mistakes. It also is essential for becoming more independent, more capable of responsibility — better able to try for what we care about.

When not willing to admit we are imperfect, we tend to avoid any activity in which we might fail to excel. Life is sharply restricted. When badly afraid of making mistakes, we are less able to make our own decisions, less able (therefore) to take charge of our own life. We stand by while someone else takes authority, or we delegate authority to someone else. Then, when things go wrong, we point to him. He made the mistake. He is responsible for the mess we are in, not we. Or so we say, rather illogically.

What we overlook is this: When we delegate responsibility to someone else, we still are responsible for any subsequent mistakes. We have merely pushed our mistake nearer to the beginning of the causal sequence. After all, we are the ones who permitted (or even forced) the other person to make the decisions and choose the actions which worked out poorly. The outcome is our "fault" as much as his. We blind ourselves to this fact; but it is nonetheless a fact.

No matter what we do, we cannot avoid mistakes. We can become better, however, in recognizing our mistakes, and thus avoid repeating the same mistakes over and over. But to do this, we must reduce our fear of errors.

We can reduce our fear of errors. We can become more willing to admit mistakes and to make our own decisions. Remembering the following facts will help.

No one is omniscient. Therefore, everyone will make mistakes, a lot of them.

Fifty million Frenchmen can be wrong. So can two hundred million Americans. If we say what they say, and do what they do, we still have no guarantee of being right. We must not be lulled into believing all will be well merely because we adopt a popular course of action.

Other people's love and respect for us are rarely contingent upon our having a perfect or near-perfect performance. Indeed, the reverse is more often true — their love is partially contingent upon our making mistakes, upon our being "human."

You are familiar probably with James Thurber's essays and drawings. A part of his charm lies in describing the absurd things he had done and said. Far from trying to cover up his mistakes, he published them — and Thurber is one of our most beloved authors. You can observe this same phenomenon in your own more immediate worlds. Being right is not necessary for being beloved. Having a terrifically high "batting average" is not necessary for being respected.

These are facts which intellectually you know, but which emotionally you tend to forget. They are worth remembering.

Finally, a person's willingness to be mistaken increases with his or her basic confidence. Paradoxical though this seems at first, the greater the confidence we have in our own value, the greater our ability to see and admit our mistakes.

Therefore, whatever reminds us that we are precious (and all people are), that our existence is worthwhile and our contributions appreciated, whatever increases our self-respect will increase also our ability to accept our mistakes. This is one place where you probably can do more for others than you can do directly for yourself. Even so, there is much you can do to increase your own self-respect. The rest of this section and Section E point out some ways whereby you can heighten your self-esteem.

4. Recognize the Future.

We are human beings. In some ways we are special. One of our most especially human potentials is a capacity for recognizing the future: for knowing there is a future — not just a present and past — for realizing that *which* future materializes depends upon us, for realizing that what happens later is linked to what happens now, for planning and slanting our actions in terms of these coming days, and weeks, and centuries.

Some persons have developed little more skill here than have typical members of other species. Other persons have made themselves highly adroit. One part of this skill consists of a willingness to defer gratification, to work for future satisfactions though it means sometimes forgoing an immediately possible gratification. This ability to defer gratification turns out to be related to constructive accomplishments and to social responsibility. Persons of greater responsibility are able on occasion, and willing, to postpone some certain immediate gratification for the sake of a better future, relatively irresponsible people being unable or unwilling to forgo small immediate rewards even for the sake of larger later gratifications.[79]

5. Practice Making Your Own Decisions.

We become so accustomed to waiting for suggestions and orders or to asking other people what to do, that we hardly realize we could be making our own decisions and determining our own courses of action. Rather than relying upon our adviser to tell us what courses to take, we could make out at least a tentative program by ourselves. Rather than asking our friends to tell us what professor is "best," we could ask our friends what they like and dislike about various professors and make our own decisions here. Rather than studying only when compelled to do so by a test, we could plan our own work. We overlook many opportunities for leading our own life more fully. Watch for opportunities to make decisions and to take responsibility for your life; then accept these opportunities.

6. Whenever You Spot Adverse Occurrences, See How You Can Behave Differently to Facilitate More Valued Outcomes.

This is another way to effectively combat a feeling of helplessness and gain more effective control over your life.

Instead of searching for ways other people should change or the world should change, see how you could change. Look for the role you played in causing things to be as they are. Look for new ways of behaving which would be more apt to enhance what you value. Then set out to modify your behavior accordingly. This is worthwhile even though the respects in which you can behave differently seem insignificant. At the very least, you thereby will contribute "insignificantly" to what you value, rather than contribute to what you dislike. Further, you will have gained new skill in accepting responsibility and will have become more free.

7. Practice Being the Person You Wish to Become.

All too often we act in ways we do not want as part of our personality, and fail to practice the habits we do want as part of our self.

In a skit, a comedienne remarked that she didn't like dogs. Dogs are too stupid. They cannot even learn to fetch sticks. She knew, because she had tried to teach a dog that trick. She threw a stick and said "Fetch" — but the stupid dog just sat there. One hundred times she threw the stick, each time saying "Fetch." Did that silly beast learn to get it? He did not! He just went on sitting there, laughing at her, she said, while she lugged the stick back in her mouth. The audience laughed.

Imagine expecting the dog to learn anything under those circumstances! The audience thought this absurd. It is absurd. And yet we often behave in much the same way. We expect ourselves (and others) to learn highly complicated tricks by merely watching someone else do them.

How many times have you watched a professor develop a logical line of thought? How many times have you watched him find examples of complex principles, watched him integrate materials from various fields, watched him do all manner of complicated tricks? How many times have you watched, and done little more? And have you ever wondered why you were so slow in acquiring his skill in reasoning? Why you improved so little in following up ideas or working independently? Have you even concluded, like the comedienne, that you must be pretty stupid?

The major trouble here, and many other places too, is this: Watching is not sufficient for learning. Even very attentive watching while somebody does his tricks will not enable you to do those tricks. You must actively practice them.

Quite thought-provoking is this experiment:[112] The task was to assemble a mechanical puzzle. One group watched while the experimenter assembled the puzzle and partially described what she was doing. After each demonstration, the learner tried to assemble the puzzle; thus he gained some practice in tackling the task. With this method, an average of sixteen trials was required before the learners could assemble the puzzle correctly.

Another group did not have the benefit of watching the experimenter assemble the puzzle. Instead, the subject himself tried to solve the puzzle and described what he was doing. Mistakes in his description were corrected by the experimenter. This group took 25% *fewer* trials on the average than the first group, who had more demonstrations but less active practice.

Still another method was tried: The experimenter solved the puzzle while the subject watched what was being done. (While watching, the subject counted aloud by two's.) How well did those people learn to solve the puzzle? As you might expect, they did poorly. In fact, they learned almost nothing about the puzzle. Even after 25 or more demonstrations of the solution, 22 of the 25 individuals still did not know how to assemble the pieces.

Other methods also were used in this experiment. The most ineffectual is the one just described — that of passively observing skillful demonstrations. This might be what you would expect. And yet, how often do you try to learn under similar conditons?

Do you spend a major part of your time passively watching an expert demonstrate the skills you wish to develop? The comedienne's approach to dog-training and the experimenter's demonstrations of puzzle-solving may seem ridiculous. No less ridiculous is the same approach in college or life in general. But we do this. We really expect to get educated, if only we sit long enough and patiently enough in the right places and have the right teachers, ones who are sufficiently bright and conscientious. We place unwarranted reliance on living in the right house, being seen in the right places, happening to be in the right spot at the right moment — for the good things of life to come our way. We fancy that merely by living we will get independence, more self-reliance, greater skill in making decisions, greater clarity of thought.

But neither you nor anyone else can learn new habits by watching someone else do the tricks or by any other such passive approach. You yourself must actually do what you wish to become.

If you wish to develop independence, you must practice drawing your own conclusions, practice making your own decisions, practice noticing and accepting your mistakes. In all of life, always do what you wish to learn. This accords with the crucially important, but often forgotten, principle of learning: We learn only what we do; and what we do, we become. Live, therefore, in the ways you desire to have as part of your personality. Practice being the person you wish to become.

8. Try to Remember the Worth of Accepting Responsibility.

When we remember what can be won by an enterprise, we find it easier to embark upon and work for that enterprise. We can better tolerate the disappointment accruing from our first clumsy efforts and can continue to work for our goal.

Many values gained by developing heightened skill in accepting responsibility were sketched in Chapter 1, pages 25–27. If you skimmed that section, please read it now. You can learn a lot about yourself.

9. Fear of Failure Deepens Dependency.

Fear of failure makes us cling to other people and turn to others for support along each step. It increases the tendency to project our own liabilities onto other people and mistakenly see others as holding the key to our success and as being the cause of our failure. These tendencies in turn deepen irresponsibility.

Therefore in order to break up habits of dependency and projection, to gain freedoms and happiness, we must break up fear of failure. But this is enormously complex. Because of its importance and complexity, the next section is devoted to this single matter.

E. TAMING FEAR OF FAILURE

1. What Does Fear of Failure Do?

As already mentioned, fear of failure increases dependency, projection, and irresponsibility. Fear of failure also is the root of many other fears — fear of people, fear of success, fear of non-conformity, fear of trying. . . .

Very occasionally, fear leads to worthwhile activity. Usually fear distracts and disrupts us. When intense, fear paralyzes. Fear that we may fail acts as a strait jacket, despite which (*not* because of which) we sometimes manage to do well. Seldom can we perform as well as we could without the fear.[28, 46, 58]

Fear of failure does not mean mere dislike of failure, nor does it mean a striving to avoid failure. We are speaking, rather, of an apprehensive dread of failure and disgrace, a dark foreboding which ranges from mere anxiety to vast terror.

Let us look at this fear in operation. Do you yearn to be a witty conversationalist, but fear saying something stupid? What happens? Do you then speak more eloquently, and gracefully, with greater perceptiveness and sparkle? The opposite is more likely. When afraid of disgracing yourself, you are apt to keep very still, not even try to converse. Or else you become garrulous, with a spate of jumbled words tumbling out. Have you wished to be an adroit dancer? Perhaps you even took lessons, but then became gripped by fear. You started to worry about being awkward, about doing poorly, about being a social failure. What happened then? We are apt to do just what we feared. We lose the beat; we step on our partner's toes; we become stiff and clumsy, and make still more mistakes. Have you ever wanted to be loved? But fearful of failure and rebuff, shut yourself off from others by walls steely strong and cold — announcing that *you* did not care about such silly things? Do you ever sit down to study and suddenly find the thought charging madly about that you cannot possibly ever "get" this stuff, that you are going to disgrace yourself this time for sure? Did that fear improve the quality of your studying? Has fear of failure ever helped you much yet? Often we fail because we fear failure.[12, 59, 81] Far from spurring us on to greater achievements, fear of failure actually is a major cause of our doing poorly.

Do not confound "desire to succeed" with "fear of failure." They are radically different.[12, 28, 36, 59] They are no more the same than a fear of the dark is the same as a love of bright sunshine. Not only is a desire to succeed very different from a fear of failure, but neither one is a cause for the other. You can value and desire success without fearing failure. You can fear failure and, instead of desiring success and striving for it, desire only to avoid failure, desire to *withdraw* from the whole appalling situation.

2. How Do We Get These Nagging, Gnawing Fears?

We were not born with them, nor with many other fears. Only a few stimuli evoked startle or fear responses in us as infants: Being dropped, loud noises, flashes of light, sudden intense changes in stimulation — these apparently are all.[56, 118] The other stimuli which now evoke fear responses in us do so through learning.

We learned to fear failure. We learned it through experiences such as these: We tried new activities, but our attempts were clumsy, inept; they elicited sniggers and sharp rebuffs. We made mistakes and were called stupid, and dumb, and in other ways ridiculed. People whose esteem we deeply needed seemed to make their love contingent upon our being successful. "That's Mother's dear little child," greeted some of our finest actions. We wondered fearfully if we were expected to always do that well and we were troubled because we knew we couldn't. If we fell below standards, we were asked, "How do you expect *anyone* to love a person like *you*?" Other disconcerting threats were levied concerning what would happen should we fail to meet the criteria set up for us. We would be a disgrace to the whole family . . . a disappointment to our parents and friends . . . unworthy of the time and effort lavished upon us. As one result, our own self-respect became contingent upon uniform success.

Simultaneously, we were caused to gravely mistrust our ability to reach any worthwhile criterion. ("High school may be a cinch, but just wait until college! You'll flunk, unless you do a lot better than this." "You do the most idiotic things for a supposedly bright person." "How could anyone be so stupid!" "You're not half as good as you think." You can extend the list.)

Sometimes we were trained to have fantastically high criteria for success, high absolutely and high relative to our own capacities. We were expected to be as good as the best person we knew, in everything or in certain specified endeavors. Anything less, we felt, would be profoundly disappointing to our parents or our teachers or even ourselves. We knew we never could do all this. We greatly feared what would happen when we failed.

One such episode makes little difference. A series of such experiences, or others of similar tone, will create a fear of failure, ranging from mild anxiety to downright terror.

3. Avoid Treating Yourself in Ways Which Create Fear.

Unless your life has been very unusual, many people many times have treated you in ways like those sketched above. More tragic, you do these same things to yourself! You treat yourself in ways bound to accentuate your fear of failure. Take another look, if you will, at Section 2 above. Can you learn to avoid doing those things to yourself? To the extent that you can, you will greatly mitigate your fear of failure. To the extent that you continue to exert such pressures on yourself, you will deepen your fear of failure. The results of this fear are manifold. Let us look at some of the effects on studying, and at how we ourselves make the fear worse.

When we fear failure, we tend to reject anything which does not fit our current beliefs. New divergent views show we were mistaken on something. This confirms our fear of incompetency. Illogically, we let it prove to us that we are inadequate. We were stupid, we tell ourselves, to have been misinformed or to have drawn the wrong conclusion. We do not tell ourselves that we are bright for seeing our mistakes and getting them corrected.

We try to write a term paper. Suddenly we are gripped by fear of failure. Is the paper going to be any good at all? Will it seem hopelessly naive, ridiculously puerile? Anything from a faint misgiving to blind panic seizes us. We do not look at our first drafts with sympathy, setting out to save the good and eliminate the weaknesses. We tear the whole thing up. We try to do mathematics. More misgivings assail us. We tell ourselves that any dope could do those problems. But *we* can't! We stare at some textbook, read and reread pages, and despair of ever understanding the material. We call ourselves dumb, and decide we are just no good at anything the least bit complicated.

We suffer from strange moods and emotional states which

we do not understand, but which are all too understandable in terms of the way we have been treated by others and by ourselves. We become obsessed by grades. We may even think about them continuously — a response utterly incompatible with what we mean by "studying." We look at long tasks and scurry in the opposite direction, feeling "bored" or slightly sick. These are some of the repercussions of *fear* of failure. None of them helps you study effectively.

Fear of failing in school even results in not studying. We avoid studying in order to have an excuse for failure and prevent harsh self-criticism for failure. "Failure" is not necessarily an "E" or "F"; any grade at all can be construed as failure, depending upon the individual's own standards and personal demands.

Let us consider Bill. To Bill any grade below "B" is psychological failure; it means the person is dumb — *if* he tried. Of course if he didn't try, that's different. Bill is afraid he would make "C's" even if he did try. Consequently, he does not try. He gets a "C" and jauntily remarks, "Well, I didn't crack a book all term." He got the "C," he says, because he "didn't try" and not because he was "stupid." To give himself this out, he avoids studying. Do you ever do this? Do you ever attempt to protect yourself from failure by not trying? Most people do, at least occasionally; some people do habitually.

We cannot change the whole world, but we can change ourselves. We can refrain from making fun of ourselves; we can stop threatening ourselves; we can stop taking errors or failures as "proof" that we are stupid. Although we cannot stop everyone else from trying to frighten us, we can at least stop frightening ourselves. We can avoid deepening our fear of failure.

In other ways too we can at least partially free ourselves from this fear of failure. Some ways of achieving this are discussed below.

4. Treat Yourself with More Respect.

Although you are not perfect and never will be, by your own or anyone else's standards, you are extremely valuable. You may not be "the greatest tiger in the jungle," but through fulfilling the potentialities you do have, you can do tremendously worthwhile things and make many contributions to our world. These facts are worth remembering. Can you do so? That is a part of what we mean by "Treat yourself with more respect." Other parts are these.

Recognize your special assets and use them to their utmost. Recognize also your shortcomings. Regard shortcomings not as proof of some malignant inferiority, but as places where you can apply your skill in learning to become a somewhat different person. Similarly, regard mistakes as clues to where you profitably can do differently in the future — not as evidence that you are "worthless."

Bear in mind the things you have done well, and not merely those you have done poorly. Encourage yourself. Tell yourself you have done well, when you have. In short, treat yourself in the ways you treat your friends, and wish they would treat you.

5. Strive for Improvement, Not Perfection.

Guard against making your self-respect contingent upon a perfect performance, or the equal of the most skillful person you know. Similarly, do not define "success" as achievement of your highest ideals. Such "success," if you have much imagination, is impossible. You are bound to fail and learn to fear failure in everything you try.

Instead, define success as *moving nearer* to your ideals. Whenever you evaluate your performance, do not note merely how far you are from where you aim to be. Note also how far you have progressed from where you began. The direction in which you are moving is at least as important as where you are at the moment. Indeed it is a better indication, than your present position, of where you are heading and what you will become in the future.

When fear of failure bids fair to swamp you, try recapturing this outlook. Remind yourself: "At least I can try. And I can try to improve. No matter how low I rate myself, nor how slim the chances for success appear to be, I can try for what I hold dear. I can do my best with what I have." In all of life, no man or woman can do better.

6. Whenever You Care Tremendously about Something, Try for It — Regardless of the Apparent Odds Against Success.

For each person, some entities are so precious they are worth trying for, even when the try seems doomed to failure. Which things these are for you, you will have to decide for yourself. In general, they are whatever you care most about in life, whatever you deem most dear.

In such circumstances, the attempt itself is valuable. You may lose a large part of what you were striving for, but you will not have lost by default. Nor will you have betrayed yourself and what you cherish. At the very least, you will win the profound satisfaction of knowing you slanted your life toward the entities you hold most valuable. You will have lived for your ideals. You will have won the self-respect, the sense of peace and achievement, which come from being true to oneself and one's own ideals. These are notable successes.

In other respects too, many attempts are bound to have partial success. Let us suppose, for example, that you endeavor to become highly educated. You study wholeheartedly in an all-out try for that goal. You try to become as skilled a thinker, as understanding, as informed, as broad and deep in your interests, and as responsible as is possible for you in your world. Through practicing the habits necessary to attain those goals, you inevitably develop at least some of the attributes you value. Whenever you practice being the person you wish to become, you do become a little more that person.

7. If You Intensely Fear Failure in Some Activity, Wholeheartedly Try That Activity.

Let us return to Bill to clarify the significance of this. You will recall that when Bill studies little and gets a "C," he says that is all right because he did not try. That approach has a flaw: The lingering suspicion haunts him that even *had* he tried, he still would have made a low grade. So Bill has lost after all. Despite not studying and thereby rationalizing low grades, Bill has only a tenuous grasp on his self-esteem.

Fear of failing in a situation probably never can be alleviated by avoiding the situation and by declining to try. Such an approach leaves one feeling much as though he actually had tried and failed. It also prevents discovering that one's fears were sometimes groundless. Fear of failure can be alleviated only when one dives in and tries.

At best one succeeds. If Bill were to study wholeheartedly, he *might* make a "B" or even an "A." He thus would allay, at least somewhat, his misgivings about his intelligence and other abilities.

At "worst," he fails to make a "B" or an "A." He gets the grade he dreaded. Would this merely confirm his gloomiest suspicions about himself, thus making matters worse than ever? No, for even this outcome is no worse and causes him to think no more lowly of himself than what he was fearfully thinking anyway.

Furthermore, even this outcome *could* lead to a marked improvement in Bill's situation. Suppose in response to his low grade, Bill set out to modify his ways of studying. He then could end with new, more satisfying approaches to learning. Or he could revise his demands upon himself so they accorded more closely with his present abilities. He could build a new view of his role in the world, such that he sees he is valuable even though unable to do certain things successfully. He could discover new ways of responding to failure which remove its sting.

Failure seldom is as awful as we feared. Few events are. Only rarely is an event as grim in actuality as in our horror-stricken imaginings. By trying and "failing," Bill will discover (at least in part) the truth of that important fact.

He might discover also that studying to the best of his abilities has intrinsic values, values quite apart from getting high grades or some other extrinsic reward. He could learn, in short, that though an activity failed to achieve some of the goals for which it was intended, other valued goals were achieved through it. When we try, "failure" is almost never as complete as we feared.

In all these ways, a defeat can lead to triumphs, with our chances for happiness being better than ever — and far better than they could have been had we declined the challenge and not tried.

8. Increase Your Respect for Other People.

The greater the extent to which you actively recognize the value of other individuals, see their contributions and special assets, and treat them with genuine consideration, the greater your respect for those individuals becomes. And, in general, the more skillfully and extensively you do these things with other people, the better you can do them with yourself.[18, 19, 26, 44] In other words, there is marked transfer here. A deep respect for other persons and deep respect for yourself often (perhaps always) are reciprocally linked.[25, 37] Hence, increasing your active respect for others will increase your esteem for yourself. Enhanced self-esteem, in turn, reduces your fear of failure.

F. OTHER DISADVANTAGING HABITS AND WAYS TO CHANGE THEM

1. The Prospect of Ridicule Is Terrifying to Many People.

What is your greatest fear or worry? Cheryl worries a lot about what people will think of her. Will they like her? Will they invite her to their parties? Jon is self-conscious and easily embarrassed. "You talk too much," a friend snapped the other day. Jon was crushed. How about you?

Worrying about other people's opinions of us and being hurt by criticism are parts of fear of ridicule. Much life is spoiled by that fear. Even when mild, fear of ridicule has considerable impact.[39, 99, 110] Seldom do we realize how great is its influence.

Have you started to compliment someone and then not done so, lest someone scoff? Have you started to offer someone a seat on the bus and hastily quashed the impulse from fear of condescending smiles by other passengers? Those are people you do not even know by name and probably never will meet again — yet you fear their opinion. Have you started to help someone and then refrained, lest somebody call you a "sucker"? Or an "apple polisher"? Or ask you what you were after? Other people too suppress kindness with a frequency which might astonish you. They too fear ridicule.

And what about your interests? Do you enjoy concerts, but become apologetic when people discover you sometimes attend them? Do you attend fine plays or read classics, but carefully not mention this lest people think you are silly? Would you like to read more, but squelch the interest? You do not want to be called stuffy, or highbrow. And how about studying? Do you hide that too? To be caught studying brings blushes of shame to many a collegian. To admit actually liking to study is almost unthinkable.

What happens to your ideas? Have you started to present an idea — and then stifled it from fear or ridicule? Have you started to build a new line of thought — only to drop it quickly when someone barked, "*No* one believes that!"?

All these actions we avoid because someone *might* scoff. Much which would be gentle and considerate . . . much which would develop an uncommon breadth and depth of interests... much which would be creative and novel... we abandon from fear of ridicule. We abandon actions which are the very essence of being civilized. We place in jeopardy values unspeakably dear to us — all to avoid the mere *possibility* of ridicule, or teasing, or loss of other people's esteem.

"We dread the blows we never feel
And what we never lose is yet by us lamented!"[45]

Fear of ridicule is a force of tremendous strength, a force which can rule, and thereby ruin, life.

We hide this from ourselves. We camouflage from ourselves that we are quashing actions primarily because someone might scoff. Often we cover up by saying emphatically (too emphatically) that we too consider the activities "silly" and "pointless." You know what happens next. We come to believe our rationalizations, with the result that many activities are spoiled for us. Many valued activities we no longer can bring ourselves to do at all; many others we do sporadically and with faint heart.

Quite probably you study little and do that studying listlessly, largely because of this fear of being ridiculed. We have a deeply rooted fear of losing status, of being labelled a "bookworm" or being given some other equally ignominious title.

Is the laughter of others really so terrible? Do you care more about avoiding the possibility of ridicule than you care about attaining various other values? Do you, for example, really value more deeply not being laughed at than you value finding the world increasingly fascinating? Or being free from boredom with yourself, now and in the years to come? Or having an increased fund of information and greater skill in thinking? Or being able to make a more sizable contribution to your fellow men? Do you care so much about avoiding occasional scoffs? These are questions all of us should answer for ourselves.

When you find yourself drawing back from something largely because someone might laugh were you to go ahead, pause for a moment. Examine what rests on the other side of the balance. It is your choice. Make it. Look at what you are choosing, and at what you are choosing to reject, while still you have the choice. Not always will you choose to do what your first automatic impulse dictates.

Quite possibly you do not care very much about avoiding laughter — but only *feel* as if you do and automatically act in the ways you were trained as a child. Very possibly you value other people's friendship and respect far more than you value avoidance of their laughter. You may have these entities confused. Avoiding people's laughter and having their friendship are not the same thing, nor does either one cause the other.

Laughter at your actions does not necessarily mean contempt of you nor of your actions. Often people laugh from surprise. Often too, laughter and even ridicule are affectionate roughhouse. They are clumsy ways of expressing attention and affection in a culture that discourages many other modes of expressing affection. Such laughter (though not always so perceived) is rather like Christopher Robin's "Silly old Pooh!" followed by, "I love you so"; except we do not add that last phrase because it is too sentimental (and people might laugh!).

Extremely often too, laughter is a defense of the laugher's self-respect. It is a defense of his right to do things in the way he sees fit. *Much disparaging laughter and much ridicule are occasioned by the person's feeling that pressures are being exerted on him to change, that he is being threatened.* Belittling other people and their activities is a way of retorting, "My ways of going at life are all right! *I* am all right! I'll prove it by showing that you and your ways are silly." This points the way to a solution.

We can avoid much derisive laughter and ridicule by following this humane expedient: Never try to force another person to adopt your ways. Communicate in words and actions that you regard their cherished ways as fine for them, though perhaps not for you. This you can do in many ways. Here are some of them.

Keep your own interests and develop them, but in addition share with other people their interests and enthusiasms. . . . Never belittle and never make fun of their actions or ideas. . . . Treat their preferences and tastes with the deep respect any person's preferences deserve. . . . Respect people as unique individuals. . . . Remember that they too need to feel important in others' eyes. . . . Express whatever admiration you feel. . . . If you defend your actions and interests, make extremely clear that you are defending them *only* as right to you and for you, and not as best or right for anyone else. . . . Never behave as though your actions should be models. . . . Never flaunt your achievements, nor in any other way (and here we return to our starting point) try to force other people to adopt your practices.

Without developing some such skills as these, you can sedulously avoid every activity your associates might ridicule, but you will not have their friendship.

When you do develop practices and attitudes like those sketched above, you can do almost anything, no matter how strange the activity seems to some people, and still win and hold their friendship and esteem. You can go to concerts; you can read a lot; you can even study for hours and hours — and rarely will anyone laugh. You can do pretty much as you please and seldom be ridiculed — so long as you do not try to force other people to do likewise nor imply your way of living is the only way worth much. In giving other people the freedom to live their lives in their own ways and encouraging them to do so, undreamt-of freedom becomes possible for you and deep friendship too.

Curiously, this approach often results in your associates' adopting many of your attitudes and coming to share many of your interests. Unadulterated, un-forcing enthusiasm is singularly contagious.

2. Conflict and Anxiety During Study Have Other Roots You Can Eradicate.

In addition to those already discussed, other fears impair our skill in studying. One of the most common is a fear that making high grades will impair our social success. Making high grades, we fear, will jeopardize our chances of being popular or holding school offices, or will in some other way cause us to be left out. These fears are very real, but are largely unwarranted.

Pertinent data are available. These show that something very like the opposite of our fears actually is the case. During college years, people with high grades are not handicapped socially. In fact, people making grades of Phi Beta Kappa caliber participate in *more* college activities and other extra-curricular activities than do the average students.[13, 53, 111] They also have more than their share of school offices (are elected to more presidencies of groups, and so on). Similarly, individuals with very high marks have just as many friends and acquaintances on the average as do students with lower grades. High grades and social success in college are not negatively correlated. Instead, they tend to go together.[1]

Comparably, university students participating in various sports (archery, fencing, wrestling, water skiing, and so on) 101 to 200 hours in a 32-week period made significantly higher grades on the average than those participating in sports only a little or not at all.[115]

3. Scholastic Success and Good Personal Adjustment Go Hand in Hand.

Not only are popularity and scholastic success related. Scholastic success and good personal adjustment also are correlated; the student tends to be high on both or else on neither.[2, 50] For example, academically successful university and college students are better integrated and freer of tensions,[96, 117] freer of anxieties and more self-controlled,[35, 101] more self-sufficient, independent, and responsible,[12, 50, 72] and in general better socialized,[3] on the average, than those with low grades or who are academically unsuccessful. (As you might guess, college and university students who are married do as well academically as those not married,[55, 98] and those working part-time do as well as those not employed.[46, 114])

Results are comparable for grade school,[4] junior high school,[5] and senior high school.[6] Students with high academic success generally have more social achievements and better psychological health than those with lower grades.

The trends cut across groups; and they cut across geographic locations and time. This is a remarkably stable phenomenon.

For students of five, ten, or fifteen years ago, and for students during the 25 years preceding that, the trends held; for students of the present, the trends still hold. Exceptions do exist,[13, 83] and never are the trends so strong that one can accurately predict individually. Still, in general, and across a wide span of time, young people of high scholastic achievement tend to be more popular, have better personal adjustment, and participate in more activities than those with low scholastic achievement.

After graduation, the trends continue. One expects success as an undergraduate and success as a graduate student to be correlated, and they are — substantial correlations being found between undergraduate grades and success in graduate work for law,[63] education,[24] engineering,[67] and other fields.[52, 74] Similarly, substantial positive correlations usually are found between grades in high school and grades at the university or college,[7] and from one year to the next, and from one term to the next,[85] suggesting again the salient role in academic success played by our intellectual and personality habits.

4. High Grades Are Related to Later Success.

In more pervasive respects, the foregoing trends continue in the years after college: People who earned high grades have better chances of success than those who did not. What is construed as success depends upon the observer. But whether one takes as the criterion for "success" the amount of money one makes,[67, 105] rapidity of promotions,[9, 20] being listed in *Who's Who in America*,[53, 64] women obtaining high prestige jobs,[116] the ratings of one's classmates,[53, 66] or creativity in science and engineering,[22, 67, 108] success is positively correlated with grades in college. That is, by any of these criteria, people with high grades generally are more successful in later life than people with lower grades.

People with high grades generally are more successful after college, but not always. For example, in a study of engineering graduates over a 45-year period,[67] 25 per cent of the persons with grade-point averages in the highest tenth of the graduates advanced to the top salary level, but so also did 9 per cent of the persons with grade-point averages in the bottom tenth. High grades do not guarantee later success, nor do low grades guarantee failure. The trend simply is in that direction, and fairly markedly so. In another sense too, the data do not mean that high grades necessarily cause success. The relationship between high grades and later success might be caused by a third set of factors. For example, certain personality characteristics (such as enthusiasm for whatever one is doing, ability to work independently and efficiently, freedom from restricting fears, relatively high intelligence) could facilitate both making high grades and being successful outside college. People who develop these personality characteristics while in school would tend, as a consequence, to make high grades in college and would tend also to become successful after college. Other interpretations of the correlations also are possible. What the data do show, conclusively, is that making high grades is no hindrance to later success.

No evidence appears of a negative correlation between grades and subsequent success. Sometimes there is no relationship, and often the relationship is low, though significant; but where there *is* a relationship, the relationship between grades and later success is always positive.

At the extremes, the relationship holds most closely. The moderately good student is only a bit more likely to do well later than the moderately poor student. But the exceptionally excellent student is apt to be excellent in other ways as well, both in college and in later life.

High grades and social success in college tend to go together. High grades and vocational successes also tend to go together. These facts are slow to be recognized; but they are facts. Remembering them can allay at least some of your fear of studying.

5. Do You Fear Success?

Akin to fear of ridicule and fear of making high grades is a more subtle anxiety: the fear of success.

Fear of success can be diffuse — a feeling that in general one is not worthy of success and ought to fail. This was touched upon in connection with feelings of guilt (see pages 131–132). The fear of success can be vague, with no target; or can be highly specific; fear of success in one's vocation — one wants to be a doctor but also is afraid to be a doctor, or actor, or carpenter, or president, or engineer, or anything else a human being can strive toward; or a fear of social success — a fear of other people's love or esteem or thinking too highly of one with danger of disappointing them; a fear of having much responsibility and making inappropriate decisions and being destructively criticized; a fear of loving and being loved and of losing love — fear of success and fear of failure often go hand in hand. The kinds of fear of success are about as numerous as the kinds of people in the world.

Success necessarily involves divergence from the commonplace, success also involves conformity to various norms and expectations, and success may involve creativity. Each of these can be a source of anxiety and fear. These fears can dilute seriously what any student gains from years at the university or college; they can destroy effectiveness. They are three roots from which springs fear of success. Let us take a closer look at these three roots of fear of success: fear of any deviancy from the norms or from the average, fear (oppositely) of any conformity, and fear of creativity.

6. Fear of Differing and Fear of Conformity Can Plague You.

We live in a world with many pressures toward conformity. We strive to adapt and sometimes, instead, succumb: We become preoccupied with fitting in, with being one of the group, with at least escaping censure. We may become obsessed with being "normal," and very fearful of being different.[42, 51] A host of concomitant fears then can assail us — among them fear of success. We dare not be outstanding in any way.

Sometimes we over-correct for the urge toward conformity and fall into an opposite pitfall: We become afraid to conform. We set ourselves apart and systematically try to be different. The next thing we know we are trying to be different just for the sake of being different. We develop habits of doing things merely because they are not common or not a socially customary way. We fear conformity: We feel that if we conform in any respect, we will lose our individuality and creativity. We might even lose our identity. Feeling this way, we become engrossed with accentuating our differences, hardly daring to do anything if it is conventional.

Fighting and fearing conformity is a tremendous hindrance to growth, since much of our development ideally parallels that of other people. Fear of conforming circumscribes us and limits our individuality since much of our nature is like that of other persons. Fear of conformity also hinders our learning, especially learning from others and their experience, because much of what has been learned is codified in customs and norms. Not all differences from the norm help us become more alive; not all conformings with norms hinder our development. Not everything that people have discovered and codified leads into blind alleys or in other ways hampers human living. Indeed, much of it gives us ways to stay out of blinds and to avoid needless trial-and-error or senselessly circuitous routes. Avoiding all conformity narrows and binds as surely as adopting all-conformity.

7. Fear of Creativity is Prevalent, and Needless.

There is a variant of the fear of success with particularly devastating implications: the fear that being very creative will lead to maladjustment, or neuroticism, or social ostracism. This is a fear singularly enervating. It can discourage you from even attempting to develop your special talents. It discourages you from using some most human potentials.

Until recently few data were available on this matter. Now however, besides the studies mentioned on pages 215–217 and pages 19–21, extensive studies have been made of highly creative individuals from a wide variety of fields: anthropology, biology, psychology, and physical science;[91, 92] architecture, literature, and art;[32, 97] engineering, mathematics, chemistry, physics, and others.[14, 71, 108] The studies show us our old stereotypes were faulty; our old fears unwarranted.

Far from being unhappy, neurotic individuals, the highly creative are relatively less subject to repression, and suppression, and self-defensiveness; are more discerning, more flexible in their routes to goals, more open to richness of experience. They are relatively freer. They are neither rigid conformists, blindly bound by convention, nor blindly anti-social. Instead they are genuinely independent.

Nor do they generally become bitter introverts. Though seldom joiners of many civic or social clubs, and sometimes described as aloof or reserved,[14] in general the highly creative are as secure and sociable, as happy and comfortable with fellow human beings, as a random sample of more ordinary people.[22, 32, 71, 120] They are very far from being out of touch.

Indeed, the data show us notably creative persons are more completely in touch with the world than the average.[14, 68, 71, 75] Concerning Aristophanes' masterful Lysistrata, we are given these thoughts: " 'The contemplation of things as they are, without substitution or imposture, without error or confusion is in itself a nobler thing than a whole harvest of inventions,' said Francis Bacon. The inventions in Lysistrata are very few, but the contemplation of things as they are is steady and unafraid. This is, of course, the distinction of the great classical writers, and the reason that they live."[11]

MacKinnon summarizes: "It is quite apparent that creative persons have an unusual capacity to record and retain and have readily available the experiences of their life history. They are discerning, which is to say that they are observant in a differentiated fashion; they are alert, capable of concentrating attention readily and shifting it appropriately; they are fluent in scanning thoughts and producing those that serve to solve the problems they undertake; and characteristically, they have a wide range of information at their command."[71]

Apparent too is "another pervasive trait of the creative, his preference for complexity, his delight in the challenging and unfinished. . . ."[71]

Far from killing breadth of interests and diversity, becoming a highly skilled and creative person leaves one more diversified. One does not become a narrow specialist — not if top-flight. Instead one is more abundantly alive.

8.   Are You Loath to Admit You Do Not Know Everything?

That is rare, but does occur. However, a slight modification is common: We are loath to admit we do not know everything known by our associates. This characteristic may or may not mean low respect for other people. It almost certainly means very low self-respect. What are some signs of this low self-esteem?

To such a person, books *have* to be vapid; lectures *must* be stating mainly platitudes; associates *cannot* be saying much that is new or significant; for if something were interesting or in any other way worthy of close attention, careful notes, or intensive study, this would prove the individual did not already know everything worth knowing. It would prove he had not thought everything worth thinking. Perhaps he had not even thought of everything his associates had. Such an admission is intolerable to people already low in self-esteem.

People with very low self-respect are driven to prove, over and over again, that they are "as good as the next person," or better. They must "prove" this to themselves and to others too, in order to maintain even their current low level of self-respect. Therefore, they scoff at other people's choices; they belittle other people's achievements; they criticize harshly and indiscriminately. About their own activities, they wax boastfully eloquent.

Clearly then, one way to reduce the just-try-to-tell-me-anything attitude is this: Decrease the self-contempt underlying the attitude.

With the problem so stated, you yourself will have promising ideas for its solution. You know many ways of helping a person feel more valued and worthwhile, of helping him gain more self-esteem and (consequently) gain greater receptivity to new ideas and information, an enhanced ability to learn. This knowledge you can apply to yourself as well as to your associates. This will help you more than you might guess.

Other people too can help. When conflicts and fears persist and interfere seriously with your chances for success, you may want to contact some new source for help. We mentioned psychologists, ministers, psychiatrists. All can help. So can trusted members of your family, university or college counsellors, respected friends, local health departments, mental health or crisis centers, Alcoholics Anonymous, Al-Anon, Al-a-Teen, Departments of Social Services, and others too. College counsellors and the Department of Social Services usually will know the resources available in your area and can guide you to the appropriate ones. The resource which meets your particular need also may be listed in the telephone book.

9. Rigidity Hinders Many Endeavors.

What does rigidity mean? This in part: We fall into stereotyped ways of behaving, overlooking changes in the external situation. We do the same thing over and over and over, although external conditions have changed and our stereotyped response is not working out well at all. We make many mistakes, and eliminate our mistakes more slowly. We even make the same mistake repeatedly. Rigidity seriously handicaps us in learning and in other aspects of living.[34, 49]

A poignant example of the impact of rigidity turned up in an experiment.[88] University students guessed whether a green light or red light would be shown on various trials. This is not a particularly ego-involving situation. Yet even so, the students required markedly more information before they would change a decision than they required to make the original decision. When they once made a decision, they tended to cling to it — even though evidence to the contrary was presented and even though the original decision was based on very scanty or even non-existent information.

Small ability to modify our beliefs or to change in other ways gravely limits our chances for growth. In its extreme form, rigidity paralyzes us and utterly precludes our growing.

An increase in rigidity and a decrease in adaptability often are caused in part by fear or hostility.[82] Alleviating intense fears or hostilities is at least as complicated as repairing a broken leg. For such difficulties, one is wise to collaborate with someone highly skilled along these lines — e.g., a clinical psychologist, psychiatrist, or psychoanalyst. Milder fears and hostilities you, of course, can reduce or break up by yourself. Many ways have been offered in the preceding sections.

Another way to increase flexibility is this: Expect new information and be organized for receiving it. Think of yourself as a recipient and processor of new information rather than primarily as a transmitter of information or as already completely informed.[8, 30, 70]

Another route toward increasing flexibility: Remember that entities with the same label always have marked differences. We touched upon this before. Let us examine more closely now its meaning for your life.

Are all science courses the same? Of course not, you say. Are two beginning chemistry courses the same? Never. Often, indeed, they are very different, far more different than we are apt to realize. Even the "same" course is very different when taught by different instructors. Radically different objectives and radically different skills may be involved.

The situation is analogous to sports. Tennis and badminton, for example, have many similarities. The similarities can mislead us into believing the games are essentially alike. Yet techniques advisable for one are utterly ineffective in the other. In tennis, letting your wrist "break" will ruin the shot; in badminton, it can be part of a beautiful smash.

Superficial similarities do not necessarily mean basic similarities. In sports we see this clearly; in other phases of life we often overlook it. Two people have similar skin color; we then act, sometimes, as though they had similar personalities. Two people belong to the same church; we then imagine they will behave in fundamentally similar ways. Two courses are offered by the same college department; we fancy that techniques effective in one will necessarily be effective in another. We blindly carry habits from one situation to another and expect them to work well or at least be appropriate to the new situation. This leads to senseless disappointments.

In studying, in playing, in interacting with people, be alert for the differences in similar entities. Watch for evidence on how well your habits are working out. If old successful habits are giving poor results, you are confronting a new situation with crucial differences from the old one — despite there being, perhaps, many resemblances between the two. When you get such evidence, modify your behavior. Such procedures are the foundation of flexible adaptability.

10. Is It Difficult to Study or Do Anything Else Wholeheartedly?

While studying, you probably feel like loafing. While loafing you feel, often, as if you should be studying; the pestering thought keeps returning that "this is a waste of time." How does it go at the movies? Or dancing? Or playing? Do you find yourself troubled then too by vague thoughts of work undone, of duties calling, or of other pleasures you wish you had chosen instead? So life goes.

Most of us have been so trained that we live in an almost perpetual state of conflict. Regardless of what we are trying to do, we are both doing it and not doing it at the same time. Almost continuously we feel ambivalent — liking and disliking the same activity. Only the rare adult can even play wholeheartedly.

These conflicts and ambivalence which infest our activities can be eradicated. How? How can you become free from inwardly tearing against yourself? How can you gain the ability to live with greater enthusiasm and delight? These problems are an underlying concern of this entire little book. Its suggestions are aimed toward achievement of these goals too.

Another big step toward resolving conflict is this: Face your fears and try to reduce them. Reducing any anxiety or fear brings increments in peace throughout one's life and better chances for happiness and enthusiasm.

Still further reduction in conflict and increases in wholehearted joy can be achieved through building these habits: For any particular time and situation, decide what course of action all in all seems best to you. Then embark upon that course and stick to it until you get data you did not have at the time of your original decision. Change your course when and only when you do have new information upon which to base a new decision. Through practice, you make this a habit. When you do, you will have new skills in living unfettered by conflict and ambivalence.

Practice living with enthusiasm. Whatever you are doing at any moment, do that with all the enthusiasm you can muster. When you become able to engage in one activity wholeheartedly, you will be able to engage in others too more wholeheartedly. For example, learning to play tennis with enthusiasm and free from conflict will enable you to study more wholeheartedly. Similarly, learning to study with wholehearted enthusiasm enhances your ability to do other activities with wholeheartedness. You can build a basic, generalized skill for doing whatever you are doing with wholehearted enthusiasm.

To develop such a habit, launch yourself with vigor into anything you decide to do. Whatever you begin, at least begin with enthusiasm. Then carry on with all the verve and imagination at your command. Live every moment to the fullest extent of your resources.

"A moment's halt — a momentary taste
Of *being* from the well amid the waste —
    And lo!—the phantom caravan has reach'd
The Nothing it set out from—Oh, make haste!

Ah, make the most of what we yet may spend,
Before we too into the dust descend;
    Dust into dust, and under dust to lie,
Sans wine, sans song, sans singer, and — sans end!"[60]

G. TOWARD A BETTER LIFE

Suppose a man were interested in becoming a skilled violinist. He might solicit instruction on fingering and bowing techniques. But no matter how elaborate the instruction, it would profit him little — if he had a broken arm. Obviously, he should do something about that arm.

When we start our college and university careers, most of us are in a similar predicament — except instead of a broken arm, we have battered personalities. The damage is such that we are handicapped gravely in our efforts to become educated, even though we have expert tuition.

Further, these characteristics continue to handicap us long after graduation. They jeopardize happiness and success in all of living.

You are not compelled to live your entire life with such handicaps, for you can repair the damage. Many leads have been presented on what the difficulties are. Many leads on how you can alleviate these difficulties and build a new personality have also been presented. From here, however, you must carry on by yourself. The actual breaking of these unfortunate habits and the building of new ones is nothing anyone can do for you, no matter how fervently desired. If it is to be done at all, you must do it for yourself.

Perhaps you should be forewarned: The job is not easy. The difficulty is rather the same, we imagine, as that encountered by a person thrown into deep water with millstones tied around his or her neck. The presence of the millstones (as of those personality characteristics) make it very difficult to act in the ways necessary to get free. But the presence of the millstones also makes it extremely difficult to live in the only ways possible for a person not freed. That leaves little choice but to try to get free.

Though arduous, this is a peculiarly challenging, exciting endeavor. Eventually you may even find it fun to work on these characteristics and note your gradual progress and increasing satisfaction. Certainly you will find the results a joy — the exhilaration of achievement and seeing what you can do . . . the satisfaction of growing toward your potentialities and of recognizing the possibilities of new growth . . . the joys of a real freedom . . . the refreshing beauty of peace with yourself and with your fellows . . . the new capacities for living enthusiastically. These are not trifles. They can be yours. Through striving to grow, working to eliminate handicaps, exploiting opportunities to become truly educated (not merely informed), a significant beginning will be made.

You can create a life you never have known, but only glimpsed. You can become the person you long to be. You can help build the world of your dreams into a new reality.

"No end is visible or even conceivable to this kingdom of adventure."[69]

Bon Voyage!

BIBLIOGRAPHY FOR CHAPTER 7

1. *High grades and popularity (college and university students)*
   Banreti-Fuchs, K. M. Attitudinal, situational and mental health correlates of academic achievement at the undergraduate university level. Brit. J. Educ. Psychol., 45, 227–231, 1975.

   Carew, Donald K. A comparison of activities, social acceptance and scholastic achievements of men students. Personnel Guid. J., 36, 121–124, 1957.

   Hopkins, J.; Mallison, N.; and Sarnoff, I. Some non-intellectual correlates of success and failure among university students. Brit. J. Educ. Psychol., 28, 25–36, 1958.

   Jensen, Vern H. Influence of personality traits on academic success. Personnel Guid. J., 36, 497–500, 1958.

   Lewis, Leslie. A multivariate analysis of variables associated with academic success within a college environment. Diss. Abstr., 27 (12-A), 4134, 1967.

   McCroskey, James C.; and Andersen, Janis F. The relationship between communication apprehension and academic achievement among college students. Human Comm. Res., 3, 73–81, 1976.

   Slocum, John W., Jr. Group cohesiveness: A salient factor affecting students' academic achievement and adjustment in a collegiate environment. Diss. Abstr., 28 (3-B), 1176–1177, 1967.

   Willingham, Warren W. College performance of fraternity members and independent students. Personnel Guid. J., 41, 29–31, 1962.

   Wyer, R. S., Jr. Behavioral correlates of academic achievement. II. Pursuit of individual versus group goals in a decision-making task. J. Educ. Psychol., 59, 74–81, 1968.

2. *High grades and personal adjustment (college and university students)*
   Banreti-Fuchs, K. M. Attitudinal situational and mental health correlates of academic achievement at the undergraduate university level. Brit. J. Educ. Psychol., 45, 227–231, 1975.

   Berger, Emanuel M. Willingness to accept limitations and college achievement. J. Counsel. Psychol., 8, 140–146, 1961.

   Berger, Irving L., and Sutker, Alvin R. The relationship of emotional adjustment and intellectual capacity to academic achievement of college students. Ment. Hyg., N.Y., 40, 65–77, 1956.

   Brar, Jarnail S. Relationship between extroversion-introversion, neuroticism and academic achievement. Indian Educ. Rev., 11, 105–110, 1976.

   Drinkwater, Ruby Straughan. The relationship between certain factors and academic success in the School of Pharmacy at Southwestern State College. Diss. Abstr., 28 (12-A), 4871, 1968.

   Faunce, Patricia Spencer. Withdrawal of academically gifted women. J. College Student Personnel, 9, 171–176, 1968.

   Glennen, Robert E. Intrusive college counseling. Coll. Student J., 9, 2–4, 1975.

   Jones, J. B. Some personal-social factors contributing to academic failure at Texas Southern University. In Sutherland, R. L.: Holtzman, W. H.; Koile, E. A.; and Smith, B. K. (Eds.) Personality Factors on the College Campus: Review of a Symposium. Austin, Texas: Hogg Foundation for Mental Health, 1962.

   Jones, John G. The relationship of self-perception measures and academic achievement among college seniors. J. Educ. Res., 63, 201–203, 1970.

   Mehryrar, A. H.; Hekmat, H.; and Khajavi, F. Some personality correlates of self-rated academic success. Percep. Motor Skills, 40, 1007–1010, 1975.

   Pace, Lawlis T. Roommate dissatisfaction in a college residence hall as related to roommate scholastic achievement, the College and University Environment Scales, and the Edwards Personal Preference Schedule. Diss. Abstr., 28 (8-A), 2989, 1968.

Rogers, William Alfred. Intellective-nonintellective characteristics and academic success of college freshmen. Diss. Abstr., 28 (3-A), 973–974, 1967.

Sinha, Durganand. A psychological analysis of some factors associated with success and failure in university education: intelligence, anxiety and adjustment of academic achievers and non-achievers. Psychol. Studies, 11, 69–88, 1966.

Smith, Paul Edward. The relationship of life change, neuroticism, and academic performance among junior college adults. Diss. Abstr., 37 (A-12), 7475, 1977.

3. *High grades and social maturity (college and university students)*

Ellis, Dwight W. The relationships between personality, attitude, achievement, and performance of college students undertaking individualized studies. Diss. Abstr., 37 (10-A), 6429–30, 1977.

Faunce, Patricia Spencer. Personality characteristics and vocational interests related to the college persistence of academically gifted women. J. Couns. Psychol., 15, 31–40, 1968.

Frank, Austin C.; and Kirk, Barbara A. Differences in outcomes for users and nonusers of university counseling and psychiatric services. J. Couns. Psychol., 22, 252–258, 1975.

Johnson, Edward G., Jr. A comparison of academically successful and unsuccessful college of education freshmen on two measures of "self." Diss. Abstr., 28 (4-A), 1298–1299, 1967.

Kisch, Jeremy M. A comparative study of patterns of underachievement among male college students. Diss. Abstr. 28 (8-B), 3461–2, 1968.

McDonald, Robert L.; and Gynther, Malcolm D. Nonintellectual factors associated with performance in medical schools. J. Genetic Psychol., 103, 185–194, 1963.

Smith, Paul Edward. The relationship of life change, neuroticism, and academic performance among junior college adults. Diss. Abstr., 37 (12-A), 7475, 1977.

Trachtman, Joan P. Cognitive and motivational variables as predictors of academic performance among disadvantaged college students. J. Couns. Psychol., 22, 324–328, 1975.

Wyer, R. S.; Weatherly, D.; and Terrell, G. Social role, aggression, and academic achievement. J. Personality Soc. Psychol., 1, 645–649, 1965.

4. *High grades and popularity, adjustment, social maturity (elementary school)*

De Anda, Natividad. The relationship of children's self concepts to their locus of control, academic achievement, and social status in the classroom. Diss. Abstr., 38 (2-A), 622–23, 1977.

Lerner, Richard M.; and Lerner, Jacqueline V. Effects of age, sex, and physical attractiveness on child-peer relations, academic performance, and elementary school adjustment. Devel. Psychol., 13, 585–590, 1977.

Lewis, John; and Adank, Richard. Intercorrelations among measures of intelligence, achievement, self-esteem, and anxiety in two groups of elementary school pupils. Educ. Psychol. Meas., 35, 499–501, 1975.

Moriarty, A. Coping patterns of preschool childlren in response to intelligence test demands. Genet. Psychol. Monogr., 64, 3–127, 1961.

Murphy, L. B. The Widening World of Childhood: Paths toward Mastery. New York: Basic Books, 1962.

Phillips, B. N. Sex, social class, and anxiety as sources of variation in school achievement. J. Educ. Psychol., 53, 316–322, 1962.

Porterfield, O. V.; and Schlichting, Harry F. Peer status and reading achievement. J. Educ. Res., 54, 291–297, 1961.

Reiss, Steven; and Dyhdalo, Nestor. Persistence, achievement, and open-space environments. J. Educ. Psychol., 67, 506–513, 1975.

Simon, William E.; and Simon, Marilyn G. Self-esteem, intelligence and standardized academic achievement. Psychol. Schools, 12, 97–100, 1975.

5. *High grades and popularity, adjustment, social maturity (junior high school)*

Airoldi, Norman; Peterson, Barbara; and Webb, Dwight. Junior high school athletes excel in scholarship. Personnel Guid. J., 45, 1021–1024, 1967.

Carter, Donald E.; DeTine, Susan L.; Spero, June; and Benson, Forrest W. Peer acceptance and school-related variables in an integrated junior high school. J. Educ. Psychol., 67, 267–273, 1975.

Carter, Harold D. Overachievers and underachievers in the junior high school. Calif. J. Educ. Res., 12, 51–56, 1961.

Pierce, James V. Personality and achievement among able high school boys. J. Indiv. Psychol., 17, 102–107, 1961.

Prendergast, Mary A.; and Binder, Dorothy M. Relationships of selected self-concept and academic achievement measures. Meas. Eval. Guid., 8, 92–95, 1975.

Sattabanasuk, Thirapan. Junior high student performance and related student and parent characteristics. Diss. Abstr., 29 (4-A), 1052–1053, 1968.

Spencer, William A. Interpersonal influence, academic performance, sex and self-concept of ability. Child Study J., 7, 59–70, 1977.

Tenopyr, Mary L. Social intelligence and academic success. Educ. Psychol. Meas., 27, 961–965, 1967.

6. *High grades and popularity, adjustment, social maturity (high school)*

Berenberg, Martin B. Achievement, attendance, discipline, and self-concept of ninth-grade students in traditional and alternative programs. Diss. Abstr., 38 (1-A), 193, 1977.

Davids, Anthony. Psychological characteristics of high school male and female potential scientists in comparison with academic underachievers. Psychol. Schools, 3, 79–87, 1966.

Gill, Lois J.; and Spilka, Bernard. Some nonintellectual correlates of academic achievement among Mexican-American secondary school students. J. Educ. Psychol., 53, 144–149, 1962.

Horowitz, Herbert. Prediction of adolescent popularity and rejection from achievement and interest tests. J. Educ. Psychol., 58, 170–174, 1967.

Jones, John Goff. Relationships among identity development and intellectual and nonintellectual factors. Diss. Abstr. 28 (3-A), 941, 1967.

Jones, John G.; and Strowig, R. Wray. Adolescent identity and self-perception as predictors of scholastic achievement. J. Educ. Res., 62, 78–82, 1968.

Lloyd, Jean. Intrinsic intellectual motivation in relation to measures of school achievement for tenth grade students. Diss. Abstr., 37(9-A), 6090A, 1977.

Marjoribanks, Kevin. Affective and environmental correlates of cognitive performance. J. Educ. Research, 71, 3–8, 1977.

Metha, Perin H. The self-concept of bright under-achieving male high school students. Indian Educ. Rev., 3, 81–100, 1968.

Pfeifer, C. Michael; and Sedlacek, William E. Predicting black student grades with nonintellectual measures. J. Negro Educ., 43, 67–76, 1974.

Ryan, F. R.; and Davie, James S. Social acceptance, academic achievement, and aptitude among high school students. J. Educ. Res., 52, 101–106, 1958.

Shaw, Merville C.; and Grubb, James. Hostility and able high school under-achievers. J. Counsel. Psychol., 5, 263–266, 1958.

Werts, Charles E. The many faces of intelligence. J. Educ. Psychol., 58, 198–204, 1967.

7. *Relationship of college grades to high school grades*

Chissom, Brad S.; and Lanier, Doris. Prediction of first quarter freshman GPA using SAT scores and high school grades. Educ. Psychol. Meas., 35, 461–463, 1975.

Gallessich, June Marie. Factors associated with academic success of freshmen engineering students of the University of Texas. Diss. Abstr., 28 (5-A), 1677–1678, 1967.

Iglinsky, Clyde L. Intellectual and non-intellectual factors affecting academic success of college freshmen. Diss. Abstr., 29 (5-A), 1423–4, 1968.

Johnson, Richard W.; Keochakian, Simon V.; Morningstar, Mona; and Southworth, J. A. Validation of freshmen orientation test battery. Educ. Psychol. Meas., 28, 437–440, 1968.

Lewis, John; and Welch, Margaret. Predicting achievement in an upper-division bachelor's degree nursing major. Educ. Psychol. Meas., 35, 467–469, 1975.

Leyman, Laretha. Prediction of freshman and sophomore grade-point averages of women physical education major students. Educ. Psychol. Meas., 27, 1139–1141, 1967.

Morgenfeld, George R. The prediction of junior college achievement from adjusted secondary school grade averages. Diss. Abstr., 28 (8-A), 2987–2988, 1968.

Nyberg, V. R.; and Baril, R. G. SACU test variables as predictors of university GPA. Alberta J. Educ. Res., 19, 303–308, 1973.

Passons, William R. Predictive validities of the ACT, SAT and high-school grades for first semester GPA and freshman courses. Educ. Psychol. Meas., 27, 1143–1144, 1967.

Richards, James M., Jr.; Holland, John L.; and Lutz, Sandra W. Prediction of student accomplishment in college. J. Educ. Psychol., 58, 343–355, 1967.

Rothney, J. W. M.; and Sanborn, M. P. Wisconsin's research-through-service program for superior high school students. Personnel Guid. J., 44, 694–699, 1966.

Schoemer, J. R. The college pushout. Personnel Guid. J., 46, 677–680, 1968.

8. Adams, J. S. Reduction of cognitive dissonance by seeking consonant information. J. Abnorm. Soc. Psychol., 62, 74–78, 1961.

9. American Telephone and Telegraph Company, Personnel Research Section. College Achievement and Progress in Management. Bell Telephone Magazine, Spring 1962.

10. Anant, Santokh. Generation gap — real or imagined? A study of the values of college students and their parents. Manas, 23, 17–22, 1976.

11. Aristophanes. Lysistrata: A New Version by Gilbert Seldes. New York: The Heritage Press, 1962.

12. Atkinson, J. W.; and Feather, N. T. (Eds.) A Theory of Achievement Motivation. New York: Wiley, 1966.

13. Baird, Leonard L. The achievement of bright and average students. Educ. Psychol. Meas., 28, 891–899, 1968.

14. Barron, F. Creativity and Psychological Health. Princeton: Van Nostrand, 1963. Also, the psychology of creativity. In Barron, Frank, et al. (Eds.) New Directions in Psychology. Vol. 2, New York: Holt, Rinehart and Winston, 1965.

15. Berger, Emanuel M. Willingness to accept limitations and college achievement. J. Counsel. Psychol., 8, 140 –146, 1961.

16. Bhatnagar, K. P. Academic achievement as a function of one's self-concepts and ego-functions. Educ. Psychol. Rev., 6, 178–182, 1966.

17. Bloxom, Bruce. Effects of anger-arousing instructions on personality questionnaire performance. Educ. Psychol. Meas., 28, 735–745, 1968.

18. Boshier, Roger. A study of the relationship between self-concept and conservatism. J. Soc. Psychol., 77, 139–140, 1969.

19. Brown, Robert D. Effects of structured and unstructured group counseling with high- and low-anxious college underachievers. J. Couns. Psychol., 16, 209–214, 1969.

20. Butler, Richard P. Relationship between college performance and success as an Army officer. J. Vocational Beh., 9, 385–391, 1976.

21. Cattell, R. B.; Sealy, A. P.; and Sweney, A. B. What can personality and motivation source trait measurements add to the prediction of school achievement? Brit. J. Educ. Psychol., 36, 280–295, 1966.

22. Chambers, J. A. Creative scientists of today. Science, 145, 1203–1205, 1964. Also, Relating personality and biographic factors to scientific creativity. Psychol. Monogr.: Gen. and Applied, 78, #584, 1964.

23. Coleman, James C.; and Hammen, Constance L. Contemporary Psychology and Effective Behavior. Glenview, Ill.: Scott, Foresman and Co., 1974.

24. Colvin, Gerald F. The value of selected variables in predicting academic success in graduate education at the University of Arkansas. Diss. Abstr., 29 (1-A), 55–56, 1968.

25. Conner, Jack M. Development and growth of understanding self and others. Diss. Abstr., 29 (2-A), 477, 1968.

26. Coopersmith, Stanley. Studies in self-esteem. Sci. Amer., 218, 96–106, 1968.

27. Costin, Frank. Do student ratings of college teachers predict student achievement? Teaching Psychol., 5, 86–91, 1978.

28. Crandall, Virginia C. Personality characteristics and social and achievement behaviors associated with children's social desirability response tendencies. J. Personality Soc. Psychol., 4, 477–486, 1966.

29. Culbert, S. A. The Organization Trap. New York: Basic Books, 1974.

30. Deutsch, Morton; Krauss, R. M.; and Rosenau, N. Dissonance or defensiveness? J. Personality, 30, 16–28, 1962.

31. Dreger, Ralph M. General temperament and personality factors related to intellectual performances. J. Genetic Psychol., 113, 275–293, 1968.
32. Drevdahl, J. E.; and Cattell, R. B. Personality and creativity in artists and writers. J. Clin. Psychol., 14, 107–111, 1958.
33. Earls, Jim H. Human adjustment to an exotic environment: The nuclear submarine. Arch. Gen. Psychiatry, 20, 117–123, 1969.
34. Ehrlich, H. J. Dogmatism and learning. J. Abnorm. Soc. Psychol., 62, 148–149, 1961.
35. Faunce, Patricia Spencer. Personality characteristics and vocational interests related to the college persistence of academically gifted women. Diss. Abstr., 28 (1-B), 338, 1967.
36. Feather, N. T. Level of aspiration and performance variability. J. Personality Soc. Psychol., 6, 37–46, 1967.
37. Fey, W. F. Acceptance by others and its relation to acceptance of self and others: a reevaluation. J. Abnorm. Soc. Psychol., 50, 274–276, 1955.
38. Fielstra, C. An analysis of factors influencing the decision to become a teacher. J. Educ. Res., 48, 659–667, 1955.
39. Fish, Barry; and Karabenick, Stuart. The effects of observation on emotional arousal and affiliation. J. Exper. Soc. Psychol., 14, 256–265, 1978.
40. Form, W. H. The social construction of anomie: a four-nation study of industrial workers. Amer. J. Soc., 80, 1165–1191, 1975.
41. Frank, Jerome D. Persuasion and Healing: A Comparative Study of Psychotherapy. Baltimore: Johns Hopkins Press, 1961.
42. Freud, Sigmund. Five Lectures on Psychoanalysis. (Translated and edited by James Strachey.) New York; W. W. Norton, 1977.
43. Gessner, P. K. Evaluation of instruction. Science, 180, 566–570, 1973.
44. Gibson, John E. Are you an optimistic pessimist? Modern Living, July-August, 10 and 11, 1966.
45. Goethe, J. W. Faust. (Translated by Bayard Taylor.) New York: Hartsdale House.
46. Gotoo, Keiichi; and Sugiyama, Yoshio. Experiments on the relationship between anxiety and psychological stress in serial rote learning. Jap. Psychol. Res., 2, 158–163, 1960.
47. Hardy, Robert C.; and Eliot, John. Comparison of external and internal individuals' ability to perceive viewpoints of others. Percep. Motor Skills, 44, 941–942, 1977.
48. Hepner, Harry Walker. Psychology Applied to Life and Work, p. 312. (Fifth ed.). Englewood Cliffs, N.J.: Prentice-Hall, Inc., 1973.
49. Higginbotham, Timothy E. Irrationality in college students. Rational Liv., 11, 34, 1976.
50. Holland, J. L. The prediction of college grades from personality and aptitude variables. J. Educ. Psychol, 51, 245–254, 1960.
51. Horney, Karen. Collected Works. New York: W. W. Norton, 1963.
52. Hsia, Hsio-Hsuan. A study of selected intellective factors related to academic performance in graduate school. Diss. Abstr., 28 (9-A), 3508, 1968.
53. Husband, Richard W. What do college grades predict? Fortune, 55, 157–158, 1957.
54. Jarman, Betty Jane. The effect of parental messages on the career patterns of professional women. Diss. Abstr., 37 (7-B), 3580, 1977.
55. Jensen, Vern H.; and Clark, Monroe H. Married and unmarried college students: Achievement, ability, and personality. Personnel Guid. J., 37, 123–125, 1958.
56. Jersild, A. T., and Holmes, F. B. Children's fears. Child Devel. Monogr., No. 20, pp. ix–358, 1935.
57. Jones, Mary Cover. A laboratory study of fear. Pedagogical Sem., 31, 308–315, 1924.
58. Kanekar, Suresh. Academic performance in relation to anxiety and intelligence. J. Soc. Psychol., 10, 153–154, 1977.
59. Karabenick, Stuart A.; and Youssef, Azkhour I. Performance as a function of achievement motive level and perceived difficulty. J. Personality Soc. Psychol., 10, 414–419, 1968.
60. Khayyam, O. Rubaiyat. (Fourth translation by E. Fitzgerald.) New York: Thomas Y. Crowell Co., 48 and 24 quatrains.

61. Kipnis, D.; Castell, P. J.; Gergen, M.; and Mauch, D. Metamorphic effects of power. J. Appl. Psychol., 61, 127–135, 1976.
62. Klein, George S. Psychoanalytic Theory. New York: International Universities Press, Inc., 1976.
63. Klein, Stephen P.; and Evans, Franklin R. An examination of the validity of nine experimental tests for predicting success in law school. Educ. Psychol. Meas., 28, 909–913, 1968.
64. Knapp, R. M. The man who led his class in college — and others. Harvard Graduate Mag., 24, 597–600, 1966.
65. Kohn, M. L.; and Schooler, C. Occupational experience and psychological functioning. Amer. Sociol. Rev., 38, 97–118, 1973.
66. Langlie, T. A.; and Eldredge, A. Achievement in college and in later life. Personnel J., 9, 450–454, 1931.
67. LeBold, William K.; Thoma, Edward C.; Gillis, John W.; and Hawkins, George A. A study of the Purdue engineering graduate. Engineering Bull. Purdue Univ., 44, #1, 1–298, 1960.
68. Lee, Young-Hi Kwum. Creativity and sensitivity to diverse cues. Diss. Abstr., 28, (4-B), 1684–1685, 1967.
69. Leigh-Mallory, G. Diary at Camp IV on the 1922 Everest Expedition. Quoted by Ullman, J. R., in Kingdom of Adventure, p. 102. New York: William Sloan Associates, Inc., 1947.
70. Leventhal, H. The effects of set and discrepancy on impression change. J. Personality, 30, 1–15, 1962.
71. MacKinnon, D. W. The nature and nurture of creative talent. Amer. Psychologist, 17, 484–495, 1962. Also, What makes a person creative? Saturday Review, 45, 15–17, and 69, 1962.
72. McDonald, Robert L.; and Gynther, Malcolm D. Nonintellectual factors associated with performance in medical school. J. Genetic Psychol., 103, 185–194, 1963.
73. McKeachie, W. J. Motivation, teaching methods, and college learning. In Jones, Marshall R. (Ed.). Nebraska Symposium on Motivation, 1961. Lincoln, Neb.: Univ. Nebraska Press, 1962.
74. Mann, Sister M. Jacinta. Relationship among certain variables associated with college and post-college success. Diss. Abstr., 19, No. 2, 253–254, 1958.
75. Maslow, A. H. Toward a humanistic biology. Amer. Psychologist, 24, 724–735, 1969.
76. Menninger, Karl. Whatever Became of Sin? New York: Hawthorn Books, Inc., 1973.
77. Menninger, Karl Augustus; and Holzman, Philip S. Theory of Psychoanalytic Technique. New York: Basic Books, 1973.
78. Miller, N. E. Theory and experiment relating psychoanalytic displacement to stimulus-response generalization. J. Abnorm. Soc. Psychol., 43, 155–178, 1948.
79. Mischel, W. Preference for delayed reinforcement and social responsibility. J. Abnorm. Soc. Psychol., 62, 1–7, 1961.
80. Moore, E. H. Professors in retirement. J. Geront., 6, 243–252, 1951.
81. Moulton, R. W. Effects of success and failure on level of aspiration as related to achievement motives. J. Personality Soc. Psychol., 1, 399–406, 1965.
82. Murthy, Vinoda N. Attempted suicide and goal-setting behaviour. Trans. All-India Inst. Ment. Health, 6, 69–78, 1966.
83. Musselman, Gerald C.; Barger, Ben; and Chambers, Jay L. Student need patterns and effectiveness in college. J. Clin. Psychol., 23, 108–111, 1967.
84. Nicholi, Armand M. An Investigation of Harvard Dropouts. Washington, D.C.: U.S. Dept. of Health, Education, and Welfare, Bureau Res., June 1970.
85. O'Donnell, Patrick I. Predictors of freshman academic success and their relationship to attrition. Diss. Abstr., 29 (3-A), 798, 1968.
86. Oskamp, Stuart. Relationship of self-concepts to international attitudes. J. Soc. Psychol., 76, 31–36, 1968.
87. Prociuk, Terry J.; and Breen, Lawrence J. Internal-external locus of control and information-seeking in a college academic situation. J. Soc. Psychol., 101, 309–310, 1977.
88. Pruitt, Dean G. Informational requirements in making decisions. Amer. J. Psychol., 74, 433–439, 1961.

89. Reik, T. Listening with the Third Ear. New York: Farrar, Straus, & Co., 1949, p. 304.
90. Robbins, P. R. Level of anxiety, interference proneness, and defensive reactions to fear-arousing information. J. Personality, 31, 163–178, 1963.
91. Roe, Anne. A psychological study of physical scientists. Genet. Psychol. Monogr., 43, 121–235, 1951. Also, A Psychological study of eminent psychologists and anthropologists, and a comparison with biological and physical scientists. Psychol. Monogr., 67, #352, 1953.
92. Roe, Anne. The psychology of the scientist. In McCollom, Ivan N.; and Badore, Nancy Lloyd (Eds.). Exploring Psychology. New York: Thomas Y. Crowell, 1973.
93. Roth, Thomas; Kramer, Milton; and Lutz, Thomas. The effects of sleep deprivation on mood. Psychiatric J. Univ. Ottawa, 1, 136–139, 1976.
94. Roth, Thomas; Kramer, Milton; and Roehrs, Timothy. Mood before and after sleep. Psychiatric J. Univ. Ottawa, 1, 123–127, 1976.
95. Rothaus, Paul; and Worchel, Philip. The inhibition of aggression under non-arbitrary frustration. J. Personality, 28, 108–117, 1960.
96. Ryle, Anthony; and Lunghi, Martin. A psychometric study of academic difficulty and psychiatric illness in students. Brit. J. Psychiatry, 114, 57–62, 1968.
97. Sallery, Robert D. H. Artistic expression and self-description with Arabs and Canadian students. J. Soc. Psychol., 76, 273–274, 1968.
98. Samenfink, J. Anthony; and Milliken, Robert L. Marital status and academic success: A reconsideration. Marriage Fam. Liv., 23, 226–227, 1961.
99. Samuel, William; Baynes, Keith; and Sabeh, Charlotte. Effects of initial success or failure in a stressful or relaxed environment on subsequent task performances. J. Exper. Soc. Psychol., 14, 205–216, 1978.
100. Sarason, S.; Davidson, K.; Lighthall, F.; Waite, R.; and Ruebush, B. Anxiety in Elementary School Children. New York: John Wiley, 1960.
101. Sassenrath, J. M. Anxiety, aptitude, attitude, and achievement. Psychol. Schools, 4, 341–346, 1967.
102. Schafer, Roy. A New Language for Psychoanalysis. New Haven and London: Yale Univ. Press, 1976.
103. Schaller, George B. Mountain gorilla displays. Natural History, 72, 11–16, 1963.
104. Scoville, Wilber E. Effects of employment on the academic performance of selected college freshmen. Diss. Abstr., 27 (12-A), 4140, 1967.
105. Seifer, Daniel M. Relationships of selected personal characteristics to income achievement of college graduates. Diss. Abstr., 27 (9-A), 2694–2695, 1967.
106. Shepard, J. M.; and Panko, T. R. Alienation. Sociol. Quarterly, 15, 253–263, 1974.
107. Tanay, Emanuel. Psychiatric study of homicide. Amer. J. Psychiatry, 125, 1252–1257, 1969.
108. Taylor, C. W.; and Ellison, R. L. Biographical predictors of scientific performance. Science, 155, 1075–1080, 1967.
109. Tedeschi, James; Burrill, Dwight; and Gahagan, James. Social desirability, manifest anxiety, and social power. J. Soc. Psychol., 77, 231–239, 1969.
110. Teichman, Y. Emotional arousal and affiliation. Exper. Soc. Psychol., 9, 591–605, 1973.
111. Terman, Lewis M.; and Oden, Melita H. Genetic Studies of Genius. Vol. V, The Gifted Group at Mid-Life. Stanford, Calif.: Stanford Univ. Press, 1959.
112. Thompson, L. The role of verbalization in learning from demonstration. Doctoral dissertation. New Haven, Conn.: Yale University, 1944.
113. Trigg, Linda J.; and Perlman, Daniel. Social influences on women's pursuit of a nontraditional career. Psychol. Women Quarterly, 1, 138–150, 1976.
114. Trueblood, Dennis L. Effects of employment on academic achievement. Personnel Guid. J., 36, 112–115, 1957.
115. Varnes, Paul R. An investigation of college intramural athletic and recreational participation and academic success. Diss. Abstr., 29 (3-A), 825, 1968.
116. Vaughter, Ressa M.; Ginorio, Angela B.; and Trilling, Barbara A. The failure of trait theories to predict success. Signs, 2, 664–674, 1977.
117. Wagman, Morton. University achievement and daydreaming behavior. J. Couns. Psychol., 15, 196–198, 1968.
118. Watson, J. B. Psychology from the Standpoint of a Behaviorist. New York: J. B. Lippincott Co., 1924, pp. 232–233.

119. White, Kathleen M.; and Waranch, Larry. The undergraduate as professor. Teaching Psychol., 5, 88–91, 1978.
120. Windholz, George. The relation of creativity and intelligence constellations to traits of temperament, interest, and value in college students. J. General Psychol., 79, 291–299, 1968.
121. Wyer, R. S.; and Terrell, G. Social role and academic achievement. J. Personality Soc. Psychol., 2, 117–121, 1965.
122. Zigler, Edward; and Hunsinger, Susan. Our neglected children. Yale Alumni Mag., 41, 11–12, 1978.

ADDENDUM

Relaxation Training – An Exercise to Lessen Anxiety

Background

Relaxation training is discussed in Section E, 6 of Chapter 5 and considerable background information about the process is given there.

The following procedure was used by 75 junior and senior students majoring in education, special education, or psychology. Each completed at least eight sessions (most complete 10 to 12 sessions) at a rate of two to three training sessions per week.

The purpose was for the students to learn to control their ability to relax. Training sessions were repeated with increasing emphasis on cue words and images, until the student could decrease heart rate by approximately ten per cent in two minutes; 80 per cent achieved this goal in ten sessions. Although heart rate is not the most satisfactory measure of relaxation, it is easily measured without cumbersome equipment. All students also reported subjective feelings of relaxation. Many reported increased self-confidence in interpersonal interactions, less fear and trauma in dealing with physicians and dentists and tests, and decreased anxiety. The decrease in anxiety was so pronounced that one student, for example, was able with her doctor's permission to stop taking a tranquilizing drug.

The protocol does not have to be followed word-for-word; it is an example you can follow or build upon. If you find one or several procedures especially relaxing, e.g., the floating image or a particularly relaxing memory, feel free to embellish the protocol or change it in any way which makes it more effective for you. This protocol is flexible and can be adjusted in any way, almost, so it fits *you*.

Instructions for Using This Exercise

There are several ways you can conduct this exercise profitably; each, however, assumes that you *listen* to the training exercise. Simply reading the exercise to yourself will not improve your ability to relax. A popular and effective technique is to have a friend read the exercise either to you or to a group of your friends.

To get the most out of the exercise, try to insure that you and your friends are as comfortable as possible during the reading. In addition, caution your reader to read slowly; there is a temptation to rush through material when one is reading out loud.

Alternatively, if you want to learn how to relax in privacy, you can record the exercise on a cassette tape, using your voice or a friend's. This alternative has proved popular for those who cannot always coordinate their schedule with a friend's schedule. It has the additional advantage of allowing you to replay the exercise at your convenience. The exercise, when read slowly, will take between 15 and 20 minutes, so use at least a C40 (20 minutes per side) cassette tape.

As you listen to this exercise, keep in mind that the closer you attend and follow the instructions, the sooner you will learn to relax in even the most anxious situations. Try to resist the temptation to go to sleep during the actual training exercise. It is all right to go to sleep after the exercise, but you will find that the training will be most effective if you are *not* fatigued or unable to pay attention.

RELAXING TRAINING EXERCISE
(to be read out loud):

To begin, it is important that you feel comfortable. Loosen any tight clothing and remove any uncomfortable jewelry. (Pause.) Move your body around until you feel comfortable. (Pause.)

The purpose of this training exercise will be to help you recognize and control relaxation by means of comparing tension and tension release. As an example, close your eyes and you will immediately feel the tension release following the cessation of brightness, movement, and color. Keeping your eyes closed for a few seconds, you can feel the relaxation begin to flow through your body. The purpose of this exercise is to give you a boost in learning how to get that feeling of relaxation to occur whenever you want. (Pause for about 5 seconds.)

Now open your eyes again. Feel that tension building back up again. It's not a bad tension but it's a small example that you have the ability, at least to a small degree, of controlling how your body feels. It's easier to focus on your body's internal feelings with your eyes closed so please close your eyes for the remainder of the exercise.

Concentrate now on the tension and release associated with breathing. Take a deep breath and hold it. Focus on the feeling of tension and anxiety building up. Hold it — it's building — you can feel tenseness building up. Now let go — all at once — not slowly. Don't force it — just let it flow out.

Notice that as your breath flows out and you begin breathing again, you feel more relaxed. Notice that each time you exhale, more tension fades and you feel more relaxed than you did before.

Now, each time you exhale, say the word "calm" to yourself; and look at each breath as a step toward greater relaxation. Go ahead now and breathe naturally for a minute or so, focusing on the increasing calm each time you exhale and say the word "calm." (Pause for about 60 seconds.)

Notice, also, that as you relax, your muscles begin to feel heavier and heavier; it's a pleasant heaviness. As you learn to relax your muscles, your mind will become more serene. As the tension flows out of your muscles, tension flows out of your mind. It is a pleasant feeling. As tension slips away, your mind feels clearer, sharper, more aware. The fogginess disappears. As you relax, you feel joy because tension was confusing things; and now it is going and you begin to feel clear, and light, and serene, and more aware. (Pause for about five to ten seconds.)

We are going to ease away the tension in your body

now by going through several more tensing/relaxation cycles. We'll start with your dominant hand: the right one if you are right-handed (your left if you are left-handed).

As I mention the various parts, I want you to tense them to the point where the tension is uncomfortable. Don't hurt yourself or cause cramps, just tense and hold it for about five to ten seconds; then release it — all at once. It is necessary that you let go all at once and let the tension leave of its own accord.

Let's start now with your hand. Tense it. Hold it. Focus on the feeling of hardness, of tension, of tightness; your fingers are digging into your palms. Now release it; let it go. Let it melt away. Feel the tension flow out and, as it flows out, feel the warmth replacing it. A nice comfortable warmth as the life-giving blood flows into the muscles and skin. As the warmth flows in, it brings a tingling feeling, a pleasant feeling, the feeling associated with waking up after a restful night's sleep.

Let's tense that hand again, but this time when you tense it, try to maintain the relaxation in the rest of your body. Just focus on your hand and tense it. As you learn to control your body's ability to relax, you will learn to control the tension and relaxation in various parts of your body. Right now practice *just* tensing your hand. All right. Go ahead and tense your hand. Hold it for a slow count of ten; notice the contrast between your hand and the rest of your body as you count toward ten. When you reach ten, relax, let it all go. Let the relaxation from the rest of your body flow in as the tension is released. Just relax and let the pleasantness flow in. (Pause for about ten seconds.)

Now let's practice with your other hand. Tense it; squeeze hard; feel the tension building up; your fingers are pushing into your palms. Harder! Now let it go. Feel your fingers straighten out as the tension leaves them and the warmth flows in. Focus on that warmth, let it flow throughout your hand. It is pleasant and comfortable, a friend. It's a friend that you will be using today and tomorrow; don't fight it; just enjoy. Go ahead and enjoy it for a few seconds. (Pause for 15 to 20 seconds.)

Now that you are becoming more skilled at controlling your tension and relaxation, we are going to practice with your whole body. We'll begin with your toes and move up your body. As I mention each part, I want you to tense it and then, moving up, I want you to continue tensing each part until your whole body is tense, and then, on my signal, you'll let it all go at once. Total, complete relaxation. To get the most out of it, focus on the feeling; flow with the relaxation; don't fight it; enjoy it. As you let go, physically exhale all the tension that has built up.

Let's begin with your toes. Tense them. Your left toes and your left foot; your right toes and your right foot. Now feel the tension moving up both of your calves. Tense your calves by pointing your toes down or up, whichever is comfortable. Now tense your thighs; allow the tension to move upward into your buttocks and pelvis.

As the tension moves up, focus on each muscle as it becomes tense. It's moving into your stomach. . .and now clench both of your hands. Feel the tension moving up your forearms, and biceps. As the tension moves from your shoulders and stomach into your chest, take a deep breath and hold it to increase the tension in your chest. It's moving into your jaw; clench your teeth; into your face, your eyes; squint them, feel the tension flowing into your eyebrows, up your forehead to the top of your scalp. Now hold it.

When I count three, relax, all at once, and exhale. One. Two. Three. Release. Breathe out. Let your muscles droop, let them relax. (Pause five seconds.) Just continue breathing naturally; focus on your breathing. Each time you exhale, feel a little more tension leave. As you relax more and more, you will feel heavier and heavier, but it is a nice heaviness. You feel pleasant.

Imagine a bit of goosedown floating on a windless day. As your tensions and anxieties flow out, imagine you are like that bit of down, seeming to float, drifting. It is a pleasant and comfortable feeling — no tension — no worries — no fears.

For the next minute, imagine that you are that piece of soft down. As you inhale and exhale, imagine that you are floating up and down. As you become more relaxed, your breathing will slow down; you don't need all of that energy right now, so just breathe easily and only when necessary. Breathe smoothly. (Pause for about 60 seconds.)

As you continue relaxing, you may notice that as your body begins to feel more relaxed, your mind is also relaxing. It is not becoming dull or unresponsive; it is becoming clearer and brighter. You are becoming more aware of your whole body, *your* body, and it feels pleasant to be relaxed. Try to imagine your blood flowing to every part of your body, to every single organ and muscle, to every single cell in your body, bringing relaxation; total, warm, life-sustaining relaxation to your whole self.

Some people like to find a place in their body where they can store that warmth so that whenever they begin to feel anxious or tense, they can call on the warmth to flood the tension and help them face the situation both more relaxed and more aware. Some like to store their warmth in their chest; others at the back of their head; others like to store it in their stomach or in the tip of one of their fingers. This is a difficult skill but many report that it is worth the effort.

As you are relaxing now, let your imagination find a spot that feels comfortable and safe, and store your warmth there. The next time you are feeling anxious and tense, and anxiety is interfering with your ability to perform, just take a deep breath, repeat the word "relax" or "calm" to yourself; you will begin to feel the relaxing warmth flowing to your shoulders and your neck and your stomach and your forehead.

As you become more practiced, you will find that tension and anxiety seem to begin in specific places; and as you practice relaxing, you will become better at focusing the warmth and serenity on those areas of tension. You will find that petty annoyances will not turn into bothersome headaches or stomachaches. The warmth of relaxation is healing; it is a beautiful, comfortable feeling.

To help you become even more relaxed, let's take your awareness and let it move up your body from your toes and, for each group of muscles, pause and let the relaxation flow in; let any tension that you find there, melt. Let the warmth flow in and ease the tension.

Focus on your toes and your feet, first one and then the other. More relaxed, it's a pleasant, warm, comfortable, beautiful feeling. If you feel any tension, just let it go. Now move slowly up your calves, just relaxed, comfortable. (Pause five seconds.)

Now your knees and your thighs; relaxed, waiting, resting, recuperating, refreshing; they are so relaxed you can almost feel the blood moving through them. (Pause five seconds.) Now focus on your right hand and forearm; let them droop, let them relax. Let the tension just flow smoothly out your finger tips. (Pause five seconds.) Now do the same for your left hand, just let it relax. Focus on the warmth and let your body relax on its own. Don't force it. Just allow it to relax.

Now I want you to take special care and focus on your shoulders and the muscles that run up your neck. With each breath, imagine that the tension is flowing out; focus on the feeling of relaxation; let it spread out through your shoulders and neck, and up your neck to your scalp and head. Just focus on that feeling of relaxation now as you become more and more relaxed. (Pause ten seconds.)

Let the relaxation and warmth move up into your jaw now, just let the tension flow out; let your jaw droop just a little; don't try to keep your mouth tightly closed, just let it relax. The relaxation is spreading throughout your face, it's a beautiful feeling. (Pause ten seconds.)

As you finish this training session, I want you to concentrate on how good it feels to be so completely relaxed. It's a quiet kind of joy, the kind of peaceful feeling we occasionally have in the morning as we wake up. It is the joy you felt as a child when waking up on a beautiful summer morning. There is no hurry; just lie back and enjoy the feeling. Relaxed. . .calm. . .serene. . . . You are at peace with yourself, your surroundings, your hopes and dreams. You are at peace with your mind, and today, and from now on, you are going to keep that serenity with you, that peace of mind. Go ahead now and just enjoy the serenity for a while. (Pause for about 60 to 100 seconds.)

I shall count backward from ten now and as I do so, I want you to allow the muscle tension to return. Not too much. Not too fast. And don't let the serenity leave. Let the serenity and awareness exist together. Be aware, be confident, be serene. As I count backward let your eyes open when I reach five, and when I reach one, kind of stretch and feel the good feeling. Ten, Nine, Eight, Seven, Six, open your eyes, Four, Three, Two, One.

Go ahead and stretch and turn the tape off, if necessary.

Index

Page numbers in *italics* indicate pages in the Bibliographies.

243

Everyday life, learning during, 47, 78, 80, 81, 85–86, 107–108
Examinations
  as a challenge, 138–140
  causes of nervousness during, 100–101, 123, 130–140
  effects of anxiety while studying for, 100–101
  essay type, 121–122, 124–127
  objective type, 127–131
  pervasiveness of, 117–118, 124
  preparation for, 73, 117–147
  reduction of nervousness during, 121–144
  reviewing for, 119–123
  unfairness of, 131–132
  usefulness of, 117–119, 134, 139
  uses of, 117–119, 124, 134, 138–139
Eye strain, 40–41, 55

Facts as tools, 9–10
  as aids to understanding, 86
  as means to share interests, 27
  as way to increase interest, 15–17
Failure
  coping with, 143–144
  fear of. See *Fear of failure.*
  what to do after, 143–144
  See also *Success.*
Fantasy, 11–13, 195–196
  and marriage choice, 11–12
  and vocational choice, 12–13
Fatigue
  effects of, 123, 136
  reduction of, 110–113. See also *Concentration, improvement of; Sleep.*
  relation to clear thinking, 123
  relation to concentration and conflict, 153–155
  signs of, 54, 191–192
  See also *Tension.*
Faust, 213
Fear
  generalization of, 101, 181–184, 223–224
  in infants, 206
  of conformity, 218–219
  of deviancy, 218–219
  of failure, 204–211
    and being loved, 205, 206–207
    and desire to succeed, 205–206, 208–209
    and habits of dependency and projection, 204
    causes of, 205–208
    definition of, 205
    effects of, 100–101, 204–208
    reduction of, 207–211
  of mistakes, 199–201, 208–209, 220–221

Fear (*Continued*)
  of rejection, 159–161, 199–201, 212–214, 215–216
  of success, 132, 218
Figures and graphs, 49, 96, 97, 181
Flexibility, and routes toward, 222–223
  See also *Rigidity.*
Folklore, and fallacies, 16–17, 22, 86, 179, 194–195, 214–220
Foreign languages. See *Languages.*
Forgetting. See *Retention.*
Freedom
  achieving of, 25–31, 201–202, 204
  and fear of failure, 204–205
  and responsibility, 25–27, 201–202
Friend, being a, 23–25, 137, 159, 161–163, 190–191, 221
Friendship
  and studying, 134, 159–163, 213–220
  building, 23–25, 27–29, 137, 159, 161–163, 190–191, 221
  essence of, 161, 196–197, 212, 213–215
  fear of losing, 159–161, 199–201, 204–207, 212–215
Frustration
  and aggression, 182–184, 190
  example of, 11–13
  See also *Anxiety.*
Futility, sense of, 27
Future, recognition of, 201

Generalization. See *Transference.*
Goals
  choosing own, 4–6, 8, 36, 37, 187–188
  dangers of low, 143–144, 169–170
  efficiency in reaching, 4–7, 168–172
  how to formulate, 6–7, 37, 165–166, 169–170, 172
  importance of knowing own, 4–6, 30–31, 36, 37, 167–170
  need for specific, 4, 6–7, 37
  of education, 7–31, 46–48, 218–220
  reasonable, 135, 165–166, 169–170, 208–209
  striving for and fear of failure, 205–207, 208–211
Godden, Rumer, 51
Goethe, J., 213, *230*
Gorillas, chest-beating of, 191
Grades
  and education, 132–133, 145–146
  and fear of failure, 205–209
  and later success, 215–218
  and marriage, 216
  and various successes, 214–218
  as goal in college, 124
    an alternative to, 132–135
    as cause of failure, 132–139
  high, fear of, 215–218